In this insightful book, Gift Mtukwa argues convincingly that for Paul, "work serves to shape Christian communities into the self-giving character of Christ. Clearly written and exegetically rock-solid, the book unfolds a coherent theology of work in Paul's Thessalonian correspondence, one that spotlights work as an expression of love for others. What's more, Dr. Mtukwa's African reading of these texts enables the communal role of labour in African societies to shed light on Paul's understanding of work as a community-forming practice. Dr. Mtukwa's reading of Paul implies that we cannot fully grasp Paul's ecclesiology apart from his understanding of work. At the same time, it leads God's people to see work for the sake of others as a vital aspect of what it means to embody the gospel in their world.

Dean Flemming, PhD
Professor of New Testament and Missions,
MidAmerica Nazarene University, Olathe, Kansas, USA

In the finest tradition of contemporary biblical scholarship, Gift Mtukwa builds upon and moves beyond recent attempts to understand the apostle Paul's approach to the challenges facing the Christian church he had planted in the ancient city of Thessalonica. As an African scholar and pastor, Dr. Mtukwa calls attention to the relevance of "work" in communities within traditional societies. His insights should encourage Western readers to leave aside (for a while, at least) more esoteric theological preoccupations in order to appreciate Paul's emphasis on the mundane but crucial role of labour in the formation and cultivation of thriving Christian communities. As he notes, "without work, there can be no community."

George Lyons, PhD
Emeritus Professor of New Testament,
Northwest Nazarene University, Nampa, Idaho, USA

Gift Mtukwa provides us with a biblical and theological foundation from the Thessalonian correspondence that demonstrates the value of work in forming and maintaining community. He argues against largely Western individualistic readings of the work passages in the Thessalonian correspondence and rightly approaches this topic from a communal perspective. His methodology, African biblical hermeneutics, highlights the importance of recognizing the contextual situatedness of the reader. An analysis of the relationship between work and community in traditional African societies forms the backdrop against which the Pauline view of work and community is investigated.

Dr. Mtukwa provides an excellent and in-depth analysis of the Jewish, Greco-Roman, and Christian influences that shaped Paul's understanding of work. Following the self-sacrificial love of Jesus encapsulated in the gospel message, he shows how Paul presents himself as a model to his readers and hearers on how to build community in a multi-ethnic context. Viewed in this holistic manner, Dr. Mtukwa cogently argues that the value of work goes beyond economic benefits. He shows that a right understanding of work negates a sacred-secular dichotomy and demonstrates that work is positive and has value in building the community of God. This is an excellent resource for the student as well as the scholar.

Elizabeth Mburu, PhD
Langham Literature Regional Coordinator, Anglophone Africa
Associate Professor of NT and Greek,
Pan Africa Christian University, Nairobi, Kenya
Extraordinary Researcher, North-West University, Potchefstroom, South Africa

The so-called Western world has too often deformed the concept and practice of "work," contorting it into a privatized, secularized, materialized mutant, far removed from the gracious gift that God assigned the Edenic pair as work-worship. The result has been to create two sad extremes: work as a necessary but abhorred burden, or work as an obsession. In other words, "idle" or "idol."

African theologian Gift Mtukwa has incisively cut through misguided myths with his analysis of the interrelationship between "work" and "community," both in the contemporary Essene community and the Greco-Roman world that interplays the two. He then focuses on Paul's epistles to the Thessalonians, exhibiting exegetically that Paul's manual work not only financed his ministry, but modelled an ethic that resulted in fusing together the early Christian community. This he parallels with the African work ethos where work is done communally, with joy and music, embracing community rather than segmenting it.

This book is an important addition to the growing body of biblical "work" studies, especially because it links work to its central community formation intent through perceptive African eyes. It also defies traditionalist objections which falsely bifurcate service as "God or mammon."

Fletcher Tink, PhD
PhD Director in Transformational Development,
Asia Graduate School of Theology, Manila, Philippines

This fresh look at the relationship between work and community in the Thessalonian correspondence takes its perspective from beliefs and practices from African cultures. The author uses African biblical hermeneutics, in contrast to the Western individual approaches to manual labour which are commonly adopted in interpreting these letters, to show that work is done for others and to build community. This helps us to see Paul's mission in a new light, because the exhortations to work are therefore a call to participate in the mission of God in Thessalonica. On this understanding, work becomes a demonstration of love for others and a commitment to holy community. The interpretive problem of the prohibition of the disorderly from the common meal (that those who do not work should not eat) is explained on the basis that enjoying the benefits of community requires one to contribute manual labour.

Sarah Whittle, PhD
Research Fellow in Biblical Studies,
Nazarene Theological College, Manchester, UK
Postgraduate Support Advisor,
University of St Andrews, UK

Work and Community in the Thessalonian Correspondence

An African Communal Reading of Paul's Work Exhortations

Gift Mtukwa

MONOGRAPHS

© 2021 Gift Mtukwa

Published 2021 by Langham Monographs
An imprint of Langham Publishing
www.langhampublishing.org

Langham Publishing and its imprints are a ministry of Langham Partnership

Langham Partnership
PO Box 296, Carlisle, Cumbria, CA3 9WZ, UK
www.langham.org

ISBNs:
978-1-83973-239-3 Print
978-1-83973-520-2 ePub
978-1-83973-521-9 Mobi
978-1-83973-522-6 PDF

Gift Mtukwa has asserted his right under the Copyright, Designs and Patents Act, 1988 to be identified as the Author of this work.

All rights reserved. No part of this publication may be reproduced, stored in a retrieval system or transmitted, in any form or by any means, electronic, mechanical, photocopying, recording or otherwise, without the prior written permission of the publisher or the Copyright Licensing Agency.

Requests to reuse content from Langham Publishing are processed through PLSclear. Please visit www.plsclear.com to complete your request.

Unless otherwise stated, Scripture quotations are from the New Revised Standard Version Bible, copyright © 1989 National Council of the Churches of Christ in the United States of America. Used by permission. All rights reserved.

Scripture quotations marked (NIV) are taken from the Holy Bible, New International Version®, NIV®. Copyright © 1973, 1978, 1984, 2011 by Biblica, Inc.™ Used by permission of Zondervan.

Scripture quotations marked (ESV) are from The Holy Bible, English Standard Version® (ESV®), copyright © 2001 by Crossway, a publishing ministry of Good News Publishers. Used by permission. All rights reserved.

Scripture quotations marked (NASB) are taken from the New American Standard Bible®, Copyright © 1960, 1962, 1963, 1968, 1971, 1972, 1973, 1975, 1977, 1995 by The Lockman Foundation. Used by permission.

Scripture quotations marked (TLV) are taken from the Tree of Life (TLV) Translation of the Bible. Copyright © 2015 by The Messianic Jewish Family Bible Society.

British Library Cataloguing-in-Publication Data
A catalogue record for this book is available from the British Library

ISBN: 978-1-83973-239-3

Cover & Book Design: projectluz.com

Langham Partnership actively supports theological dialogue and an author's right to publish but does not necessarily endorse the views and opinions set forth here or in works referenced within this publication, nor can we guarantee technical and grammatical correctness. Langham Partnership does not accept any responsibility or liability to persons or property as a consequence of the reading, use or interpretation of its published content.

Contents

Acknowledgements xi

Abstract xiii

List of Abbreviations xv

Chapter 1 1
Background of the Study, Survey of Scholarship, and Methodology
   1.1 Thesis Statement 1
   1.2 Justification of the Study 2
   1.3 Survey of Scholarship 5
   1.4 Historical-Critical Issues Related to Work and
       Community in Thessalonian Correspondence 16
       1.4.1 Ancient City of Thessalonica – Economic and
            Political Background 16
       1.4.2 Paul's Ministry at Thessalonica 19
       1.4.3 Authorship, Audience, and Date of Writing 22
       1.4.4 Conclusion 27
   1.5 Methodology 27
   1.6 Suggested Contribution to Knowledge 32
   1.7 Limitations of the Study 33
   1.8 Working Definitions 34
   1.9 Outline of the Study 36

Chapter 2 37
Work and Community in African Worldview
   2.1 Introduction 37
   2.2 African Worldview or Worldviews? 38
   2.3 God and Ancestors in the African Context 39
   2.4 African Idea of Community 42
   2.5 Individual and Community Obligations 43
   2.6 Age Sets, Work Parties, and Community 47
   2.7 Work and Community in the Household 51
   2.8 Conclusion: Work and Community in the African
       Traditional Society 55

Chapter 3 57
  Work and Community in the Dead Sea Scrolls and the Qumran Community
  3.1 Introduction 57
  3.2 Qumran Community and the Dead Sea Scrolls 58
  3.3 Wealth and Work in the Dead Sea Scrolls 61
    3.3.1 Wealth in the Damascus Document (CD) and the
          Rule of the Community (1QS)...61
    3.3.2 Work and Community at Qumran 65
    3.3.3 Work and Community: Archaeological Evidence 66
    3.3.4 Work and Community in the Scrolls: Obligations
          for the Community Members..70
    3.3.5 Synthesis – Dead Sea Scrolls on Work and Community ...77
  3.4 Conclusion on Dead Sea Scrolls and Qumran Community
      on Work and Community 78

Chapter 4 81
  Work and Community in the Greco-Roman Perspectives
  4.1 Introduction 81
  4.2 Work and Community in the Greco-Roman Household 82
  4.3 Work and Community in Epicurean Philosophical School 86
  4.4 Work and Community in Greco-Roman Associations 94
    4.4.1 Definition, Purpose, and Membership of Associations 94
    4.4.2 Financial Obligations in Association...................................98
    4.4.3 Responsibilities Inside and Outside Associations............101
    4.4.4 Summary of Work and Community in Associations 103
  4.5 Conclusion – Work and Community in Greco-Roman
      Perspectives 104

Chapter 5 105
  Work and Community in First Thessalonians
  5.1 Introduction 105
  5.2 The Work of the Apostles and the Beginning of
      Community Life at Thessalonica in 1 Thessalonians 2:8–9 106
    5.2.1 Introduction 106
    5.2.2 Work as Sharing Community Life: "*Mgeni siku
          mbili, ya tatu mpe jembe*" 107
    5.2.3 The Workshop as Platform for Paul's Preaching 111
  5.3 Brotherly/Sisterly Love, Work, and Community in
      1 Thessalonians 4:9–12 117
    5.3.1 Introduction 117

  5.3.2 Φιλαδελφία and Community Life 118
  5.3.3 Φιλαδελφία Demonstrated 124
   5.3.4 The Implication of Proper Behaviour to All Humanity ..131
 5.4 Work in Service of the Community in
  1 Thessalonians 5:12–14 135
  5.4.1 Introduction 135
  5.4.2 Are the Injunctions General or Specific?...........................136
  5.4.3 Recognition of Community Workers 137
  5.4.4 Censoring of οἱ ἄτακτοι 146
 5.5 Conclusion 149

Chapter 6 151
Working, Eating, and Community Life in 2 Thessalonians 3:6–15
 6.1 Introduction 151
 6.2 Literary Context of 2 Thessalonians 3:6–15...............................152
 6.3 The Problem of Walking in Idleness 153
 6.4 Paul as the Paradigm for the Community
  2 Thessalonians 3:7–9 155
 6.5 Paul's Διδαχή on Work and Eating in 2 Thessalonians 3:10:
  "A Lazy Person Kills the Whole Community"...........................164
  6.5.1 What is the Occasion for the ἄτακτοι? 166
  6.5.2 Meals in Early Christian Communities 168
  6.5.3 Exclusion of the ἄτακτοι from Participation in
   Communal Meals 171
 6.6 Paul's Paradigm and Its Application 2 Thessalonians 3:11–12 ...174
 6.7 Discipline on Account of Refusing to Work in
  2 Thessalonians 3:13–15 181
 6.8 Conclusion 189

Chapter 7 191
Conclusion
 7.1 Summary and Conclusions 191
 7.2 Contributions 197
 7.3 Further Studies 197

Bibliography...199

Acknowledgements

I would like to express my most profound gratitude to Dr. Sarah Whittle, my primary supervisor, for her unceasing encouragement and patient guidance throughout the research. Her valuable feedback has shaped the ideas in this document. I am also indebted to Dr. Kent Brower, my secondary supervisor, for his encouragement and helpful feedback throughout this study. His wife Mrs. Francine Brower's hospitality during my time in Manchester was terrific.

I wish to express my gratitude to the faculty, staff, and students of Nazarene Theological College, Manchester, for help, encouragement, and fellowship. I particularly remember our time over coffee during the PhD residence. Special appreciation Dr. Deirdre Brower-Latz, Dr. Dwight Swanson, Dr. Svetlana Khobnya, Dr. John Wright, Dr. David Rainey, Dr. Tom Noble, Dr. Geordan Hammond, and Dr. Mi Ja Wi for conversations that helped shape ideas in this thesis. Special appreciation to Dr. Dean Flemming and Dr. George Lyons for reading some sections of this thesis. I am also indebted to Dr. John Jeacocke who proofread this, his comments made the language much clearer.

Special thanks to Dr. Peter Rae and Don and Bonnie Irons for making it possible to study at NTC. Langham Partnership provided funds that made it possible for me to travel back and forth to Manchester and buy books which I could not get in local libraries here in Kenya. Liz and Malcolm McGregor, my Langham care givers, for their support and prayers throughout this study. I am indebted to Dr. Jerry Lambert, the IBOE staff and Dr. Filimao Chambo and the Education and Clergy Development office for Africa Region for a scholarship for part of my tuition fees. Dr Gabriel Benjimann and the REC office (Africa Region) has also supported me in many ways.

I appreciate the Administration of Africa Nazarene University, especially Prof. L. T. Marangu, Dr. Stanley M. Bhebhe, Prof. Rodney Reed, and the entire Management of ANU for according me a Sabbatical with which I used to conduct this research. ANU has done much more than giving me a sabbatical, it has provided a conducive working and studying environment for me. Thanks also goes to the School of Religion and Christian Ministry for bearing with me during my PhD residence in Manchester.

This is to acknowledge that Prof. Mark and Rev. Nancy Pitts generously assisted my studies at NTC. Ruth Copeland and Rev. Joseph Kisoi and supported me in various ways while I was a student at NTC. My fellow students – Jacob Lett, Nabil Habiby, Samantha Chambo, James Sedlacek, Ezekiel Shibemba, Joshua Bloor, Julianne Burnett, Lindy Williams, Richard Liantonio, Joe Houston, Kelly Yates, Justin Bradbury, J. R. Woodward, Sègbégnon Mathieu, and Andrew and Gina Pottenger to mention only a few – you taught me more than you can imagine. As they say, it takes a village to raise a child; it certainly takes a village to get a PhD. I would like to offer my appreciation to Tyndale House for the two months I spent at their library. Members of their staff were very kind and their entire community of readers – thank you for your hospitality. I would also extend special appreciation to the faculty, staff, and students of Trinity College Bristol for their hospitality while I was in Bristol. The staff and residents of Hodgkin house for the time I lived in Bristol. The University Church of the Nazarene for their prayers and encouragement during my research. The inspiration to study work came from this faith community.

I also owe a debt of thanks to my lovely wife Judy and our son Nathan for putting up with many hours alone as I worked on this research. Only God knows how much they had to endure many hours which I spent in different libraries around the world. Special appreciation goes to members of my family the Chidavaenzi family, Motsi/Mtukwa family, and the Gikanga family for their unceasing support and prayers – truly as we say in Africa "it takes a village to raise a child." Most of all I am grateful to Almighty God for the strength and provision to accomplish this project.

Abstract

This study makes use of African biblical hermeneutics to investigate Paul's work exhortations in the Thessalonian letters. It investigates the relationship between work (labour) and community in the Thessalonian correspondence (1 Thess 2:9; 4:9–12; 5:12–15; and 2 Thess 3:6–15), arguing that Paul's exhortations towards work have as their goal community formation. Work is here defined as a purposeful communal activity done in the power of Spirit by God's people to honour God and for the benefit of the worker and their co-creatures. By means of a consideration of the role of work in community in traditional African society, where even the ancestors remain obliged to offer work to the community, we propose the hypothesis that work is crucial to community formation. We will test this across a range of evidence contemporary to Paul before turning to the Thessalonian correspondence to discuss fresh insights.

The sectarian Dead Sea Scrolls revealed that members were required to contribute "knowledge, power and wealth" (1QS 1 11–15), which, we will argue, included the fruit of and potential for work. Work was required to manage community resources. A study of the household and the voluntary associations of the first century, with reference to trade guilds, demonstrates the keen relationship between work and community, as trades were regulated and those who worked hard were honoured. We also explore this relationship within a philosophical school – Epicureans – and found that work and community do not have a positive relationship since most members had either benefactors or slaves who laboured on their behalf.

Paul's ministry in Thessalonica was carried out in a workshop, where he also had an audience for the gospel. He worked out of consideration for others in the community – not to be a burden (1 Thess 2:9). Moreover, work is a demonstration of love for others in the community – both internal and external (1 Thess 4:9–12). Individuals offered themselves to others through their varied acts of service (1 Thess 5:12–15). Further, this study sheds light on Paul's instruction about the ἀτάκτοι; the disorderly should be forbidden from eating at communal meals, as participation in the communal meal requires one to contribute the result of their labour (2 Thess 3:6–15). Yet even this restriction is itself a promotion of community. The evidence shows that for Paul work is integral to community formation. Indeed, without work, there can be no community. However, in contrast to African tribal exclusivity, community life in Thessalonica was open to outsiders who were willing to contribute their labour.

List of Abbreviations

1QS	Rule of the Community
1QSa	Rule of the Congregation
1QH	Thanksgiving Hymns
BDAG	Greek-English Lexicon of the New Testament
CD	Damascus Document
DSS	Dead Sea Scrolls
GLNT	A Manual Greek Lexicon of the New Testament
HALOT	A Concise Hebrew and Aramaic Lexicon of the Old Testament
LSJ	A Greek-English Lexicon
LXX	Septuagint
NT	Novum Testamentum
SLGNT	Shorter Lexicon of the Greek New Testament
TBDAG	The Brill Dictionary of Ancient Greek
TDNT	Theological Dictionary of the New Testament
TLNT	Theological Lexicon of the New Testament
UBS	United Bible Societies

Apocrypha

1–2 Macc	1–2 Maccabees
3–4 Macc	3–4 Maccabees

CHAPTER 1

Background of the Study, Survey of Scholarship, and Methodology

1.1 Thesis Statement

In African traditional society work and community have a positive relationship. Human work is not peripheral but essential to the building of community.[1] In the words of Herbert Applebaum, "work is a cooperative effort of mankind [sic]."[2] This work examines this assertion with respect to Paul's work exhortations in the Thessalonian correspondence. Much of what has been said about Paul and work has centred on Paul himself as an apostle. The concern is usually what informed Paul's work ethic. Some scholars have argued that Paul's view of work arose from his Jewish background. Others have equally emphatically credited it to the Greco-Roman influences at work in his upbringing in the diaspora. As important as Paul's influences are, equally important is the subject of how work fits with his concern to build a community. This question has been largely left unanswered. This study is interested in the role work plays in community formation within the Thessalonian correspondence.

---

1. George Rupp says, "While work exemplifies instrumental action, it also offers distinctive strengths for addressing the question of community in contemporary pluralistic societies . . . The sense of community that may eventuate from such shared commitments accordingly is not restricted to the bonds of traditional communities." (Rupp, "Communities of Collaboration," 192–208.) Similarly, Herbert Applebaum asserts that "Working together and sharing an occupation creates a special type of relationship" as such "Workgroups solidarity is not only an end-in-itself, but can contribute to quality of life" (Applebaum, *Concept of Work*, 572).

2. Applebaum, *Concept of Work*, 589.

1.2 Justification of the Study

Paul's focus on human work is theologically essential to his overall theological understanding of the people of God.[3] Human work is a crucial aspect in the shaping of the people of God, primarily because the Spirit of God empowers it. The people of God for Paul are those who are not only in Christ but in the Spirit as well.[4] As Georg Bertram affirms, "All ἔργον in the Christian community is finally God's work through men . . . For Paul and for all believers all work is the fruit of faith."[5] To join the people of God is not to escape work, but to enlist oneself among working people. For Paul, the work of proclaiming the gospel is not the only work that is significant; everyday work contributes to bringing about the new order.[6] Paul acknowledges that work is a communal affair in which human beings join co-workers and those who benefit from their labour.[7]

An individualistic perspective often colours interpretations of Paul. Andy Johnson has described the problem in reading Paul's texts as "entrenched commitment to an individualism that understands the self as an autonomous construction of the individual."[8] Yet as Malina notes, the New Testament writings reflect a "strong group orientation" and in the place of individualism we have "dyadism."[9] Paul as an apostle of Christ is concerned here not only about personal virtues, although these are important; his central concern is "the life of the community."[10] Paul as a founder and leader of congregations exhorts these communities as an insider.[11] He wrote to Christian communities not

---

3. William A. Beardslee asserts "For Paul . . . vocation and work are grounded in an understanding of God's will, so that although his message about work may seem to reflect a new pre-occupation with human effort, it is really based on a profound faith in God's purpose." Beardslee, *Human Achievement*, 15.

4. The Thessalonian letters bear testimony to this reality. God is the one who gives his Holy Spirit to the Thessalonian believers (1 Thess 4:8). The believers are those who have been sanctified by the Spirit (2 Thess 2:13). There is justification here for the assertion that whatever the believer does, he or she, does it in the Spirit.

5. Georg Bertram, "Ἔργον, Ἐργάζομαι, Ἔργ," *TDNT* 2:635–52.

6. Beardslee, *Human Achievement*, 41.

7. See Applebaum, *Concept of Work*.

8. Johnson, "Sanctification," 290.

9. Malina, *New Testament World*, 67.

10. Furnish, *Theology and Ethics*, 84.

11. Furnish, 84.

necessarily to tell them about himself but about themselves; thus, what he says about himself should be evaluated in terms of how it builds his communities.[12]

Mark Batluck has questioned the collectivist approach, arguing that the individualistic approach is present in Paul's letters. He asserts that there are more first-person pronouns in the undisputed letters of Paul: 436 versus 315 appearances.[13] For Batluck, "the burden is on the interpreter to explain the hundreds of uses of the first-person singular before asserting that Paul is collectivistic."[14] However, statistics by themselves do not provide compelling evidence; one has to investigate each individual case before deciding whether or not it supports an individualistic reading.

In fact, in the Thessalonian correspondence, the bulk of the pronouns are in the plural form; that is, seventy-two plurals and only two first-person singular. The only occurrence of the first-person pronoun is found in 1 Thessalonians 2:18, which occurs incidentally. Paul is talking about how the missionaries wanted to visit the Thessalonians: "As for us" (Ἡμεῖς δέ) (1 Thess 2:17), which is followed by διότι ἠθελήσαμεν ἐλθεῖν πρὸς ὑμᾶς (1 Thess 2:18). Paul emphasizes how he personally wanted to come to Thessalonica (ἐγὼ μὲν Παῦλος). It is evident, even in this case, that Paul's visit is part of the group visit. The second singular is found in 2 Thessalonians 3:17 where Paul refers to his hand with the adjective ἐμῇ.

This study takes the communal nature of Paul's society seriously and seeks to ascertain how his exhortations on work fit that context. It is crucial because the individualistic reading of texts such as, for example, "If any will not work, let him not eat" (2 Thess 3:10) leads, as Jewett puts it, to a manifestation of "Christian capitalistic principles and individual enterprise."[15] Philip F. Esler is right to note that individualistic reading of Paul's first-century letters are anachronistic; for him, these readings are a result of the inappropriate ethnocentric assumptions of modern Western interpreters.[16] It is our assumption here that the African communal worldview has much to contribute to our understanding of what Paul's exhortations imply. Within the African

---

12. Gager, *Reinventing Paul*, 33.
13. Batluck, "Paul, Timothy," 44.
14. Batluck, 44.
15. Elliott, *What Is Social-Scientific Criticism?*, 50.
16. Esler, *First Christians*, 24; Elliott, *What Is Social-Scientific Criticism?*, 50.

worldview work and community go hand in hand. As such this study will test the hypothesis of the connection between work and community in Paul's Thessalonian letters. The study concludes that there is a positive relationship between work and community in Paul's exhortation and that Paul's aim in these exhortations is communal formation.

There is an erroneous view of work that only sees it as an occupation that brings about economic benefits. This view has to a large extent prevented interpreters from seeing what George Rupp calls the "more inclusive purposes" work "participates in realizing."[17] This study is primarily concerned about those all-inclusive purposes, which include work's role in the formation of community. This thesis takes seriously these "more inclusive purposes" as it seeks to investigate ways in which work participates in community formation in the Thessalonian correspondence.

Most major studies which have focused on the subject of work in Pauline thought have treated 2 Thessalonians as pseudonymous.[18] This study presupposes we read both letters as authored by Paul and try to see the role work plays in community formation in both letters. If what Paul says in the two letters about work and community coheres, the study may challenge the recent scholarly consensus on the authorship issue. Instead of focusing on what Paul said about himself, the study focuses on what Paul said about the community through what he said about work. The question the study is answering is: What is the relationship between work and community in the Thessalonian correspondence? What role if any does work play in community formation? In what follows we will provide a brief survey of scholarship.

1.3 Survey of Scholarship

Pauline scholars have dealt with the issue of Paul and his ministry, and his tent-making job, in important studies.[19] Helen-Ann Mcleod Hartley notes concerning the literature in this area that, "among significant developments in Pauline scholarship in recent years has been an increased appreciation of

---

17. Rupp, "Communities of Collaboration," 202.
18. Hock, *Social Context of Paul's Ministry*, 48.
19. Hartley, "We Worked Night"; Hock, *Social Context of Paul's Ministry*; Malherbe, *Paul and the Thessalonians*; Beardslee, *Human Achievement*.

the cultural, religious and political milieu of Paul's world."[20] All this literature sheds light on our investigation; however, this study is concerned not only with Paul and the importance of work for him personally but the importance of work in community formation. This study will focus on the connection between work and community in Paul's Thessalonian correspondence.

W. A. Beardslee's purpose was to determine if human labour achieves something of value, in light of the "real work" of proclaiming the gospel.[21] He argued that vocation and work are grounded in God's will. Even though work may reflect human effort, it is based on deep faith in God's purposes.[22] Beardslee understood God's purposes manifested in Christ to be crucial. Paul did not believe any particular work to be superior to any other as long as it was done in obedience to Christ; it is this that gives work enduring significance and ultimate value.[23] Beardslee laments the secularization of the meaning of vocation and concludes, "to Paul, there is only one calling, the service of Christ. . . . Paul knows himself to be laid hold of by Christ as a 'whole man,' brought into subjection to Christ."[24] However, as Miroslav Volf has shown, conceiving of work as a vocation is problematic because of its static nature; i.e. that once one is called to a particular station, one should not seek change.[25] As such, we are inclined to follow Volf in thinking of work as work in the Spirit rather than as a vocation.

Beardslee's study is significant, especially in that he sees meaning in human work.[26] He makes a distinction between so-called secular human work and ministry (work of proclaiming the gospel). All work can have meaning, even though the only calling Beardslee knows is the call to preach the gospel.[27] This notwithstanding, Beardslee does not go further to ask if work plays any role in the formation of the people of God. He is true to his purpose in the

---

20. Hartley, "We Worked Night," 1.
21. See Beardslee, *Human Achievement*.
22. Beardslee, 14.
23. Beardslee, 15, 19.
24. Beardslee, 14.
25. Volf, *Work in the Spirit*.
26. He asserts, "In the church, God has created a situation in which men can truly work, and work with enduring results," Beardslee, *Human Achievement*, 41.
27. According to Beardslee, Paul, "finds that not only the great 'work of proclaiming the gospel, but also the daily round of labour by any believer, participates in a new order already being created by God through Christ.'" Beardslee, *Human Achievement*, 41.

sense that his desire was to validate his hypothesis; namely, that human work has value, and it achieves something of value. Our quest is to see if human work has a place in the formation of the people of God. If work is significant in any way, one such way might well be community formation.[28]

Ronald F. Hock breaks ranks with some of the major scholars in Pauline studies.[29] He prefers sources in the Greek-speaking eastern Mediterranean context as a background for understanding Paul's secular work as a tent maker.[30] Hock examined numerous examples of rabbis who combined their secular employment with their study of the Torah. He concluded that rabbis from the second century onwards worked because their economic status required it, not because of their self-understanding of their rabbinic vocation. What we know about the rabbis suggests that they did not attempt to link their work to some motivating theology. They understood work as merely instrumental. Thus, secular work had no other role than to provide economic support to make their rabbinic vocations viable.[31] Hock further notes that Paul's working should not be seen as "Jewish regard to toil, or as arising from ecclesiological problems due to eschatology . . . but as reflecting Paul's clear familiarity with the moral traditions of the Graeco-Roman philosophers."[32] Here the pendulum swings drastically to one side and Paul's other two identities – his Jewish heritage, and life as a follower of Christ – are disregarded.

Following moral philosophers, Paul did not want to be a burden, since his householders did not have sufficient means to support Paul and his co-workers. Hock argues that Paul's working was essential for his apostolic self-understanding.[33] Paul's conception of work can be paralleled with the writings of Cynics such as Dio Chrysostom and Musonius Rufus.[34] Paul avoided being

---

28. Rupp, "Communities of Collaboration," 192–208.

29. See Bruce, *Paul*, 108. Bruce asserts that "Many Rabbis practised a trade . . . Paul scrupulously maintained this tradition as a Christian preacher." Gunter Bornkamm agrees: "With Paul . . . theological training in Judaism was combined with learning and practice of an occupation" (Bornkamm, *Paul*, 24).

30. Hock, *Working Apostle*.

31. Hock, *Social Context of Paul's Ministry*, 23.

32. Hock, 47.

33. Hock writes, "The relation between Paul's tent-making and his self-understanding as an apostle is evident from his reference to the 'necessity' (ἀνάγκη) that pressed upon him (v. 16). This was the necessity to preach the gospel (εὐαγγελίζεσθαι v. 16)." Hock, *Social Context of Paul's Ministry*, 61–62.

34. Hock, *Social Context of Paul's Ministry*, 44.

a burden primarily by utilizing his trade but also by gifts from churches he founded. At times Paul is found lodging with one who shared his trade, as happened in Corinth, where Aquila was a tentmaker.[35] As a result, "The earnings from Paul's tent-making would have gone for necessities: food, clothing, perhaps even part of his householder's rent."[36]

Hock's overall conclusion is that "far from being at the periphery of his life, Paul's tent-making was actually central to it. More than any of us had supposed, Paul was *Paul the Tentmaker*. His trade occupied much of his time."[37] Hock notes that though Paul's tent-making was the primary means of his livelihood, the proceeds were not enough, "so that hunger and thirst and cold were at times his lot."[38] Hock portrays Paul as a philosopher, and does not pay sufficient attention to other influences that could have been at work in Paul's self-understanding. The Jewish heritage does not feature in Hock's *Paul the Tentmaker*.[39]

Helen-Ann M. Hartley, who has also taken issue with Hock's one-sided view on Paul's tent-making activities, challenges Hock's conclusion:

> His representation of a Jewish view of work is problematic. Other possible explanations of Paul's working strategy, such as the discussion of the problem of work in the Hebrew Bible (for example in Genesis 3:17–19, and in the Wisdom literature) and in Judaism prior to Paul, may well have had an important impact on Paul's thinking.[40]

Hock in arguing for a Greek context in understanding Paul the tentmaker fails to differentiate the working context and the ideas that inform actual work.[41]

---

35. Hock, 30–31. He goes on to say, "Paul found lodging in a household; and instead of simply becoming its resident intellectual, as was his apostolic right, he refused to be a financial burden and so found work making tents and other leather products in order to be self-sufficient." (Hock, 37).

36. Hock, 31.

37. Hock, 67.

38. Hock, 67–68.

39. Adolf Deissmann is of the opinion that Paul may have dictated some of his letters from the workshop. Adolf Deissmann, *Light from the Ancient East*.

40. Hartley, "We Worked Night," 15; Hock, *Social Context of Paul's Ministry*, 30–31.

41. Hock, *Social Context of Paul's Ministry*, 18.

Hartley finds it problematic that Hock should call Paul, *The Tentmaker*. For Hartley, Paul was "surely first and foremost, an apostle not a tentmaker." Moreover, "Paul's manual work was . . . a means to an end, a way of serving the gospel."[42] We agree with Hartley in seeing work as having higher ends. Our assessment is that Hock is only concerned about why Paul worked and what influences motivated his work. He does not go further to ask whether work plays any role in the formation of the people of God. He rightly observes that being a tentmaker was necessary for Paul's self-understanding as an apostle but does not ask why work was crucial for his communities of faith.

Hartley's critical study primarily aims to counter Hock's assertion that Paul's working had nothing to do with his Jewishness.[43] As a result, she is primarily concerned about the influences on Paul's working, rather than on work itself, and its role in forming the holy people of God. Hartley studies work under the rubrics of "divine work" and "human work."[44] Her assessment of the evidence reveals that God is indeed a worker; God does the work of creation. Scripture declares in unequivocal terms "the works of YHWH." God's work in history is also emphasized.[45] To Hartley, there is ambivalence when looking at human work, which can be either cursed or blessed, depending on whether it is done in disobedience or obedience to God.[46]

Concerning Paul's working strategy, Hartley acknowledges that certain features match the Greco-Roman context, especially the difficulties in working Paul mentions in his letters. She then concludes that the evidence examined demonstrates that "there was a clear distinction between the activities of the gods and that of humans."[47] This becomes her basis for questioning Hock's categorization of Paul's working strategy as non-Jewish. Hartley proceeds to examine Pauline texts that mention work in Galatians, Thessalonians, Corinthians, Romans, and Philippians. Her purpose was "to demonstrate how all-pervasive the theme of work is for Paul."[48] Even though she sees am-

---

42. Hartley, "We Worked Night," 15.

43. Hartley, 22. Her other aim is to restate the significance of, "Paul's working strategy without overstating its potential importance," Hartley, 22.

44. Hartley, 30.

45. Hartley, 86.

46. Hartley, 87.

47. Hartley, 136.

48. Hartley, 167.

Background of the Study, Survey of Scholarship, and Methodology   9

bivalence in Paul's understanding of work, she acknowledges, "work for Paul was valuable."⁴⁹ However, work was important only "in as much as it enabled him to present his message to his communities without being a burden upon them."⁵⁰ Hartley also sees work in Paul as work "with and for God" and not "for the good of imperial establishment."⁵¹ As to whether Paul actually makes a distinction between work done for God and for the imperial establishment, Hartley does not comment.

In 1 Thessalonians Paul presented himself as the model that the Thessalonians were to follow. In 2:9 Paul says he and his co-workers worked night and day (νυκτὸς καὶ ἡμέρας ἐργαζόμενοι) in order not to be a burden to the Thessalonians.⁵² Hartley perceives the reason for Paul's working as grounded in his message of the self-sacrificial love of Jesus, which he saw as irreconcilable with seeking financial gain at the cost of those to whom he preached.⁵³ In relation to 1 Thessalonians 4:10b–12, Hartley sees Paul's admonitions as grounded in the gospel that he preaches. The Thessalonians are to conduct themselves in a manner worthy of the gospel they have received. In verse 11, they are not to need anybody's help; hence, they are to attain a measure of independence. For Hartley, in Paul's view, "The imminence of the parousia is not an excuse for idleness." To do nothing made one "a nuisance and a burden to other people."⁵⁴

In 2 Thessalonians 3:6–15 Paul takes on the problem of the ἄτακτοι. Hartley makes various suggestions regarding the meaning of ἀτάκτως without taking any position.⁵⁵ For Hartley, Paul offers himself as an example to be followed, since to follow Paul is to follow Christ.⁵⁶ Hartley is to be commended for showing interest in community life and work, unlike other studies

---

49. Hartley, 167.
50. Hartley, 167.
51. Hartley, 167.
52. Hartley, 173–74.
53. Hartley, "We Worked Night," 175. Hartley says, "Here Paul encourages the Thessalonians to reflect the character of God, and thus he speaks to the Gospel and not to the presuppositions of his Culture" (Hartley, 176).
54. Hartley, "We Worked Night," 179.
55. These range from eschatological excitement appeals to the utopia prior to the Adam and Eve story, the accusation of Jews as lazy due to Sabbath observance. Hartley, "We Worked Night," 179–80.
56. Hartley, "We Worked Night," 180.

which simply focus on Paul and totally neglect the community to which he wrote. However, Hartley does not follow through in all her engagement with the texts she analyzes; she is narrowly concerned with Paul's work under the category of human work.

At the end of her study, Hartley concludes that even though Paul shared common aspects with his Greco-Roman context, "it is his Jewishness which provided the decisive conceptual matrix for his portrayal of work."[57] Her work is commendable in many respects. First, the that fact that she links divine work and human work is crucial. This means that theology is not divorced from the world of work. This understanding is essential for a Judeo-Christian tradition. Second, Hartley links Paul's working with his understanding of the gospel. However, this leans to the instrumental side; Paul worked so as not to be a burden to his Christian communities. We argue that there is more to Paul's working than just avoiding becoming a burden.

Since Hartley's concern was with the influences on Paul's understanding of work, she gives no attention to the place of work in the formation of Christian communities. Work itself does not get a thorough treatment. It is revealing that she calls Paul's working a working "strategy." We contend that "strategy" does not do justice to human work, especially as Paul understood it. Hartley acknowledges concerning work, "It is an arena within which the worker (as an individual and communally with others) serves God and participates in God's continuing creative work."[58] However, she does not develop this idea. In our estimation, this is significant for Paul's understanding of work. The influences of Paul's work are critical; however, one needs to go beyond the influences and ask, does work play any role in the formation of the community?

Catherine Jones's study of the impact of Paul's manual labour on Paul's apostleship in 1 Corinthians is also important to this study.[59] Jones is right to recognize that Paul's manual labour was the occasion for calling his apostleship into question at Corinth.[60] For Jones, Paul's response is to present his weakness "not as something that hinders his apostolic ministry, but rather, as a facet of his life that affords the best platform from which to display the

---

57. Hartley, 211–12.
58. Hartley, 87.
59. Jones, "Theatre of Shame."
60. Jones, 219.

glory of the Lord."⁶¹ Jones characterizes Paul as "Paul, the manual labourer."⁶² Perhaps the most controversial part of Jones's study is her claim that Paul did not get support from the Corinthians and, as such, in 1 Corinthians 9:1–18 Paul is defending his entitlement to such support. She claims that her reading is based on a literal reading of 2 Corinthians 9:6.⁶³ Jones does not reconcile the contradiction in her argument, however: on one hand Paul turns a vice (manual labour) into a virtue; on the other hand, he claims support from the Corinthians.⁶⁴ The other question that arises is, if the Corinthians did not offer Paul support, on what basis would they call into question his apostleship?

A recent study from Kei Eun Chang⁶⁵ looks at communal life in terms of "private interests" (τὰ ἴδια) and "common good" (τὸ συμφέρον) at Corinth through Greco-Roman perspectives. Chang argues that Paul makes use of τὸ συμφέρον as an "ethical device" to deal with division at Corinth.⁶⁶ For Chang, Paul operates within this Greco-Roman framework of seeking "common good" rather than "idionistic (individualistic) concerns."⁶⁷ The individual is able to meet their needs within the context of what is in the best interest of the community. The individual interests are not subservient to those of the community as they are in Platonic and Aristotelian thought.⁶⁸ Both interests are equally important and are addressed.⁶⁹ Chang's interest is "unity" and how division presents a problem in the Christian community; moreover, unity has a "salvific thrust."⁷⁰ The book is not about work and contribution to the community as is our concern in this study. We are, however, captivated by the axis of community and individual. Chang's work is a communal reading of Paul's teaching on keeping unity in the community that ultimately leads to salvation.⁷¹ This study will seek to demonstrate the importance of individual

---

61. Jones, 221.
62. Jones, 230.
63. Jones, 198.
64. Jones, 226.
65. Chang, *Community*.
66. Chang, 1–2.
67. Chang, 138.
68. Plato, *Commentatio ad Legg*, 9.875d.
69. Chang, *Community*, 4–16.
70. Chang, 4–5, 208.
71. Chang, 220.

contribution through work for the life of the community and as such it builds on Chang's work.

An important question that needs to be addressed is whether the problem of idleness was socially or eschatologically motivated. Scholars in the nineteenth and twentieth centuries believed that wrong eschatological views were behind the problem of idleness in 2 Thessalonians 3:6–15.[72] This is given as the main reason Paul addresses eschatological problems in the letter.[73] Nicholl has questioned this view based on an apparent lack of identification of eschatology and idleness in both 1 and 2 Thessalonians, concluding "There is, in fact, no convincing evidence of a link between the eschatological problem and the idleness in 2 Thessalonians."[74] For Nicholl, Paul does not address false eschatological views when he addresses the issue of idleness.[75]

However, Nicholl sees the eschatological problems in their initial stages, whereas the problem of idleness is interpreted as a full-blown issue. Paul expects the audience to understand that work was not cursed, but that toil was introduced as part of the punishment for sin. Whereas this is indeed true, not all interpreters saw it that way. Considering that we are dealing with pagans who came from various religions in Thessalonica, who had different views concerning the golden age, it should not surprise us that some could have stopped working. Even though work was a pre-fall mandate (Gen 2:5, 15), there is no explicit teaching of its continuance after the parousia has come. To expect these early Christians to know that is to expect too much.[76] Moreover, if the problem of eschatology was a massive problem as it was at Thessalonica, would it not have affected other areas of Christian existence, including right conduct?[77] If as Nicholl claims people were "shaken, horrified and filled with despair as they considered the implication that God had abandoned them

---

72. Baur, *Paul the Apostle*, 2–232; Gottlieb, "Critical and Exegetical Handbook," 248; Lightfoot, *Notes on the Epistles*, 260; Okorie, "Pauline Work Ethic," 55–64; Richard, *First and Second Thessalonians*, 390–91; Gaventa, *First and Second Thessalonians*, 129.

73. See Nicholl, *From Hope to Despair*.

74. Nicholl, 158–60.

75. Nicholl, 158–60.

76. Nicholl, 162.

77. Scott J. Hafemann has demonstrated that "The return of Christ as savior and vindicating judge thus plays a foundational role both in Paul's own motivation for ministry and in the Thessalonians' life of faith" as such "Eschatology drives not only Paul's ethics, but also Paul's missionary activity." Hafemann, *Paul's Message and Ministry*, 192–93.

and that there was no hope remaining for them,"[78] how could they not be unaffected in their conduct by such a scenario?

Those who have questioned the eschatological view include R. Russell,[79] David C. Aune,[80] Bruce W. Winter,[81] Charles Wanamaker,[82] and Colin Nicholl.[83] Russell saw the problem as relating to manual labourers who were dependent on patrons. The reason for this dependence was that they could not find work. Russell says these people "appeared to outsiders to be idle beggars who exploited the generosity of the Christian community without any sense of reciprocal response to the new benefactors."[84] The result was that the indolent adopted new beliefs and practices and abandoned their work to rely on Christian brothers and sisters to proliferate their religious ideas. And they became a burden to those who had the means.[85] Russell believes his view is compatible with "social descriptions of Pauline Christianity."[86]

The problem with Russell's thesis, however, is that his sociological explanation does not resonate with the tone of Paul's exhortations. Could Paul have been so firm on people who could not get work? Is it unreasonable to exhort people who cannot get work to work with their own hands? It should be kept in mind that Thessalonica would have offered more economic opportunities compared to other cities in Macedonia and Achaia[87] but we do not see Paul confronting this problem elsewhere. M. J. J. Menken points out that, "His [Russell's] sociological approach explains why people are without work; another explanation is required for their unwillingness to work."[88] We conclude that Russell's approach is not sufficient to explain the situation of the "disorderly."

---

78. Nicholl, *From Hope to Despair*, 198.
79. Russell, "Idle in 2 Thess," 105–19.
80. Aune, "Trouble in Thessalonica."
81. Bruce, "If a Man Does," 303–15.
82. See Wanamaker, *Epistles to the Thessalonians*.
83. See Nicholl, *From Hope to Despair*.
84. Russell, "Idle in 2 Thess," 110–13.
85. Russell, 113.
86. Russell, 113.
87. Green, *Letters to the Thessalonians*, 30. Gow and Page, *Greek Anthology*.
88. Menken, "Paradise Regained," 273–74.

Winter proposes the patron-client social convention as the issue behind the disorderly at Thessalonica. Patron-client relationships were primarily based on "giving and receiving."[89] The one who received consequently became indebted to the giver and appropriate thanks was required for the gift. In returning gratitude, the giver was asked for more gifts. The free poor (client) were able to meet their daily needs through the gifts from the patrons.[90] A patron who became a Christian still maintained his obligation even after they changed their religion. Their clients did not suddenly stop expecting gifts from them. At Thessalonica, clients who became Christians also continued to expect their patrons to support them; the patrons could be Christian or non-Christian.[91]

Furthermore, Winter highlights the famine of AD 51, which resulted from an earthquake, as reported by the Roman historian Tacitus. This famine saw Roman citizens receiving corn dole. The Roman citizens at Thessalonica would not have been an exception in not receiving. The patrons were the leading players in providing the dole. After the famine, some clients continued to expect their patrons to support them.[92] Paul's solution was that Christians should be benefactors rather than clients. Winter sees this in how he required them to do good – that is, he wants them to do both private and public benefactions. Yet Christian benefaction was different from Greco-Roman benefaction – it was for those who were genuinely in need.[93] In other words, it was for those who could not work rather than those who could work.

Other scholars like Aune have suggested that the idlers were those who being "cut off from their *collegia* looked to the church to meet their needs."[94] The labourers who were clogged by greed and laziness felt that work was beneath them and as such took advantage of the largess of well to do Christians.[95] Nicholl questions the use of *collegia*, preferring Winter's patron-client model[96] to be the issue behind the problem but overall agrees with Aune's depiction

---

89. Winter, "If a Man Does," 306.
90. Winter, 306.
91. Winter, 306.
92. Winter, 306.
93. Winter, 306.
94. Aune, "Trouble in Thessalonica," 87–90.
95. See Nicholl, *From Hope to Despair*.
96. Winter, *Seek the Welfare*.

of the situation.⁹⁷ But could the work that clients do for their patrons not be considered work? The question that should be asked is whether there were patrons in the Thessalonian church, and Robert Jewett has rightly challenged their existence. We contend that Paul was more concerned about community building; he wished to deal with issues that did not promote community, and the "disruptive idle"⁹⁸ are the people Paul's exhortations address. The disorderly, in Paul's estimation, threatened the very fabric of the Christian community. This should not be discussed either from a sociological or eschatological perspective; no one perspective can fully account for what happened at Thessalonica.⁹⁹ People's theological views have to be lived out in the day-to-day reality of life. There is undoubtedly a relationship between the issues discussed in these two letters.

In summary, many studies that have investigated work concentrate on Paul's influences; that is, whether Paul is influenced by the Jewish or Greco-Roman context in his work habits. Other studies are so concerned with *Paul's* work that they neglect the work of the community and the role of work in community formation and enhancement of community life. While these works tend to focus on an understanding of work for him as an individual, this study intends to emphasize the communal aspects. Unlike earlier interpreters who preferred either sociological explanation or eschatological explanations for the problem of the "disruptive idle" this study takes both explanations as having contributed to the problem.

1.4 Historical-Critical Issues Related to Work and Community in Thessalonian Correspondence

We shall consider historical questions related to the ancient city of Thessalonica – the economic and political context of the city, Paul's mission, authorship, date, and audience of the Thessalonian correspondence, and the occasion which resulted in the writing of these letters. Our analysis shall be

---

97. See Nicholl, *From Hope to Despair*.
98. Gupta, *1–2 Thessalonians*, 148.
99. Gregson observes that "There are a number of possible causes for this and it seems likely that there is a mix of reasons behind this group's actions." Gregson, *Everything in Common*, 231.

limited to issues related to aspects of work and community, and the results of this investigation will pay dividends when we turn to the exegetical work.

1.4.1 Ancient City of Thessalonica – Economic and Political Background

As the location of the church that received the Thessalonian correspondence, an understanding of the city of Thessalonica is essential for our survey. Our probe would be incomplete without an exploration of what this city looked like before, during, and after the first century. Our investigation shall look at the location and economic activities of the city. We are primarily concerned about the kind of work opportunities this city would have provided to those who lived in it in the first century.

A good number of Macedonians were agrarian, and their main occupations were horse breeding and riding, shepherding, and farming.[100] In addition, there were some working and artisan class, who included fishers, farmers, carpenters, cooks, scribes, hunters, weavers, rhetors, and religious practitioners.[101] Witherington notes that "It was a city full of artisans, manual labourers, sailors, and orators."[102] Since the city provided a breadth of opportunities for work, it attracted various people, not least "laborers, tradespeople, orators and philosophers," including missionaries, like Paul and his co-workers.[103] As such, Paul and his missionary band were able to find work or means to support themselves, which in turn provided opportunities to meet people who frequented the marketplace.[104]

Thessalonica had enough economic opportunities to allow its citizens to earn their daily bread (2 Thess 3:12). Green is right to note that "Whatever the economic situation of other cities in Macedonia and Achaia, Thessalonica offered the majority of the population both work and food."[105] Speaking more specifically about the Christians at Thessalonica, Best notes that "the great

---

100. Paige, *1 & 2 Thessalonians*.
101. Green, *Letters to the Thessalonians*; Page and Gow, *Greek Anthology*.
102. Witherington III, *1 and 2 Thessalonians*, 4; Malherbe, *Letters to the Thessalonians*, 14.
103. Byron, *1 and 2 Thessalonians*, 11.
104. Byron, 11.
105. Green, *Letters to the Thessalonians*, 30; Page and Gow, *Greek Anthology*, 329; Jewett, *Thessalonian Correspondence*, 120; Hock, *Social Context of Paul's Ministry*, 34–37.

majority . . . were manual workers, whether skilled or unskilled."[106] Robert E. Evans supports this characterization from Paul's remarks in 2 Corinthians 8:2–4 about the extreme poverty of the Macedonian Christians.[107] As such the Thessalonians were poor manual workers who had to work to earn their daily bread.

At the same time, some have suggested that there were a few patrons who could provide meeting places for the house church in the city.[108] The Acts account of the Pauline mission suggests individuals like Jason, and not a few leading women, functioned in this way (Acts 17:4).[109] Yet Luke does not reveal the kind of work Paul did, and when he mentions Paul's converts like Jason, they are not identified as manual labourers.[110] While Jerome Murphy-O'Connor believes there were wealthy patrons in the Corinthian assembly, he thinks that is not the case at Thessalonica.[111] Yet in 1 Thessalonians Paul speaks of his manual labour (night and day) in the workshop so that he would not be a burden to his converts.[112] Given that recent scholarship has affirmed that the Thessalonian Christians were drawn from mostly the artisan class, such characterization does not leave space for patrons. All the evidence used by scholars who hold this view to support the existence of patrons in Thessalonica is drawn from Acts of the Apostles, Colossians and Philemon (Acts 20:5, cf 27:2, Col 4:10, and Phlm 24). Nothing in the Thessalonian letters themselves indicate that there were any patrons.

Considering that typical artisans worked from sunrise to sunset, Paul clearly did more than an average artisan to make ends meet.[113] It is quite in order to assume that there were some (not patrons) within the Thessalonian church who had means that the idlers were taking advantage of.[114] When Paul speaks about the Christians in Macedonia (Thessalonica included) he

---

106. Best, *First and Second Epistles*, 176.
107. Evans, "Eschatology and Ethics."
108. Murphy-O'Connor, *St. Paul's Corinth*.
109. Russell, "Idle in 2 Thess," 111.
110. Malherbe, *Letters to the Thessalonians*, 64.
111. Murphy-O'Connor, *Paul*.
112. Hock, *Social Context of Paul's Ministry*, 31; Weima, *1–2 Thessalonians*, 29; Murphy-O'Connor, *Paul*, 72.
113. Murphy-O'Connor, *Paul*, 72.
114. Evans, "Eschatology and Ethics," 91–92.

mentions their "extreme poverty" and their giving which was "beyond their means" (2 Cor 8:2–3).[115] Also, the way Paul talks about his work as an artisan reveals that he was part of the working class (skilled or unskilled) of Thessalonica with whom he worked and preached the gospel.[116] We maintain that the Thessalonian Christians lived among the middle and lower class of society who received meagre income for their work.[117]

The Thessalonian economy experienced exponential growth during the first century.[118] This growth is supported by immigration from different areas including Rome: as well as mention of growth and beauty of the city, the massive building projects undertaken suggests an increase in the economic levels.[119] The location of the city between the port and Via Egnatia resulted in Thessalonica being a significant trading centre for food, mining products, timber, and other products sold in the Balkan Peninsula.[120] Consequently "The city became a focal point of east-west as well as north-south communications in the empire."[121] However, even though there was economic prosperity in the city, only a few elites had access to it; the Roman establishment favoured only a few, while a majority of the lower class languished in poverty.[122] The Thessalonian Christians, as Jewett puts it, "stemmed from this low level of society, witnessing the economic advancement of others, but participating in it only marginally themselves."[123]

The city of Thessalonica had professional associations; these include that of the purple dyers, muleteers, garland (wreath) makers, and gladiatorial school.

---

115. Miquez, *Practice of Hope*. However, as James Jeffers has noted the Thessalonians were not wholly destitute as they were able to give towards the Jerusalem collection. Jeffers, *Greco-Roman World*, 196.

116. Jewett, *Thessalonian Correspondence*. Many early Christians experienced "status inconsistency"; they were mostly mobile meaning they had the means to travel but were either slaves, women, artisans, traders who may have had wealth, but other factors diminished their overall status. Jeffers, *Greco Roman World*, 194.

117. Jeffers, *Greco-Roman World*, 194.

118. Rostovtzeff, *Social & Economic History*.

119. Jewett, *Thessalonian Correspondence*, 21.

120. Jewett, 21.

121. Jewett, 21.

122. Scheidel and Friesen, "Size of the Economy," 61; Meggitt, *Paul, Poverty*; Longenecker, *Remember the Poor*; Friesen, "Poverty in Pauline Studies", 343. The advantage with this taxonomy is that it has some level of differentiation. Friesen, "Poverty in Pauline Studies," 323–61.

123. Jewett, *Thessalonian Correspondence*, 122.

There were others that also doubled up as religious associations, including merchants, and those engaged in maritime activities, such as transportation and fishing.[124] Even though voluntary associations often attracted people from the lower social classes with just a few wealthy patrons, at Thessalonica, the situation was different; all social classes were well represented.[125] Some scholars have suggested that Paul converted a worker's guild, which was composed of mostly men.[126] It is likely that the guild in question could have been a leather guild, examples of which could be seen at Phrygia, Pisidia, and Lydia.[127] At the same time, to limit Paul's church only to the worker's guild is to go beyond what the evidence allows. Paul's church may have started with the guild, but it went on to attract other people who were not members of the guild.

In summary, Thessalonica was the principal city of the province of Macedonia. Its location on the Via Egnatia and its proximity to the harbour on the Thermaic Gulf ensured its prosperity. This city provided economic opportunities to its citizens and those who were attracted by its opulence. Even though the city had much wealth, it was concentrated in the hands of the few. Most of the Thessalonians lived below the poverty line; and it is among the majority that we find most of Paul's converts. Let us now discuss Paul's ministry in this city.

1.4.2 Paul's Ministry at Thessalonica

Having looked at the economic opportunities offered by the city, let us now turn to Paul's ministry at Thessalonica. We have two primary sources of this information; that is, Paul's Thessalonian letters, which constitute our primary source, and Acts of the Apostles, which is our secondary source. The way Paul established the church at Thessalonica is significant for this study, for his work is not only a mission strategy but also offered an example for his followers.

Paul was at Thessalonica between AD 49 and AD 50.[128] Luke reports that after his ministry in Philippi, Paul and his entourage came to Thessalonica

---

124. Nigdelis, "Voluntary Associations," 17–19; Ascough, "Of Memories and Meals," 49–72.

125. Ascough, "Of Memories and Meals," 50.

126. Ascough, 53.

127. Phrygia, Pisidia, and Lydia are locations where leather guilds were found. IGRR 907; I Pisidia 93; SEG XXIX, 1183; Witherington, *1 and 2 Thessalonians*, 37–38.

128. Murphy-O'Connor, *Paul*, 73.

"where there was a synagogue of the Jews" (Acts 17:2). According to Luke, visiting the synagogue was Paul's custom "and on three Sabbaths he reasons with them from the Scriptures" (Acts 17:2). Some scholars have concluded based on the phrase "on three Sabbaths" that Paul's ministry was conducted within the confines of three weeks.[129] This conclusion is unwarranted; Paul's ministry could have included in the words of Weima "a post synagogue ministry."[130] It is also possible that Paul could have worked even before he spoke in the synagogue. The invitation to address the synagogue gathering would have come after Paul interacted with some synagogue leaders who were convinced that he could address the audience on a Sabbath.[131] Paige estimates Paul's stay to have been in the range of two to six months and not three weeks.[132] There are several reasons that suggest that Paul stayed longer at Thessalonica. The reasons include the fact that sufficient time must be granted to allow for trips from Philippi since Paul says he received gifts from the church in Philippi at least more than once (Phil 4:16). In addition, Paul and his co-workers worked day and night to support themselves and mutual affection between Paul and his converts required time to develop. Paul also had ample time to set an example for his converts.[133]

The workshop was a conventional setting for discussing intellectual ideas.[134] As a result, Paul chose to work as a tentmaker (leather worker) which would assure him work consistently. Murphy-O'Connor has noted that Paul "would have been welcomed in any short-handed workshop. Paul had chosen to arm himself with a skill that virtually guaranteed him jobs on every road he walked and on every sea he sailed."[135] Furthermore, "The workshop provided Paul with an address, a stable base and a web of ready-made contacts deriving from his employer, the clients, and his fellow workers."[136] Paul, like Socrates in Simon the shoemaker's workshop, was "busy at tent making and busy at

---

129. Lake, *Text of the New Testament*; Lüdemann, *Paul*.

130. Weima, *1–2 Thessalonians*, 26.

131. Witherington, *1 and 2 Thessalonians*, 38–39.

132. Paige, *1 & 2 Thessalonians*, 33.

133. Richard, *First and Second Thessalonians*, 10; Malherbe, *Letters to the Thessalonians*, 60; Weima, *1–2 Thessalonians*, 26; Williams, *1 & 2 Thessalonians*, 4.

134. Hock, *Working Apostle*; Weima, *1–2 Thessalonians*, 29.

135. Murphy-O'Connor, *Paul*, 30.

136. Murphy-O'Connor, 73.

Background of the Study, Survey of Scholarship, and Methodology 21

preaching the gospel."[137] Paul mentions in his two letters how he worked with his own hands (1 Thess 2:9; 2 Thess 3:8).

Paul left the city rather abruptly because of Jewish opposition (Acts 17:10). His missionary work was not complete, and consequently he sent a messenger, Timothy, back to Thessalonica to check on his converts.[138] The report was somewhat ambivalent: on one hand they diffused the light of the gospel (1 Thess 1:6–8), but on the other, they seem to have misunderstood Paul's message about the eschaton.[139] As a result, some have "stopped working because they were convinced that they had enough to live on until Christ appeared in glory."[140] Some also worried about the status of those who had recently died,[141] their concern being that they have missed the coming of Christ.[142]

Many charlatans were up and about in the Roman empire "peddling their religious or philosophic wares"[143] and Paul has to remind the Thessalonians of his conduct while he was with them, how he and his companions worked day and night so as not to be a burden. In light of this, the Thessalonians are to live a "life worthy of God" (2:12).[144] Paul is at pains to differentiate his ministry from these charlatans. He makes use of the charlatans' language to differentiate his ministry from the Sophists who did many of the things he avoided. Paul specifically mentions that he did not use flattery, ill motives, and deception (δόλῳ), neither did he preach for glory (δόξαν) (1 Thess 2:1–12).[145] Elsewhere we have demonstrated that Paul's mission was cruciform ministry based on the example of Jesus including his willingness to do manual work.[146]

But why would Paul accept gifts from Philippi at the same time as he insisted on working while in Thessalonica and Corinth? For Murphy-O'Connor it was a missionary strategy: "He would accept financial aid from a community

---

137. Hock, *Working Apostle*, 450.
138. Bruce, "St Paul in Macedonia," 331.
139. Bruce, 332.
140. Murphy-O'Connor, *Paul*, 5.
141. Mitchell, "1 and 2 Thessalonians," 55.
142. Murphy-O'Connor, *Paul*, 90.
143. Bruce, *Paul and His Converts*.
144. See Bruce, *Paul and His Converts*.
145. Green, *Letters to the Thessalonians*, 118.
146. Mtukwa, "Paul's Cruciform Mission," 1–14.

only after he had departed, never while he was still present. Distance made the difference."¹⁴⁷ Also crucial for Paul was that the "Philippian gift represented a community effort."¹⁴⁸ It was not one individual supporting Paul as his client; all members of the church had participated, albeit in different proportions. This way Paul would not be indebted to any particular individual.¹⁴⁹ Paul's concern was that he would not become "the captive of the wealthy section of the community, to the detriment of the poorer members."¹⁵⁰ Paul's relationship with the Philippian church, which was a mutual partnership rather than a patron-client relationship, also influenced Paul's decision. It is evident here that Paul's strategy from the beginning promoted communal participation.¹⁵¹

In summary, Paul and his fellow workers came to Thessalonica to proclaim the good news of Jesus Christ. He stayed in the city longer than the three weeks mentioned in Acts of the Apostles. This would create time for him to work, provide an example for his followers, and receive a gift from Philippi. This gift was received from the community and was not an opportunity for individuals to show off. The workshop provided Paul with a launchpad for his ministry; as a result, the mission began among working artisans but was not limited to them. Paul differentiates his person and strategy from the charlatans who were motivated by money and glory. Paul's ministry was a cruciform ministry anchored on the example of Jesus Christ. Paul intended to create a community and the strategy he adopted advanced that goal.

1.4.3 Authorship, Audience, and Date of Writing

We have found that Paul's ministry in Thessalonica included work for multifaceted reasons. Let us now consider the questions of authorship, date, and audience of the Thessalonian correspondence. We intend to demonstrate that Paul penned the two letters to the Thessalonians. We shall demonstrate our theory of authorship to show why we believe Paul wrote the two letters. It is also assumed here that there is no substantial difference between the two letters in their concern for work and building of community.

---

147. Murphy-O'Connor, *Paul*, 94.
148. Murphy-O'Connor, 94.
149. Murphy-O'Connor, 178.
150. Murphy-O'Connor, 94.
151. Mtukwa, "Reconsideration of Self-Support," 90.

1.4.3.1 Authorship

Paul adopted a strategy used in his time when he wrote letters to his churches. The letters he wrote functioned as a "substitute for his presence within the community." Thus "the letter offered a scripted performance – Paul's words delivered orally by someone else who read what Paul's scribe had written."[152] As Paul wrote the letters to the Thessalonians, he continued a conversation that he had started when he made contact with the Thessalonians.[153] That Paul wrote 1 Thessalonians is widely acknowledged. Robert Jewett's comment is worth noting: "No one in the current scholarly debate doubts its authenticity."[154]

The same, however, cannot be said of 2 Thessalonians, particularly in recent history. Johannes E. C. Schmidt in 1801 was the first to question the Pauline authorship of 2 Thessalonians.[155] Scholars have questioned Pauline authorship primarily based on vocabulary, literary style, tone, and theology.[156] However, it has to be noted that no one doubted its authenticity as Pauline in the early church.[157] John A. Bailey represents those who question Pauline authorship based on tone; he writes "The tone of II Thessalonians is official and formal; instead of the 'we give thanks,' of 1 Thess i. 2, ii. 13, there is the 'we are bound to give thanks' of II Thess i. 3, ii. 13."[158] However, Malherbe has shown the supposed tone of 2 Thessalonians is not impersonal as is often suggested. The formal language could be explained by the new situation that has arisen in the church.[159] Even M. J. J. Menken, a proponent of pseudonymity, acknowledges that tone alone is not evidence enough to doubt Pauline authorship of 2 Thessalonians.[160] For Menken the argument is weighty only when it is considered alongside other arguments. One does not need to restrict an author like Paul to only one tone; certainly he is capable of having different tones just the same way people speak with different tones. As Weima

---

152. Friesen, "Second Thessalonians," 189–212.
153. Marxsen, *Der erste Brief an die Thessalonicher*.
154. Jewett, *Thessalonian Correspondence*; Weima, *1–2 Thessalonians*, 40; Kümmel, *Introduction*, 185.
155. Schmidt, "Vermuthungen," 380–86, cited in Friesen, "Second Thessalonians," 189.
156. Krentz, "2 Thessalonians," 515–25.
157. Weima, *1–2 Thessalonians*, 47.
158. Bailey, "Who Wrote II Thessalonians?," 131.
159. Malherbe, *Letters to the Thessalonians*, 367.
160. Menken, *2 Thessalonians*, 1994.

notes, "Paul was willing and ready to adapt his tone to fit better the specific historical context that he is addressing."[161] In this study, Pauline authorship is assumed but the thrust of our argument does not depend it.

1.4.3.2 *Audience*

Adolf von Harnack, based on the difference in tone, surmised the theory of separate recipients for the letters. It was suggested that 1 Thessalonians was written to a gentile congregation whereas 2 Thessalonians was written to the Jewish-Christian faction.[162] It is unlikely this was the case, since such a move would have encouraged factionalism, an argument proposed by Jewett.[163] Besides, as noted by Best, we do not have textual evidence to support this assertion. Harnack's suggestion is that the "loafers" are Jews.[164] This is unlikely, as there is no evidence of Jews anywhere neglecting work because of the day of the Lord. The prophets of Israel, like Isaiah, did not envision the end of work at the consummation of time; it is war which they saw ending and its tools becoming working tools. Besides, it is unthinkable that, as Best puts it, "Former Jews, whose culture laid great emphasis on the importance of work, would be less likely than Gentiles to abandon it."[165]

Martin Dibelius revised Harnack's separate recipients' proposal by suggesting that the first letter was written to the leaders at Thessalonica while 2 Thessalonians was written to the entire congregation. 1 Thessalonians 5:27 "to all the brethren" is cited as evidence.[166] E. Earle Ellis, on the other hand, suggests the reverse of what Dibelius suggested: for him, it is 2 Thessalonians which was addressed to the leaders, while 1 Thessalonians was written to the whole congregation.[167] It is not explained how Paul would have used the tone he did for his "trusted co-workers" and how they could have been the

---

161. Weima, *1–2 Thessalonians*, 49.
162. von Harnack, "Das Problem des zweiten Thessalonicherbriefs," 560–78; Jewett, *Thessalonian Correspondence*, 17.
163. Jewett, *Thessalonian Correspondence*.
164. Best, *First and Second Epistles*, 38–39.
165. Best, 39.
166. Dibelius, *An Die Thessalonicher I-II*, 1925.
167. Ellis, "Paul and His Co-Workers," 437–52.

disorderly ones.[168] Furthermore, there is no evidence in the letters to support the hypothesis of a different audience.[169]

It is unlikely that the problem of indolence described in 2 Thessalonians 3 would be a problem of the Jewish believers; rather, it seems to be a problem likely to be espoused by the Gentile believers.[170] Besides, there is no evidence of divisions in the church in terms of Jews and Gentiles at Thessalonica.[171] Given that Paul fought vigorously against divisions in the church between Jewish and Gentile Christians there is no reason to suppose he would promote factions and encourage them by writing separate letters.[172] Foster is right to state the lack of evidence: "There is no archaeological or textual evidence on which to postulate the existence of two ethnically segregated communities of believers in Jesus at Thessalonica in the first or second centuries (or beyond)."[173] We can conclude that the two letters were written to the church at Thessalonica rather than to a faction of the church. The church was comprised of both Jews and (majority) Gentiles.

1.4.3.3 *Date of Writing*

The question of date of writing is closely linked with the authorship question. 1 Thessalonians is generally accepted to have been written by Paul in AD 50 from Corinth.[174] The date of writing for 2 Thessalonians had been debated since its authorship was questioned. Those who accept the letter as Pauline date it as late AD 50 or early AD 51 Corinth. On the other hand, those who question its authenticity advocate for a later date. They consider the letter to be a forgery which was written by someone other than Paul after AD 70, about thirty to forty years after 1 Thessalonians.[175] Bailey is even more precise in that he dates 2 Thessalonians in the 90s, "the last decade of the first century."[176]

---

168. Jewett, *Thessalonian Correspondence*, 23.
169. Malherbe, *Letters to the Thessalonians*, 352.
170. Lucian, *Lucian*; Durant, *Story of Philosophy*; Aristotle, *Politics*, i, 2.
171. Jewett, *Thessalonian Correspondence*.
172. Best, *First and Second Epistles*, 39; Foster, "Who Wrote 2 Thessalonians?," 166.
173. Foster, "Who Wrote 2 Thessalonians?," 161.
174. Witherington III, *1 and 2 Thessalonians*, 10; Beale, *1–2 Thessalonians*, 14; Marshall, *1 and 2 Thessalonians*, 20–23; Furnish, *1 Thessalonians*, 30; Weima, *1–2 Thessalonians*, 38–39.
175. Best, *First and Second Epistles*, 58.
176. Bailey, "Who Wrote II Thessalonians?," 143.

However, one wonders why a supposed forger would write a letter with the same contents to the same community which received a genuine letter of Paul. It ought to be queried how the Thessalonians received such a letter. Byron asked, "How would they react to a previously unknown letter from Paul that suddenly surfaced after a significant delivery delay?"[177]

The other problem has to do with the *Sitz im Leben* the letter was written to address. How can a letter that was written thirty to forty years later address the same concerns (persecution, eschatology, and idle church members) as 1 Thessalonians?[178] Donfried succinctly captures the problem when he states that it is "difficult to imagine a setting where a letter specifically addressed to the Thessalonians by Paul would be relevant and convincing to a non-Thessalonian church some thirty or more years after the Apostle's death."[179] We can postulate that 2 Thessalonians was written about six to twelve months after the writing of the first letter which puts the dates in Autumn of AD 50 to Spring of AD 51. The place of writing would still be in Corinth.[180] We contend that the situation deteriorated between the writing of 1 Thessalonians and 2 Thessalonians, and as such a different response was required.[181]

1.4.3.4 Summary

In summary, the Thessalonian letters were written by Paul[182] to a church he had founded in the metropolis of Thessalonica. The letters were written sometime between AD 50 to AD 51. The recipients of these letters were a predominantly Gentile congregation and not a group of leaders as has been suggested by some scholars. If our contention is true, this means that Paul's work exhortations are applicable to each and every member of the congregation and not just to the leaders.

---

177. Byron, *1 and 2 Thessalonians*, 215–16.

178. Weima, *1-2 Thessalonians*, 53–55.

179. Donfried, *Paul, Thessalonica*, 66; Still, *Conflict at Thessalonica*, 58; Malherbe, *Letters to the Thessalonians*, 373–74; Witherington, *1 and 2 Thessalonians*, 11.

180. Paige, *1 & 2 Thessalonians*, 41; Jewett, *Thessalonian Correspondence*, 53–60; Malherbe, *Letters to the Thessalonians*, 350.

181. Malherbe, *Letters to the Thessalonians*, 351.

182. The results of this thesis are still valid even if 2 Thessalonians is considered Deutero-Pauline.

1.4.4 Conclusion

In conclusion, Paul wrote the two letters we call 1 and 2 Thessalonians from Corinth to the church he founded in the metropolis of Thessalonica. The city had a thriving economy, and it attracted various people who were seeking economic opportunities. All who needed work could find it. It also offered social groups with which one could identify. In addition, there were options in the religious arena. Paul's ministry began in a workshop among working artisans but grew beyond this group. Since Paul left town before he had finished nurturing his converts, he continued to socialize them through the two letters he writes to the Thessalonians. His converts are predominantly Gentile, with a few Jews. These people had faulty eschatological views and were taking advantage of Christian love within the community. Paul through his letters sought to correct this. In so doing we see him forming a community and demonstrating the importance of work in community building. Let us now consider the method we shall use for this study.

1.5 Methodology

The study will begin by looking at evidence of the relationship between work and community in traditional African society in order to generate a hypothesis on the extent to and ways in which work and community might be related. Our working hypothesis is that work can be shown to play a role in community formation. Following this, ancient texts, culminating in Paul's letter to the Thessalonians, will be addressed partly by historical-critical issues and partly by means of an African biblical hermeneutic (hereafter, ABH) in which the texts are read against "the contextual background of the present reader."[183] This approach is not being used in any way to advance the interpreter's "interests."[184] It allows us to interpret the biblical text "within the social, cultural, and religious contexts of Africa."[185] Furthermore, ABH "seeks to make a to and fro move from: reader – text – context (as in the traditional approaches) to new

---

183. Loba-Mkole, "Rise of Intercultural," 1350.
184. Oeming, *Contemporary Biblical Hermeneutics*, 7.
185. Nyiawung, "Contextualising Biblical Exegesis," 3–4.

context (Contextual text) – new reader (African reader)."[186] Our goal is to read the texts from a particular contextual background and thus gain fresh insights.

In ABH, the focus is on the reader; however, not in the sense that the reader brings meaning but, in the sense, that the reader can gain an understanding of the biblical text within their own social milieu. It is assumed in this study that meaning resides in the text and not with the reader, as is the case in the extreme forms of contextual approaches or reader-response criticism. The key is that social systems are indispensable for the African biblical interpretation since it uses "appropriate and relevant African contextual factors which are related to the realities of the African context in order to understand and interpret texts."[187] The social location of the "new" reader is important in this method; in addition, this study takes the social location of the original readers seriously. It is assumed here that unless we can understand what the text meant to the original readers; we cannot understand what it means to the new reader.[188]

A criticism levelled against ABH, as with all contextual approaches, is that it "does not necessarily address issues from a universal standpoint."[189] From this perspective, the method is seen as a subjective method with no consideration for objectivity. Yet it must be noted that no approach can be absolved from this criticism since every interpreter approaches the text from where they are situated, irrespective of one's awareness. As Nyiawung asserts, "the gospel is universal, yet its application is contextual."[190] Many African readers believe that the Bible is a record of God's self-disclosure to humanity; however, that message has been transmitted with the aid of the Jewish culture set in a different time in history.[191] ABH has the advantage of being intercultural; in other words, other cultures have a contribution to make to the interpretive process.[192]

---

186. Nyiawung, 3–4.
187. Nyiawung, 3–4; Manus, *Intercultural Hermeneutics*, 11.
188. Contra Nyiawung, "Contextualising Biblical Exegesis," 5.
189. Nyiawung, "Contextualising Biblical Exegesis"; Gunn, "Narrative Criticism," 226.
190. Nyiawung, "Contextualising Biblical," 8.
191. Obeng, *African Anthroponymy*, 22.
192. Manus, *Intercultural Hermeneutics*, 34.

ABH is related to intercultural exegesis, which is a "constructive exegesis dialogue between an original biblical culture and that of a receptive audience."[193] Intercultural biblical hermeneutics ensures that the "African context and the African people are not merely regarded as a field to apply exegetical conclusions, but they stand as the subject of interpretation, equipped with genuine epistemological privilege."[194] Even though culture is a human product, it is still the amphitheatre of God's revelation and as Kabiru wa Gatimu notes "the Bible is not, culturally and ideologically, an innocent text. Though it is the word of God, it is also expressed in human language, culture and worldview that inevitably generate diverse interpretations."[195]

A word needs to be said about our use of the term African context or worldview. Some might object given that Africa is a massive continent with different cultures and people groups. As Edward W. Fashole Luke notes about Africa it "presents pictures of diversity, unity and variety . . . precisely because Africa has a rich and varied complexity of cultural, economic, political, linguistic, social and religious ideas, practices and rites."[196] Indeed Africa does not have "an identical culture" and "it brings together rich and diverse, but related cultures and worldview."[197] Still, in John Mbiti's opinion when one examines the thinking or the philosophy behind the different religious beliefs and practices, they are confronted with the same philosophy which, in his words, is nothing other than "philosophy in the singular."[198] J. V. Taylor had long noted that in Africa there is a "basic world-view which is fundamentally the same."[199] Ruel B. Khoza following Edward Blyden has noted that Africans "have special distinctive modes of behaviour, expression and spiritual self-fulfilment."[200]

The African worldview is the context that provides the lenses through which the author of this study reads the text. The concept of community is an integral part of this worldview. Having taken the world behind the text, the

---

193. Loba-Mkole, "Rise of Intercultural," 1359.
194. Loba-Mkole, 1362.
195. Gatumu, *Pauline Concept*, 8–9.
196. Gatumu, 8–9.
197. Gatumu, 8–9.
198. Mbiti, *African Religions*, 1–2.
199. Gatumu, *Pauline Concept*, 8–9.
200. Khoza, *Attuned Leadership*, 312.

world within the text seriously, we will also take the world seriously in front of the text, that is the world of the reader. It emerges that traditional African society has a close affinity to the biblical text. In his book, *Africa's Roots in God*, Yankson affirms the similarity between ancient Israelite and African cultures. He writes concerning the Akans of Ghana, "Since the Akan people have kept their ancient Mesopotamian culture [Babylonian] intact, it will be helpful to interpret Biblical culture through African eyes instead of seeing them through European eyes."[201] Similarly, Gerlinde Baumann has pointed to the possibility of equivalences between the ancient Egyptian concept of *Maat*, the Old Testament deed-consequence nexus, with *Ubuntu*.[202] Even though Paul does not share the same worldview with ancient Egypt, to a great extent even the communal worldview of the New Testament relates to the African context.

The ideas of kinship and *Ubuntu* cannot be ignored in any contextual analysis in the African context. Such ideas lend themselves to the communal readings of the text such as this study is attempting. As Louis Jonker has noted concerning the communal approach, it "provides the opportunity of discovering how the hermeneutical and exegetical contributions from our own contexts enrich the (what one could call) communion of biblical interpretation."[203] The benefit of such an approach is that it will "eradicate the individualistic and exclusivist tendencies in biblical scholarship."[204] This then is not another hermeneutic but a hermeneutical outlook which pays attention to all other exegetical methods and tools.[205]

In addition, Paul's teaching on his work and that of the Thessalonians will be investigated using historical-critical methods.[206] ABH is not opposed to proper biblical exegesis but rather it makes use of "people's culture and life experiences as complementary to conventional critical tools of biblical exegesis."[207] Historical-critical methods will help us to look at the text as we

---

201. Yankson, *Africa's Roots*.
202. Baumann, "Ancient Egyptian Ma'at," 1–4.
203. Jonker, "Towards a 'Communal' Approach," 79.
204. Jonker, 83.
205. Jonker, 83.
206. Chang, *Community*, 25. Chang has successfully made use of this method in 2 Corinthians.
207. Gatumu, *Pauline Concept*, 8–9.

have it, to understand the historical situation addressed particularly in its setting in the Greco-Roman world, and what might Paul's message be to the implied readers.

We will situate Paul within three identities; that as a Jew, as a Greco-Roman, and as a follower of Jesus.[208] Ben Witherington III sees Paul's identities saying he was "a Jew, he was a Roman citizen, and he was a Christian."[209] Rather than see Paul only as influenced by one world, we will take each of these worlds seriously and demonstrate that all Paul's worlds influenced him. However, we are cognizant of the fact that no single identity can be the basis for understanding Paul and even when the three are put together, a lot more remains impenetrable.[210] Paul's Christian identity is often neglected when scholars speak of Paul's worlds. As Morna Hooker notes, it was his "encounter with the risen Christ, which made him rethink many of his assumptions."[211] In this study, we affirm that Paul was a follower of Christ and that his message was "the gospel of Christ" and "his mission is to be an apostle." As such his ethical message corresponds to both his "message and mission."[212]

From the Jewish texts, we shall consider the Dead Sea Scrolls and the Qumran community as a background to our reading of the Thessalonian correspondence. This research assumes the link between the Dead Sea Scrolls and the Qumran community. We are cognizant of the fact that this connection is contested.[213] We are in support of the scholars who see a connection between the scrolls and the Qumran community. Even though we see a connection between the scrolls and the Qumran Community, we are aware that Qumran represented only part of the larger movement called Essenes.[214] We shall look at how the Dead Sea Scrolls and the Qumran community relate work and community. The Qumran scrolls and community provide a Jewish attempt at forming a community that shares life together. As such it provides the closest parallel to the house churches that Paul formed across the Mediterranean.

---

208. Furnish, *Theology and Ethics*.
209. Witherington III, *Paul Quest*, 52–53. He says this in the chapter in which he discusses the "The Trinity of Paul's Identity."
210. Witherington, *Paul Quest*, 87.
211. Hooker, *Paul*, 38.
212. Furnish, *Theology and Ethics*, 50.
213. Knibb, *Qumran Community*.
214. Collins, *Beyond the Qumran Community*, 59.

As for the Greco-Roman perspective, we shall look at how various Greco-Roman writers perceived work either positively or negatively. After that, we shall look at the relationship between work and community in the household, philosophical school – Epicurean – and voluntary associations. In comparing the biblical text, we shall ensure that we do not engage in what Samuel Sandmel termed "parallelomania," which is the tendency to see parallels and immediately "proceed to describe source and derivation as if implying literary connection flowing in an inevitable or predetermined direction."[215] As to how Paul's writings should be compared to the works of rabbinic Judaism, Richard B. Hays, following Philip Alexander, suggests that, "it is more valid methodologically to use Paul as a background source for the study of rabbinic traditions than vice versa."[216] Rabbinic Judaism, early Christianity, Qumran Community, and Philo's writings represent, "adaptations of the religious cultural heritage represented by Israel's Scripture."[217]

Adolf Deissmann's distinction between analogical and genealogical similarity is helpful. He sees analogical as those predicated on the same religious experiences and based on the universality of the human psyche, whereas genealogical are those of dependence, in which case there is borrowing from one source to another.[218] More recently Atsuhiro Asano has fruitfully used the Japanese group to understand community identity in the book of Galatians.[219] The value of our comparators lies in the fact that Paul is a product of both the Jewish worldview and the Greco-Roman worldview. The data from associations will be heuristically applied to early Christian communities.[220]

1.6 Suggested Contribution to Knowledge

This African reading will prove fruitful with its communal perspective. We will read the Pauline work exhortation using African biblical hermeneutics.

---

215. Sandmel, *Parallelomania*, 1.
216. Hays, *Echoes of Scripture*, 11.
217. Hays, 11.
218. Huttunen, *Paul and Epictetus*.
219. See Asano, *Community-Identity Construction*.
220. We agree with Kloppenborg who poignantly asserts that "To employ data from ancient associations heuristically avoids a long and perhaps pointless debate as to whether Christ groups were associations, or extensions of synagogues, or extended households." Kloppenborg, "Membership Practices," 188.

This research will demonstrate that Paul sees work as more than just instrumental – that is, merely to provide one's physical needs. Rather, Paul sees a significant role for work in the formation of the people of God. Whereas most studies focus on social and economic problems in the community that require people to work, our focus here is the value of work for the community becoming the people of God.

Unlike earlier studies that focused on Paul's influences for his practice of work, this study concentrates on the rhetoric of Paul's exhortations on work to see what role he envisions for work in community formation. Once we see the role work plays in the Christian community, the role of individual contribution to communal life will become clear. The study demonstrates that Paul's understanding of work contributes to forming a community into the image of the holy God whose work is constitutive of his character as revealed in Christ. Since this study reads both 1 and 2 Thessalonians together, another potential contribution lies in helping us to read Paul's letters together as letters penned by Paul a few months after each other.

1.7 Limitations of the Study

This is an African reading; this approach to the text is not a study on various kinds of work but work in general. The study will not discuss what form of work is appropriate for the people of God, but will simply bracket work as any meaningful work that promotes overall well-being for the one working and the community. The study will build upon Paul's theology as reflected in his writings; however, its primary focus is the Thessalonian correspondence. The study is not a theology of work per se. It concentrates on the role of work in community formation. Paul has much to say about work in his other letters, but this study only focuses on the two epistles to the Thessalonians. We believe that focusing on the two letters helps us see the place of work in community formation within a particular Christian community. Since 1 and 2 Thessalonians have the largest concentration of sayings about work, we have deemed it necessary to focus on the two letters.

1.8 Working Definitions

It is critical that we define what we mean by work. Pope John Paul II in his *Laborem Exercens* defines work as "any activity by man, whether manual or intellectual, whatever its nature or circumstance."[221] Clearly, this definition is too broad and does not separate work from all other activities.[222] Everything is absorbed as work; a broad definition like this will not help us. Witherington defines work as "any necessary and meaningful task that God calls and gifts a person to do and which can be undertaken to the glory of God and for the edification and aid of human beings, being inspired by the Spirit and foreshadowing the realities of the new creation."[223] This definition separates work from activities that are done for leisure since work is seen here as "necessary and meaningful." However, it is limited in the sense that it does not include other creatures; it only sees God and other human beings as recipients of work.

Volf defines work as follows:

> Work is honest, purposeful, and methodologically specified social activity whose primary goal is the creation of products or states of affairs that can satisfy the needs of working individuals or their co-creatures, or (if primarily an end in itself) activity that is necessary in order for acting individuals to satisfy their needs apart from the need for the activity itself.[224]

This definition is specific in that it mentions that in work there is the creation of products and we can also add services since in offering services people work. The needs Volf has in mind include those of our co-creatures (human and non-human) – hence work is socially responsible.[225] It is interesting to note that Volf speaks about the Spirit in his theology of work, but he does not say that in his definition something which Witherington does. We shall define work as follows: Work is a purposeful communal activity done in the power of the Spirit by God's people to honour God and for the benefit of the worker and their co-creatures. This definition resonates with the African perspective in that it recognizes work as a communal activity.

---

221. Pope John Paul II, *On Human Work*.
222. Volf, *Work in the Spirit*, 7.
223. Witherington III, *Work*.
224. Volf, *Work in the Spirit*, 7.
225. Volf, 7.

It is also essential that we define what we mean by community. Much goes under the banner of community. Ferdinand Tonnie's distinction between "community" (*Gemeinschaft*) and "society" (*Gesellschaft*) is helpful.[226] Our concern is not with *Gesellschaft* but with *Gemeinschaft*. The εκκλῆσια which is the assembly of the people of God that remains an assembly regardless of being gathered together or dispersed is a community (*Gemeinschaft*). The members of the community are linked with each other in and outside their meeting by way of "reciprocal social interaction."[227]

Reciprocal interaction is a *sine qua non* for any would be community. Yet a Christian community is not just about reciprocal human relationship but is first and foremost participation in divine grace. Such a community is a real fellowship (κοινονία) in which "God's revelation is cruciform, [so] the life of the apostle and the ethos and identity of the community are to be cruciform also."[228] Unlike human communities that are established by "social engineering," like the Epicurean community, the Christian community is a "matter of participation in divine love in the power of the Spirit and testifying of that love and power to others."[229] The divine love in the community is the basis for participation which is "a mode of being together with others" which results in something totally new.[230] As such, "A community thus becomes the ongoing repository, as it were, of the participation of those who have constituted and who presently constitute it."[231] In a real community, an individual does not lose oneself in the group but participates as an individual who is enriched through participation in the life of the community.[232] This, however, is often a critique against the African concept of community. Consequently, when society becomes a community, "participants act spontaneously in accord with others in imaginative ways to satisfy common needs and realize common purposes."[233]

---

226. Schwartz, "Chinese Culture," 117.
227. Stegemann and Stegemann, *Jesus Movement*, 264.
228. Barton, "Christian Community," 3.
229. Barton, 3.
230. Deutsch, "Community as Ritual," 22.
231. Deutsch, 22.
232. Deutsch, 23.
233. Deutsch, 24.

1.9 Outline of the Study

The first chapter of this study looks at the thesis statement, the research question, the rationale of the study, the methodology of the study, limitation and scope, outline and the survey of scholarship. Chapter 2 examines the background of the traditional African society to expose the context in which the Pauline view of work and community is being investigated. Here we explore ideas of African worldview – kinship, *Ubuntu*, God and ancestors, age sets, work parties and community, and work in the household – and we conclude the chapter by responding to the critique levelled at the idea of kinship. Chapter 3 of the study presents the Jewish texts on work and community with particular reference to the Dead Sea Scrolls and Qumran community. Chapter 4 discusses the Greco-Roman perspective on work and community, beginning by looking at perceptions of work and then looking at the household and the voluntary associations as an example of particular communities querying what role work plays in community formation.

Chapter 5 looks at 1 Thessalonians with particular reference to 1 Thessalonians 2:8–9, the work of the apostles, and the beginning of community life at Thessalonica. Then the chapter considers 1 Thessalonians 4:9–12, which juxtaposes brotherly love, work, and community. Finally, the chapter addresses 1 Thessalonians 5:12–14 and work in the service of the community. Chapter 6 is devoted to 2 Thessalonians 3:6–15: its literary context; the problem of walking ατάκτως; Paul as community paradigm (2 Thess 3:7–9); Paul's διδαχή on work and eating (2 Thess 3:10); Paul's paradigm and its application (2 Thess 3:11–12); and discipline on account of refusing to work (2 Thess 3:13–15). Chapter 7 concludes the work with summary, conclusions, and recommendations for further research.

CHAPTER 2

Work and Community in African Worldview

2.1 Introduction

Having set the context for our study, let us now look at the relationship between work and community in African worldview. The African context will help us frame the question we need to ask of the text (Thessalonian correspondence) as well as state our hypothesis. The hypothesis for this study is that there is a relationship between work and community. This relationship can be seen in either the actual work that is done together or the results of work that are used to bring people together. We shall investigate an African understanding of God, ancestors, kinship, and *Ubuntu* to see if there is a connection between work and community, with particular reference to the Shona, Kikuyu, Luo, Zulu, Ibo, and Yoruba speaking people. The idea of work parties (invitations to share work, food, dance, and music by people of the same age set) is of interest in this study since in it we see the coming together of community to work and accomplish a particular task. We are also interested in traditional African attitudes towards work. This analysis of the African context is integral to African biblical hermeneutics; the context in which the Bible is to be interpreted must be understood adequately.

2.2 African Worldview or Worldviews?

Africa is a diverse continent consisting of diverse people groups with different traditions. The question arises, should we say African worldview or African worldviews? Worldview is defined here as "a set of presuppositions . . . which we hold . . . about the makeup of our world."[1] We can speak of a single African worldview that most Africans especially those who live south of the Sahara share.[2] Such a worldview is different from say Western or Asiatic worldviews. As Dumisani Thabede has rightly noted, "The world is differently defined in different places."[3] The Afrocentric worldview has its origin in the philosophical underpinnings of traditional Africa.[4] Even though the influences of colonization by Europeans and Arabs have had an impact on this worldview, "the philosophical integrity of traditional Africa has survived among continental Africans."[5]

There are elements that can be identified as core of the African worldview. Among such concepts are "life, person and community."[6] Africans generally believe in the unity of all things – human beings, plants, animals, stars, moon, and everything else.[7] Van der Walt supports this view when he states "They [Africans] do not face the world objectively and at a distance but live in it. No objects exist outside reality. They touch and are attuned to things and the earth. They experience everything intensely and are part of everything."[8] As such all aspects of reality are interrelated, that is art, religion, politics, economics, and family life.[9] Religion functions primarily in terms of helping

---

1. Sire, *Discipleship of the Mind*, 30.

2. Van der Walt, *Afrocentric*; E. Fuller Torrey, *Witchdoctors and Psychiatrists*; Kamalu, *Foundations of African Thought*; Gyekye, *Essay on African Philosophical Thought*.

3. Thabede, "African Worldview," 235.

4. Thabede, 235.

5. Thabede, 235. For the critics who claim that Africa is diverse with various tribes even in the same country, Thebede responds that these arguments are often not used on Europeans who have different ethnic groups and yet people still refer to them as the West or Western civilization. He further notes "when it comes to African culture, and minor differences are used to divide Africans, while the same differences in other groups are ignored in favour of unifying factors." Thabede, "African Worldview," 237.

6. Sindima, *Africa's Agenda*, 198.

7. Moyo, "Material Things," 50.

8. Van der Walt, *Afrocentric*, 89. The same view is supported by Tempels, *Bantu Philosophy*; see also Kenyatta, *Facing Mount Kenya*, 74.

9. Ferkiss, *Africa's Search for Identity*, 36; Mwikamba, "Search of an African Identity," 9.

people have access to earthly possessions (life, health, power, and wealth) and also maintaining social harmony and order.[10] John Mbiti rightly noted that Africans are "notoriously religious" and for them "religion permeates all the dimensions of life."[11] Having given the justification of a single African worldview, we are now ready to discuss God and ancestors in the African context.

2.3 God and Ancestors in the African Context

People always shape themselves after the gods they worship.[12] In this section, we would like to investigate how the work of God and ancestors is expressed. Africans acknowledge in their creation stories that God is indeed a creator.[13] God's most notable work is that of making or creating the world. Speaking of the Akamba's understanding of the work of God in creation Mbiti asserts that "God first creates, originates, moulds and makes; then He gives shape, supplies details and adds distinctiveness and character."[14] God's work of creation is not only true of the Akamba but of most African communities; for them, God is known as the one who moulds.[15] The Yoruba God *Olodumare* delegates the creation of the world to lesser divinities *Orisa-nla* or *Obatala*.[16] Unlike in Mesopotamian creation myths where the gods delegate because they do not want to work,[17] for the Yoruba it is done so that each and every entity participates in the work that is being done. Even where God delegates, he still oversees the work done. These lesser divinities are said to be in the "ontological category of spirits" according to Mbiti.[18]

God's work of creation is not done once and for all; there is a sense in which it continues throughout the universe. For instance, the Twi of Ghana hold that "God never ceases to create things."[19] However, it is not only in

---

10. Parratt, *Reader in African Christian Theology*, 60.
11. Mbiti, *African Religions*, 1.
12. Beale, *We Become*, 12.
13. Mbiti, *African Religions*, 38.
14. Mbiti, 38.
15. Aringo, "Work in the Old Testament," 172.
16. Ferdinando, *Triumph of Christ*, 28; Ilogu, *Christianity and Ibo Culture*, 169.
17. Hallo and Younger, "Epic of Creation"; Wenham, *Rethinking Genesis*, 8.
18. Mbiti, *African Religions*, 76–78.
19. Mbiti, 38.

creation that God's work is seen: rather, his work continues in the area of providence among most African communities. God is known to be the one who provides daily needs for people. Even though people must work to provide for their daily needs, God is somehow involved in ensuring that there is food. Mbiti is right to note that "He provides life, fertility, rain, health, and other necessities needed for sustaining creation"; however, Mbiti is wrong in saying that God works "entirely independent of man."[20] Humanity is required to work, and God ensures that work is productive. Human beings, of course, cannot take credit for what God has done since all that happens is done by God albeit through humans.

This aspect is most evident in hunting, especially among the Ila, Zulu, Ndebele, Shonas, and others, where the hunters have to go hunt but God is seen as the one who brings the animal to be killed.[21] Even Mbiti acknowledges that among the Acholi, Kakwa, and Tiv, God is the one who taught the first human beings how to make a living by cultivating the land, cooking food, and preparing beer.[22] Keith Ferdinando has noted that "it is through them [humans] that harmony is accordingly sought and maintained with the natural environment."[23] Each entity (God included) is expected to play its part in ensuring the equilibrium of the world.[24] The African worldview is one with the Hebrew tradition is seeing God as a worker.[25]

God is not the only one who works in African myths; ancestors also have work to do. Ancestors play an important role in traditional African thinking. In most African communities – the Yoruba, Kikuyu, Shona, and Zulu – ancestors are those who have lived a good life, have had children and lived up to a good old age. The ancestors do not merely rest among their fathers (contra Hebrew tradition) but are expected to continue to contribute in some way to the community.[26] D. B. Barrett has highlighted some of the roles of the ancestor when he says "The ancestor-cult . . . represents the hierarchical

---

20. Mbiti, 38.
21. Mbiti, 45.
22. Mbiti, 94.
23. Ferdinando, *Triumph of Christ*, 32.
24. Ferdinando, 37.
25. Adamo, *Explorations*, 86.
26. Ferdinando, *Triumph of Christ*, 33; Fortes and Goody, *Religion, Morality*, 76–77; Ilogu, *Christianity and Ibo Culture*, 187.

social system carried into the spirit world; it validates the traditional political structure; it ensures fertility, health, prosperity, and the continuity of past and future in family life; it is a sanction for the respect of the living elders."[27] Besides, the ancestors play a significant role in the maintenance of harmony, and they work for the welfare of their community to which "they belonged and still belong."[28] Their most prominent role is to "solidify and mystically bind together the whole family."[29] In return for their service the ancestors are given food and libations as "tokens of the fellowship, communion, remembrance, respect and hospitality, being extended to those who are the immediate pillars or roots of the family."[30] It follows that every member of the African community has a responsibility to the community of which they are a part.

A few African communities hold that in the original state of man there was no need to work since humankind at that time did not eat or drink.[31] The natural outcome of this is that when the state of blessedness ended, food was introduced and work then came with it. In this sense, work is not original with creation. However, only a few tribes (Bambuti, Tswana, Fajulu) have creation myths that indicate this scenario. Most, like the Ashanti and Yoruba, indicate that it is actually labour (pounding *fufu*/yam for the Yoruba) that drove God into the heavens. It is said that two women were busy pounding and their stick went too high into the air, and God was pushed further into the sky.[32] The Zulu believe that it is God who instructed them to work the farm from the beginning when he said: "Let there be men and let them cultivate food and eat!"[33] In some tribes like the Acholi, it was God who taught the first humans all that they needed to live including cultivating the fields, cooking food, and making beer.[34]

In summary, most creation myths of the African people speak of God working – that is, creating the world and also sustaining it. In addition to God, ancestors also have work to do. Becoming ancestors is not escaping

---

27. Barrett, *Schism and Renewal*, 120.
28. Ferdinando, *Triumph of Christ*, 34; Mbiti, *African Religions*, 104.
29. Mbiti, *African Religions*, 105.
30. Mbiti, 105.
31. Mbiti, 94.
32. Mbiti, 94; Adamo, *Explorations*, 86.
33. Mbiti, *African Religions*, 94.
34. Mbiti, 95.

work, it is instead to continue to labour for the human community. Some African tribes perceive work as originating at creation; others consider it to be a later introduction. Regardless of their place of work, they all understand that work is now part of what it means to be human, ancestor, and God. As such, no one is exempt from work. Having discussed God and ancestors in the African tradition, we are now ready to discuss the African kinship idea, which undergirds social relations among Africans.

2.4 African Idea of Community

Community in Africa is defined as "the willingness of human beings to belong to one another in love."[35] The community is essential in traditional African thinking. Life is unthinkable outside of the community.[36] John Mbiti has eloquently summarized the African thinking when he says "I am, because we are; and since we are, therefore, I am."[37] The Zulu of South Africa convey this idea when they say *Umuntu ngumuntu ngabantu*. This means "a person is a person by or through other people."[38] In other words "African existence is existence in community, and apart from one's community, one is a non-entity."[39] The individual identity is wrapped up in that of the community, and there cannot be an individual without the community and the community without the individual.[40] As Magesa notes "his or her well-being can be assured only in the context of the well-being of the community."[41] However, Benezet Bujo is right in asserting that "It is not membership in a community as such that constitutes identity: only common action makes the human person a human person and keeps him from becoming an 'unfettered ego.'"[42] As such, one becomes human only in solidarity with the community in performing good things and inversely they become non-human in performing harmful

---

35. Shorter, *African Christian Spirituality*, 27.
36. Moyo, "Material Things," 53; Kirwen, *Missionary and the Diviner*, 72.
37. Mbiti, *African Religions*, 105.
38. Kunene, *Communal Holiness*, 142–43. Shona "munhu munhu nevanhu" Kikamba "mundu ni andu" Swahili "mtu ni watu".
39. Moyo, "Material Things," 52.
40. Sindima, *Africa's Agenda*, 195; Oduyoye, "Value of African Religious Beliefs," 110–11.
41. Magesa, *African Religion*, 279.
42. Bujo, *Foundations*, 115.

things.[43] This is clear in a Baganda proverb which says "A lazy person kills the whole community."[44]

Those who desire to be alone are often shunned and looked upon suspiciously. People consider themselves a part of a group and to isolate oneself is evil of the highest proportions, which is only commensurate with being a witch[45] – those perceived to cause misfortune and calamity.[46] Edmund Ilogu reports that among the Ibos "group life with its web of social life is very strong, and the ties of relationship far spread, and the pattern of life is communalistic."[47] This sense of community is known by various African words such as *Ubuntu* in Nguni, *Utu* in Swahili, *Unhu* in Shona, and *Umundu* in Kikuyu. Leonard Tumaini Chuwa notes "The word is found in most Bantu languages and shares the same construction, or same root, or same phonetics, or the same concept."[48] The idea of *Ubuntu* conveys goodness, the moral ideal that is displayed by the person with *Ubuntu*.[49] The values associated with *Unhu* include "group solidarity, conformity, compassion, respect, human dignity, and collective unity."[50] The concept of *Ubuntu* "places great importance on working for the common good."[51] Individuals within the community have obligations that they must fulfil, just as the community has obligations to the individual. We now turn to the discussion of the individual and communal obligations.

2.5 Individual and Community Obligations

In Africa the community expects the individuals to do their obligations to others within the kinship group. Such kinship obligations control "the behaviour, thinking and whole life of the individual in the society of which he

---

43. Bujo, 115.
44. Bujo, 115–16.
45. Ferdinando, *Triumph of Christ*, 23.
46. Währisch-Oblau and Wrogemann, *Witchcraft*, 19.
47. Ilogu, *Christianity and Ibo Culture*, 24.
48. Chuwa, *African Indigenous Ethics*, 12.
49. Gelfand, *Genuine Shona*, 140. He also notes for the Shonas "A person with *unhu* behaves in a good way, respects his parents and sets a good example. He shows respect to a stranger, particularly one older than himself." Gelfand, *Genuine Shona*, 39
50. Kunene, *Communal Holiness*, 148; Broodryk, *Ubuntu*, 26.
51. Khoza, *Attuned Leadership*, 317.

is a member."[52] The individual is not only conscious of themselves in the group, but also learns of his "duties, his privileges and responsibilities toward himself and towards other people . . . Whatever happens to the individual happens to the whole group, and whatever happens to the whole group happens to the individual."[53] Being a member of the clan provides "closer human cooperation" especially in times of great need.[54] African traditional community functioned as a mutual society in which human behaviour was linked to human need. As such, members of the community were moved by human need.[55]

A young man looks forward to a time when he can leave his father's house and establish his own house with his wife and start a new family. Among the Shona, the word *kusununguka* (freedom) is used for such a person. In a sense, one is not totally free when dependent on one's parent. A similar word *kugarika* (to be at peace) is also relevant here; for one who is settled and prosperous, having all that one requires for survival is one who is at peace.[56] Gelfand is right to equate *kugarika* with the concept in Greek philosophy of "freedom from want."[57] Even though parents provide help for a young man to get a wife and possibly a plot of land, the individual has a part to play to make his own home. His responsibility includes building a house, which the new family will call home. Under normal circumstances he cannot go back to his mother's house to get food; he has to acquire his own food and feed his family.[58] As Bujo has noted, "One cannot expect everything from the community, for each has his own work to do."[59]

The Swahili convey this belief when they say "if you want to have peanuts, get yourself a roasting pan."[60] The Baganda say "You cannot quench your thirst with water for which you have gone begging."[61] For most African communities, one who can work for self but continually begs, cannot attain

---

52. Mbiti, *African Religions*, 102.
53. Mbiti, 106.
54. Mbiti, 104.
55. Shorter, *African Christian*, 27.
56. Gelfand, *Genuine Shona*, 142–43.
57. Gelfand, 143.
58. Kenyatta, *Facing Mount Kenya*, 34.
59. Bujo, *Foundations*, 121.
60. Bujo, 120.
61. Bujo, 120.

the status of adulthood and therefore cannot start a family.[62] Even if these things are done for oneself, they relieve the community from having to take care of someone who should take care of themselves. As such the first obligation one must fulfil is that of providing for oneself. And, one does not only provide for oneself but for members of the community who cannot provide for themselves. Africans understand that their labour should be useful to the community, as noted by Sindima:

> In traditional society production for its own sake is an alien idea; neither does it make sense to enjoy the fruits of one's labour all by oneself. While sharing presupposes production, it is not a mere function of production, but rather the opposite: production emerges from the fact of sharing. Everyone works to share the fruits of labour with others. Every uncorrupted [not westernized] African works not for him or herself but to assist parents, friends, and others.[63]

All African communities not only encourage but require that individuals share their belongings with members of their community. They believe that what one has comes from God through the ancestors and as such, they expect each person so endowed to share with those in need. One can detect a cycle of sharing starting with the supreme God, to the living dead (ancestors), to the living individuals, and finally to the needy. To hold on to things tightly is considered anti-social and such behaviour is consistent with a witch or wizard.[64] The Shona have a saying that states that *ukama igasva hunozadziswa nokudya* ("relationships are fulfilled by sharing food"). This means that if one is genuinely related, then they must share with their relatives. The other side of this is that this makes those who are not members of one's kinship group non-persons. As such one can do harm to those who are not of his kinship group and such actions are considered honourable.[65] Those with access to

---

62. Bujo, 120.
63. Sindima, *Africa's Agenda*, 202–23.
64. Moyo, "Material Things," 52.
65. A. E. Ojie has noted that "the pervasiveness and ubiquity of ethnicity has profoundly disenabled the realization of the ideal democratic ethos in Nigeria. Panaceas were advanced as the curative for the conflict-ridden and nebulous political atmosphere," in Ojie, "Democracy, Ethnicity," 546–69; Sithole, "Class and Factionalism," 117; Mafeje, "Ideology of 'Tribalism,'" 261; Mulinge and Lesetedi, "Corruption in Sub-Saharan Africa," 56.

public resources can take them and use them to benefit their kin and often this is seen as an honourable thing.[66] As A. E. Ojie has noted "The elite ethnic bigots are determined in the perpetuation of sectarian politics [fuelled by tribalism] in order to cling to power for the purpose of the disbursement of the national cake and personal aggrandizement."[67] This serves to indicate that by no means is the African idea of community perfect; however, its positive aspects can fruitfully be used and the concept can be broadened by the gospel of Christ. Ruel J. Khoza is right to note that the African community (*Ubuntu*) is "an ideal conception, towards which we should strive rather than a state of affairs that exists already. Human weakness makes it impossible to realize the utopian state of the ideal community."[68]

It is not just the individual with obligations to the community, but the community has obligations to the individual. The chief in most agrarian African societies would ensure that every adult had a place to build a home and to grow their crops.[69] This is the reason that among the Shona people as in other tribes, one may not refer to his property as "my land" (*Munda wangu*) but as "our land" (*Munda wedu*). The possessive pronoun is always plural rather than singular.[70] Since the land is given, one does not own it, yet they can use it on behalf of the community. This was the first way to ensure that everyone's needs were met. Those who became poor for one reason or another were supposed to be cared for by the well to do. The chief also had a responsibility to provide for the poor especially from the gifts that people gave him for deciding on their cases. When a chief is given tribute (cattle, grain, or labour) he receives it on behalf of the community, in other words the tribute "functions as a system of redistribution of the community's resources. In a time of need, every community member has a claim to them."[71] This does not in any way suggest that every chief always acted in accordance to this ideal.[72]

---

66. For a treatment of Corruption in Mozambique see Chambo, "Metadidonai as Ethical," 165, 187. Chambo makes the case that colonialism and the subsequent struggle for liberation had an impact on the social structure of the African people in Mozambique. Chambo, "Metadidonai as Ethical," 180.

67. Ojie, "Democracy, Ethnicity," 561.

68. Khoza, *Let Africa Lead*, 59–58.

69. Moyo, "Material Things," 55.

70. Muzorewa, *Origins and Development*, 18–19.

71. Magesa, *African Religion*, 278.

72. Khoza, *Let Africa Lead*, 59–58.

In summary, Africans have an obligation to the community of which they are a part of. They understand that they owe their very existence to their community. As such they do all they can to promote the life force of the community. Their labour is part and parcel of the obligations they owe to the community. The same community also ensures that the individual is cared for and supported when they need the community. One obligation the community owes an individual is to provide them with a place they can settle and earn their livelihood. Yet, just as there is no culture that is perfect, in some cases, the reality does not always match the reality. At times the individual needs and rights are not always taken into consideration. A healthy balance needs to be maintained between the individual and the community.[73] In Christian theology the explanation for this is that all cultures have been marred by sin and are in need of the redemption that is available in Christ. Let us now discuss work and community as seen in African age sets.

2.6 Age Sets, Work Parties, and Community

People of the same age group form relationships that tie them together as members of the same extended family. The bond is so strong that it continues even when they are physically separated from one another. In Tanzania, among the Nyakyusa, these age groups are termed Nyakyusa society.[74] These groups are maintained by rites of passage, which mark transition from one state to another. There is a sense in which one is not entirely a member of the community when they have not gone through the rites of passage. Yusufu Turaki sees them as "covenants, bringing the neophyte into covenant relationship with the living members of the community, the ancestors and the gods and divinities."[75] Similarly, Jomo Kenyatta states concerning the Kikuyu of Kenya that once boys and girls are initiated, they join the age-grade (*riika rimwe*), which transcends the family group (*mbari*) and the clan (*moherega*). As such "They act as one body in all tribal matters and have a very strong bond of brotherhood and sisterhood among themselves."[76] The rites of passage as

---

73. Khoza, *Attuned Leadership*, 317.
74. See Wilson, *Good Company*.
75. Turaki, *Foundations*, 119.
76. Kenyatta, *Facing Mount Kenya*, 1, 72–73.

noted by Ferdinando should not be seen as rites marking individual's progress but "means by which the group integrates its members into the corporate life."[77]

Members of an age set are also known to organize days in which they offer their service to a member's parent farm. A member who lacks a farm on which to work can offer their labour to one who has within their age set and in return will get produce or land.[78] The reason for this is to avoid shame, which would occur when it is that member's turn to benefit from members of the group, and they fail to find a place to cultivate on their behalf.[79] Among the Kikuyus, the concept of *ngwatio* is the equivalent of working together as an age set. Those who took part did not receive pay; they merely offered their service for the common good.[80] Among the Shonas, the concept of *nhimbe* (work parties) is prevalent. The Shonas invited their neighbours to come and work and those who came, did so knowing they were coming to work.[81] *Nhimbe* was practised when building a hut (*imba*) as well as cultivating the fields.[82] These are usually called for at the threshing floor, and members of the neighbourhood take turns in visiting each farm, and the only form of payment is the provision of local beer and food. As Kenyatta notes "this is not looked upon as a reward for the work done, but as hospitality to one's guests."[83] When Shonas do this, they demonstrate what is known as *kunzwanana* or *kuwirirana* (good harmony).[84]

The work parties are also frequent among the Maasai who called communal work *Ematoyok*, the Luhya *Obwasio*, Luo *Konyir-Kende*, and the Akamba *Mwethya* or *Mwilaso* (young girls not initiated), Swazi *lilima*.[85] The Tiv of Nigeria also have age sets in which they help each other with physical work. The beneficiary of the work has the prerogative of providing food and beer and also being available when a member of the age set calls upon them to

---

77. Ferdinando, *Triumph of Christ*, 24.
78. Ilogu, *Christianity and Ibo Culture*, 28.
79. Ilogu, 28.
80. Bahemuka, *Our Religious Heritage*, 121.
81. Rayner, *Tribe and Its Successors*, 104.
82. Gelfand, *Genuine Shona*, 152.
83. Kenyatta, *Facing Mount Kenya*, 35, 72.
84. Murphree, *Christianity and the Shona*, 21; Gelfand, *Genuine Shona*, 151–52.
85. Bahemuka, *Our Religious Heritage*, 121; Mbithi and Rasmusson, *Self-Reliance*, 13.

reciprocate.[86] The Yoruba also have work age sets which they call *egbyevugo*, which have the characteristics of a voluntary association as they even invite the services of a patron (respected elder). P. C. Lloyd perceives the *egbe* as an "instrument of social control."[87] The *egbe* has responsibilities to perform public duties for the good of the community, which included making roads and defending the tribe against aggressors. Only the young, those between zero and nine years old, and those aged forty-five and above were exempt from manual public service.[88] The *riika rimwe* (age set) of the Kikuyu will build houses, cultivate, harvest, dig trap-pits, and other kinds of work. The Kikuyu have a saying which states "*Kamoinge koyaga ndere*" meaning "collective activities make heavy tasks easier" and which provides the theoretical framework in which the tribe works together.[89] Ilogu reports that among the Ibo, the motivation for working hard is "partly due to the influence of the age sets."[90]

For the Kikuyu there is competition between people in the adjacent fields in both singing and work.[91] Accompanying work with singing is quite common among African tribes. The Bahima of Uganda not only sing but tell stories while working, which thy call *ebyevugo*.[92] Even the modern-day concept of Harambee in Kenya provides the "only widely accepted mixture of dance, work and song."[93] Kenyatta is right to note that "the African . . . works with good spirit and enthusiasm to complete the task before him."[94] It can be said here that for the African work is not drudgery but part of what makes life enjoyable. This is captured in a Kikuyu saying: "To work in a happy mood is to make the task easier and to relieve the heart from fatigue."[95]

In Kenya, the traditional ideas of collective work among age sets have given birth to the concept of Harambee, which has become a national mantra

---

86. Bohannan, "Tiv of Nigeria," 536.
87. Lloyd, "Yoruba of Nigeria," 563–64.
88. Lloyd, 563–64.
89. Kenyatta, *Facing Mount Kenya*, 72.
90. Ilogu, *Christianity and Ibo*, 28.
91. Kenyatta, *Facing Mount Kenya*, 36.
92. Bahemuka, *Our Religious Heritage*, 130.
93. Mbithi and Rasmusson, *Self-Reliance*, 28.
94. Kenyatta, *Facing Mount Kenya*, 36.
95. Kenyatta, 48.

even on the coat of arms of the nation. The word Harambee means "collective effort" or "pull together," and as Bahemuka points out it certainly does not mean "let's watch them pull."[96] The concept of Harambee is guided by "the principle of collective good rather than individual gain,"[97] Bahemuka further states "Harambee, (self-help) reminds the society and its members that they have a responsibility towards each other to do their very best. They do this in the knowledge and understanding that, if the society prospers, all its members will share in that prosperity."[98] The people involved in a Harambee select the project they think will best serve the community, and they use locally available resources such as human labour, traditional forms of transport, thatch, stones, and bricks.[99] Harambees are a testament that work parties do not belong to yesteryears but are something that is still in the psyche of the African.

A word needs to be said about work during and after the colonial period in African countries. Literature from the colonial period mostly written by Europeans lamented the fact that Africans were not as hardworking as people in Europe. The Europeans thought that African men only worked to earn enough money to pay *lobola* (bride price) which "would go to buy more women, several heads of cattle, or to get drunk on alcohol."[100] The issue here as pointed out by Chambo is not work per se but the "western standards of work,"[101] which are predominantly capitalistic. Considering that the social organization of the people had been disrupted,[102] any value judgements on the African work ethic should not be taken seriously.

In summary, the African people can be said to not only live together but work together. Work in a way brings people together who would otherwise not come together except in tribal ceremonies and rituals. The work parties ensure that each member of the community gets the help that they require. They also ensure that every member has an opportunity to work. Anyone regardless of social status has the prerogative to call members of the community

---

96. Bahemuka, *Our Religious Heritage*, 122; Mbithi and Rasmusson, *Self-Reliance*, 13.
97. Bahemuka, *Our Religious Heritage*, 121; Mbithi and Rasmusson, *Self-Reliance*.
98. Bahemuka, *Our Religious Heritage*, 123.
99. Bahemuka, 123.
100. Matsinhe, "Masculinities," 14.
101. Chambo, "Metadidonai as Ethical," 171.
102. Chambo, 172.

to assist them with work.[103] Work in this setting is not drudgery since people sing songs of rejoicing while working. Food is an important part of the work parties, yet only those who have worked actually eat. Let us now discuss working together in the family setting.

2.7 Work and Community in the Household

Africans know that charity begins at home. Before one can be of help to other community members, one needs to start at home, that is in the family setting. In this section, we shall consider how the family unit works together. Before we do that, we need to say something about the African family. Kinship is "the most distinctive feature of African village life."[104] Families are not nuclear families but extended. These relationships are not just personal but also "serve economic, political, social, and religious function as well."[105] The kinship ties are foundational to all other social units.[106]

Any particular clan was known to practice a particular trade, which members of the family were taught through apprenticeship from a tender age. Such crafts like pottery, wood carving, cloth weaving, blacksmithing, and basket weaving were common among certain clans.[107] Ilogu remarks concerning the Ibo "In the old traditional Ibo way of life, in the absence of money economy and orientation of life along market system, economic life was largely directed by the simple necessities of the life of the extended family community, rather than of an individual."[108] This is the case, for instance, among the Tiv of Nigeria; work is not seen in market terms of remuneration but as one's responsibility owed to one's kin.[109]

Ilogu laments that, among the Ibo, communal working together within the extended family resulted in lessening "the danger of class consciousness, but with new emphasis of the market system of technological culture, individualism has been encouraged, and with it, class consciousness has started

---

103. Kunene, *Communal Holiness*, 144.
104. Ferkiss, *Africa's Search for Identity*, 32.
105. Ferkiss, 32.
106. Ferkiss, 32.
107. Ilogu, *Christianity and Ibo*, 21.
108. Ilogu, 93.
109. Bohannan, "Tiv of Nigeria," 520.

to develop."[110] However, in the tribal setting, the selfish person has no good reputation and is often considered a wizard or a witch. Such a person will not get help when they need it. As Kenyatta notes there is no such thing as a private matter since everything has social significance. Consequently, "the habit of corporate effort is but the other side of corporate ownership; and corporate responsibility is illustrated in corporate work no less than in corporate sacrifice and prayer."[111]

In most African societies, building a house is not a personal responsibility as it is in modern society. In traditional African societies (Ibo, Shona, Maasai, Kikuyu, Zulu, Luo, and others), it is the responsibility of the kin to help a member of their clan to build their own house.[112] Kenyatta reports that in addition to friends and relatives, the ancestral spirits are summoned to participate in building the house, and they also share in the beer that is brewed for the function.[113] In this vein, among the Ibo, the farm work is shared among members (both men and women) of each unit of the kinship structure.[114] Kenyatta affirms this among the Kikuyu: "Each member of the family unit knows perfectly well what task he or she is required to perform in their economic productivity and distribution of family resources, so as to ensure the material prosperity of the group."[115]

In the contemporary world, this way of doing things seems to have been eroded in the face of urbanization and the rapidly changing social structure. However, as Marc J. Swarts has noted concerning the Swahili, even in the midst of changing social structure "the community is still the locus of its members' most important relationships in all domains . . . Members take pride in each other's triumphs, and are distressed at the misfortune or maltreatment of those they regard as fellow members."[116] Through proper socialization, even where there has been rapid urbanization, it is possible to bring the values of the traditional society in the modern world. This is the

---

110. Ilogu, *Christianity and Ibo*, 94.

111. Kenyatta, *Facing Mount Kenya*, 74.

112. Ilogu, *Christianity and Ibo*, 14; Perrin-Jassy, *Basic Community*, 9; Kenyatta, *Facing Mount Kenya*, 46.

113. Kenyatta, *Facing Mount Kenya*, 46.

114. Ilogu, *Christianity and Ibo*, 14.

115. Kenyatta, *Facing Mount Kenya*, 32; Kithinji, "Search of an African Identity," 273.

116. Swartz, "Politics, Ethnicity," 236.

case primarily because of circularity in migration, which allows migrants to move back and forth between home and the host country; such migrants are able to keep their traditions alive.[117] It should also be noted that even though the African person has experienced the impact of modern civilization, the African worldview still exists side by side with western worldviews.[118] To the extent that African traditions express values, these values are much needed in modern Africa. These values are often seen during crisis moments like sickness and death.[119]

In addition to building houses, cultivating the field is another type of work that falls within the purview of the family or household. Among the Ibo, young men and their wives engage in communal farm work for the benefit of the family head known as the *Okpara* at least one day in an eight-day native week.[120] Another economic activity that occupies the Ibo is the manufacturing of household tools for their own consumption and the surplus for trade.[121] The economic life of most African communities consists of land, food, crops, and communal work.[122] Apart from eating the output from their farms, Africans also use their farm produce to conduct social feasts required of all inhabitants of the land throughout the year.[123] These feasts require contributions from all members of the community and those who fail to participate, incur wrath from the ancestors. Members of an age set, mentioned above, work hard in farms so that they have enough funds for the ceremonies.

Among the Hausa of Northern Nigeria, it is not uncommon to find two or more men and their wives and children working on the same farm and living in the same homestead, sharing common food supplies, forming what is known as a *gandu* (family farm). The most senior men in the group will assume leadership of the group.[124] Smith observes that

> officials, therefore, address their communications to junior members of the *gandu* through its head, who is also responsible

---

117. Potts, *Circular Migration*, 256–57; O'Connor, "Review: *Circular Migration*," 511.
118. Mwikamba, "Search of an African Identity," 4.
119. Mwikamba, 6.
120. Ilogu, *Christianity and Ibo*, 20.
121. Ilogu, 20.
122. Ilogu, 20.
123. Ilogu, 20.
124. Smith, "Hausa of Northen Nigeria," 140.

in their eyes for the conduct of all his dependents, for the payment of any fines they incur, for the unit's total tax, and for such labor or supplies as may legitimately be required from the group.[125]

Apart from ensuring the responsibilities of the group to outsiders are met, the official also ensures the unit has enough food provisions for a year, seeds for the next planting season, tools, houses, and bride price for young males.[126] To effectively meet all his responsibilities the *gandu* leader "controls the unit's male labor force within traditional units. At his direction, all work daily on the *gandu*."[127]

Among the Luo of Kenya, the same concept of the *gandu* is seen within the confines of the extended family where people live together on the same farm with a family head in charge of his wives, his sons and their families, his mother, brothers, and unmarried sisters.[128] Among the Shona, those who descend from a common ancestor would build houses close to each other and "work together as a group," and the eldest son would assume leadership for the group and had the prerogative of settling family issues.[129] Among the Kikuyu, men and women divide the various kinds of work within the household and children are also introduced to farm work at a tender age including having their own small gardens where they practice being agriculturalists.[130]

Emefie Ikenga-Mutuj has drawn attention to the fact that humankind in African tradition comes endowed with a package to contribute "to the life force of his family, clan and tribe, and indeed to the whole universe."[131] As such "the supreme and ultimate goal of human life is the increase of his own life force and the life forces of the family and other groups to which he belongs."[132] It is in this regard that in traditional African society every able-bodied person *Munhu* (in Shona) ought to work; such a society did not have a place for beggars and idlers, and Sindima is right that they have been

---

125. Smith, 140.
126. Smith, 140.
127. Smith, 140.
128. Perrin-Jassy, *Basic Community*, 4–5.
129. Gelfand, *Genuine Shona*, 155; Kenyatta, *Facing Mount Kenya*, 46.
130. Kenyatta, *Facing Mount Kenya*, 34.
131. Metuh, *God and Man*, 6–7.
132. Metuh, 6–7.

brought about by the "new economic order."[133] Gelfand says of the Shonas "Every member of the village will do all he can for his community, provided he is working for the good of all and thereby contributing to the universal harmony."[134] As such, one has a "sense of duty" to the village to make their modest contribution.[135] The opposite is also true; one commits a grave sin when they weaken or destroy the life force.[136] In the Kamba tribal system, each member of the extended family enhances the welfare of the *mosie*, depending on his skills and experience.[137]

In summary, for Africans, like the Greeks, the household was the basic economic unit. In this unit, the contribution of each and every member was not only expected but required. Even though in some communities there was some form of division of labour, in all tribal societies each gender had something to contribute. Even children had a part to play within the family economic matrix. When people sat to eat, they were eating their food. Work for Africans was a family affair, which required even the living dead (ancestors) to take part. The only member of the family who did not participate was the unborn, but once they were born and were able to work, they were expected to do their part.

2.8 Conclusion: Work and Community in the African Traditional Society

Our investigation revealed that God and ancestors are not exempt from work in the African setting. The Africans as such see work as something they cannot escape from. Given that the traditional African society is a communitarian society, we found that work is also done communally, and it also serves to bring members of the community together. People work in age group work parties, where they come together and accomplish a particular task for a member of the group and also share a meal. No one is paid for taking part in the work party; they are only given food and drink (beer), not as compensation but

---

133. Sindima, *Africa's Agenda*, 198.
134. Gelfand, *Genuine Shona*, 80.
135. Gelfand, 80.
136. Metuh, *God and Man*, 6–7.
137. Ndeti, "Elements of Akamba Life," 68.

an expression of hospitality. The work parties provide an opportunity for every individual to work. Work was done while singing, implying that it was something enjoyable. Similarly, the household setting provides an opportunity for members of the household to work together. Apart from building houses together, and working on the farm together, members of the same household were also known to perform the same trade, which was passed from one generation to another. The household structure ensured that no one was a "parasite"; even the young were expected to work. Our method, ABH, relies on the background painted in this chapter. The hypothesis for the study stems out of this background and ABH will draw on this material in our interpretation of the Thessalonian texts. Let us now turn to the relationship between work and community in the Dead Sea Scrolls.

CHAPTER 3

Work and Community in the Dead Sea Scrolls and the Qumran Community

3.1 Introduction

The last chapter considered work and community in the traditional African society. We were able to demonstrate our hypothesis that within the African traditional society there is connection between work and community. We now want to see if the Jewish texts of the Second Temple period (hereafter 2TP) texts uphold our hypothesis. We shall seek to examine the 2TP texts particularly the Dead Sea Scrolls (hereafter DSS) to see the relationship between work and community. The value of these texts lies in their potential for being the background for Paul's ideas on work and community. We are not, however, in any way arguing that there is an intertextual connection between these texts and the Thessalonian letters. Our investigation will focus primarily on the sectarian literature, which includes the Rule of the Community (1QS), the Damascus Document (CD), Rule of the Congregation (1QSa), and the Hodayot (1QH).[1] Particular emphasis shall be given to the Rule of the Community and the Damascus Document. To augment the picture painted in the scrolls we shall turn to archaeology to provide evidence of work done by the sectaries. In this move we are following the scholars who see a connection between the DSS and the sectarian community that lived at Qumran.

---

1. Harrington, *Wisdom Texts*, 75.

Our interest here is in the DSS and the community behind the scrolls. Here we have a Jewish community that attempted to live life together in a manner reminiscent of the communities founded by Paul. Even though there are considerable differences between the two communities, similarities can also be discerned. We shall primarily utilize the Dead Sea Scrolls and archaeological evidence to learn about the connection between work and community among the sectaries. We shall not rehearse what scholars have deliberated on concerning the relationship between the scrolls and the New Testament.[2] However, one interesting area for this study is the community of goods – that is, the practice of collective ownership.[3] Furthermore, the practice of eating communal meals could provide useful correspondences with Thessalonians, where people eat together and every member is required to work so that the meals are provided. Nevertheless, the Qumran community was much more sectarian or separate than Paul's communities – more separate from society in general, and much less interested in evangelism than Paul and his communities.

3.2 Qumran Community and the Dead Sea Scrolls

The relationship between the Scrolls and the Qumran community needs to be explained. The reason for this is that this study draws evidence of the relationship between work and community from the scrolls as well as from the archaeological evidence about the Qumran community. It is assumed here that the material remains of the Qumran community supply relevant evidence for study of work and community in the sect.[4] As such our primary source of information will be archaeological discoveries and the Dead Sea Scrolls themselves. Some scholars have questioned attributing the Dead Sea

---

2. Brooke, "Scrolls and the Study," 61–78. It is primarily in the area of self-understanding where the most significant parallels can be detected between the people of the scrolls and the early Christians. The two communities were living at the end of time. VanderKam and Flint, *Meaning of the Dead Sea Scrolls*, 321, 346; VanderKam, *Dead Sea Scrolls Today*, 199–200; Collins, "Introduction," 3–5; Schiffman, *Eschatological Community*, 6; Martínez and Tigchelaar, *Dead Sea Scrolls*, 15; Brooke, "Scrolls and the Study," 66.

3. Brooke, "Scrolls and the Study," 66; Martínez, Barrera, and Watson, *People of the Dead Sea*, 15; VanderKam, *Dead Sea Scrolls Today*, 211.

4. Here we are following Murphy's methodology of using both the texts and the material remains as evidence. Murphy, *Wealth in the Dead Sea*, 293.

Scrolls to the Qumran community. Magness has defended the connection by pointing out that the same type of ceramic pottery (unique pottery for that matter) was discovered in both the settlement and the caves. In her view, it is unlikely that a different community came to deposit the scrolls in the caves given the proximity between the two.[5] Yizhar Hirschfel, using archaeological evidence, states that "there was a connection of some kind between the deposition of the scrolls and the inhabitants of Qumran."[6]

Having set themselves apart from the Jerusalem temple,[7] the sectaries decided to separate themselves so as to restore purity for the remnant. 1QS IX (see also 4Q256 xviii; 4Q258 vii, viii; 4Q259 iii, iv; 4Q260) states that the purpose for the community was "to atone for the guilt of iniquity and for the unfaithfulness of sin, and for approval for the earth." Since this was to be done without burnt offering and fats of sacrifices, the sacrifice, became "the lips in compliance with the decree . . . like the pleasant aroma of justice and the perfectness of behaviour" (1QS IX. 5). The purpose for which the offerings and sacrifices were made was "to form a most holy community, and a house of the community for Israel, who walk in perfection" (1QS IX. 6). In some way, the concern for holiness is closely related "to the fact that it envisions the *yahad* as a substitute for the temple cult."[8] As such the community chose to live in the desert, and which in Israel's memory, is the location of the exodus,[9] a place where it was possible to intensify holiness.[10] Daryl F. Jefferies states "the hope was to portray the Qumran community as a new exodus into the desert, away from the sin of the religious communities in Jerusalem."[11]

These Scrolls show an interest in apocalyptic expectation, especially the wait for the end of time the sectarians are experiencing.[12] However, not all

---

5. Magness, *Archaeology of Qumran*, 43.

6. Hirschfeld, *Qumran in Context*, 129, 147.

7. Magness, *Archaeology of Qumran*, 37.

8. Collins, *Beyond the Qumran Community*, 73.

9. As Martínez observes concerning the people of Israel, "it is not difficult for them to transform it from a place of exile into a dwelling, a temporary residence or a stage on the path." Martínez, Barrera, and Watson, *People of the Dead Sea*, 33–34.

10. Collins, *Beyond the Qumran*, 73.

11. Jefferies believes 1QS, 1:20–25 which speaks of dividing the community into thousands, hundreds, fifties and tens is citing Deuteronomy 1:9–18. D. Jefferies, *Wisdom at Qumran*, 28. CD 13 also organizes the community in the same numbers.

12. Dimant, "Scrolls and the Study," 57.

Qumran texts uphold the belief system of the community and its *halakha*.¹³ For that reason, the sectarian nature of some of the documents is contested. Regardless, it is from these writings that we learn first-hand about the way of life of the Qumran community, an important part of this study. The Damascus Document (CD) addresses the ordinary sectaries. These include the Essenes who domiciled with their kith and kin in the Jewish villages and towns of Palestine.¹⁴ In contrast, the 1QS seems to address the sectaries who lived at Khirbet Qumran.¹⁵ Concerning these, Collins says "It reflects a more intense preoccupation with holiness, and provides for an elite group that pursues it to a higher degree in the wilderness."¹⁶ In the Damascus Document, we encounter married sectaries who seem to have slaves, did business with gentiles, including keeping cattle, and grew different crops and at the same time lived in strict conformity to the law.¹⁷ This notwithstanding, there is not much difference between two documents on their outlook on the role work plays in the community. Ultimately the two documents "should be seen as complementary branches of a larger movement, one of which aspired to a higher degree of holiness that the other."¹⁸ We are aware of the different terminologies used for the community in the CD *'edah* "congregation" and 1QS *yahad* "commune or association";¹⁹ however, the similarities far outweigh the differences. It is possible that the differences can be accounted for by the different stages of development of the same community.²⁰ Be that as it may, the differences do not affect our overall argument.

---

13. Martínez, Barrera, and Watson, *People of the Dead*, 9.

14. Knibb, *Qumran Community*; Collins, "Introduction," 1–8; Collins, *Beyond the Qumran Community*, 2. Collins is of the opinion that the similarities between *Manual of Discipline* and what we know of the Essenes from both Philo and Josephus required an identification between the Essenes and the Qumran community. He further states "The *yahad*, as described in the *Serek* texts, resembles the Essenes more closely than any other known group." See Collins, *Beyond the Qumran Community*, 2, 10.

15. Knibb, *Qumran Community*, 15; Collins, "Introduction," 2.

16. Collins, *Beyond the Qumran Community*, 6.

17. Vermès, *Complete Dead Sea Scrolls*, 35.

18. Collins, *Beyond the Qumran Community*, 6.

19. Collins, 4.

20. Vermès, "Laws of the Damascus Document," 177. We agree with Collins contra Charlotte Hempel that CD seems to be older and more original than the Rule of the Community since sects tend to become strict rather than lax in their demands. Collins, *Beyond the Qumran Community*, 6.

The Manual or Rule of the Community, which has been rightly termed by James Vanderkam "the constitution of the community," reveals much of what we know about the communal life of the sectaries.[21] It is also of importance that the Rule of the Community has a concern for the ideal community with an alternative economy; however, CD differs from the 1QS in that it concentrates on "socio-economic critique."[22]

In summary, the people behind the Qumran scrolls were part and parcel of the sizeable Essene movement. Apart from the sectaries who lived on the fringes of the wilderness of Judea, there were members of the sect who lived in the towns and villages. Following Murphy, both the CD and the 1QS share a concern for wealth, which includes work that is one's ability to make wealth. The community required those who join to bring their wealth to the community. Both documents shall form the basis for our study of the interplay of work and community in the Dead Sea Scrolls. We will now discuss wealth and work in the DSS.

3.3 Wealth and Work in the Dead Sea Scrolls

3.3.1 Wealth in the Damascus Document (CD) and the Rule of the Community (1QS)

We shall first look at the Damascus Document and then the Rule of the Community. The Damascus Document has much to say about wealth and its use. The sectaries used some of their community resources to support those who were not able to support themselves for one reason or another. For instance, the CD requires the sectary to "love himself; to strengthen the hand of the poor, the needy and the foreigner" (CD A VI. 20 =4Q266 3; 4Q267 2; 4Q269 ii; 6Q15 3, 4).[23] Besides, they also helped young men acquire skills so that they could provide for themselves and their families from their trade. They also extended help to those who had lost their property as a result of

---

21. VanderKam, *Dead Sea Scrolls Today*. Of importance to this study is the fact that both the Rule of the Community and the Damascus Document demonstrate a concern for wealth and work. Murphy has demonstrated that wealth includes more than what one owns; it includes one's ability to acquire wealth, which is the purview of work.

22. Murphy, *Wealth in the Dead Sea*, 428.

23. Martinez and Tigchelaar, *Dead Sea Scrolls*, 559.

failing to pay their debts (CD X III 9–10).[24] The practice of caring for their own fits the criteria for wealth distribution whose rationale was "covenant fidelity, sacrificial offering and communal unity in the holy spirit."[25] As such, the community's religious obligations and economic practices were in harmony.

The Rule of the Community also had an interest in matters of wealth. The community's interest in one's wealth reveals that work played a critical role. The interest in wealth is demonstrated by the fact that the novice Essene was required to not only to bring themselves but their property to the commonwealth of Israel.[26] However, one could not be denied membership because they did not have something to contribute. Since members brought their property, it follows that the community shared its property and possessions.[27] The word הון has to do not only with a person's material resources but the profits that accrue from it as well (4Q257/4QRule of the Community 3.3; 4Q258 [4QS] 4QRule of the Community 1:13).[28] The word כוה is another vital term which refers to one's ability to work and what one can earn in profit from it, and דעת which refers to mental skills one can trade for profit. Both כוה (1QS 1.19–20 =4Q255 1; 4Q256 I, II) and דעת (1QS 1.11–12 =4Q255; 4Q256 I, II) were considered by the Essenes as personal resources the same way they regarded material property.[29]

The 1QS in two passages makes it clear that contributing one's wealth relates to one's obligation to the covenant with the God of Israel.[30] For instance 1QS 1.11–15 states

> His knowledge, his energy and his wealth shall not enter the council of the Community because he ploughs in the mud of wickedness and there are stains on his conversion. He shall not

---

24. The Examiner is charged "9 He shall have pity on them like a father on his sons, and will heal all the ‹ afflicted among them › like a shepherd his flock. 10 He will undo all the chains which bind them, so that there will be neither harassed nor oppressed in his congregation" (CD XIII 9–10). Murphy, *Wealth in the Dead Sea*. Consequently, the Essenes did not have slaves in their number, a fact noted by both Philo and Josephus. Stegemann, *Library of Qumran*, 189.

25. Murphy, *Wealth in the Dead Sea*, 103.

26. Stegemann, *Library of Qumran*.

27. Stegemann, *Library of Qumran*, 176; Helyer, *Exploring Jewish Literature*, 211.

28. Stegemann, *Library of Qumran*, 176.

29. Stegemann, 177.

30. Murphy, *Wealth in the Dead Sea*, 117–18.

be justified while he maintains the stubbornness of his heart,
since he regards darkness as paths of light.³¹

It is unlikely that Isaiah 9 is echoed here, as suggested by Murphy.³² In Isaiah, the passage is a messianic text, which is not the case envisioned by 1QS. As such, one's wealth (including knowledge and energy) are offered as an indication of walking as the covenant required.³³ Thus the trio is rightly considered "the symbols of commitment" to the covenant.³⁴

The community absorbed temple prerogatives of atonement and provided the sacrifice which provided purification for Israel and guaranteed God's blessing on the land (1QS III 4–12; V 6; VIII 6, 10).³⁵ Wealth (along with judgement, righteousness, perfection of the way) is part of what the community presents as offerings (נדבה) to God in place of those required by the Levitical system. Consequently "The members of this community are themselves the priests and victims of its sacrificial system, offering themselves freely to a way of life stylized as sacrificial."³⁶ For that reason, the sectaries were required to come with their wealth. Of course, there cannot be wealth without work; the requirement for offerings presupposes that the community was a working community.³⁷

Community wealth introduced work related to the management of community resources. This was needed mainly because of those who would negligently handle communal wealth (1QS VII 6–7).³⁸ Those who mishandled community assets were required to make amends, suggesting that they still

---

31. Martinez and Tigchelaar, *Dead Sea Scrolls*, 75.
32. Murphy, *Wealth in the Dead Sea*, 117–18.
33. Murphy, 117–18.
34. Murphy, 120. The people of the Dead Sea Scrolls had enough material resources. Stegemann suggests that their resources resulted from their internal economy, which required that imports be kept at a minimum due to purity concerns. For instance, they would buy bread from a baker among their own, who of course had purchased his flour from the Essene farmer; as such, money was changing hands within the community, and consequently was staying in the community. Stegemann, *Library of Qumran*, 186. Contrary to Philo, Josephus, and Pliny the elder, who thought that the Essenes did not have private possession of the property, it was the right to ownership upon which the duty to contribute was anchored. Stegemann, *Library of Qumran*, 187.
35. Collins, *Beyond the Qumran Community*, 59.
36. Murphy, *Wealth in the Dead Sea*, 148.
37. Murphy, 154.
38. Murphy, 158.

had their own property or their work could earn the income required to make restitution (1QS VI 6–8; 16–17; 24–25).[39] The community required that the possessions of individuals should be available to the entire congregation to meet the needs of any among them.[40] Vanderkam, on the basis of 1QS 7.6–8 which prescribes punishment for one who mishandles community property, concludes that the member in question could have retained some of the property.[41] This position does not take the requirement seriously for one to give up control of private property.

We ought to avoid the modern distinctions between private and communal ownership when dealing with ancient people as suggested; for the sectarians, the property was dedicated both to God and the community and the individual could still make use of that which they contributed.[42] We contend that punishment does not need to have been property but work that one had to do as a way to earn the community property which they had mishandled.[43] Vanderkam only thinks of wealth in terms of what a sectary already owns and contributes but he does not envision how one's work can be construed as part of one's wealth. The 1QS says, "if he is negligent with the possessions of the Community achieving a loss, he shall replace it […] 7 in full." (1QS VII 7).[44] In line 8 it proceeds by stating that "And if he does not manage to replace it, he will be punished for /sixty days/" (1QS VII 8).[45] This tells us that one may have been involved in some investment with community property and lost it and the person then is given an opportunity to redeem the community wealth and fails. As such, the individual's work and productivity are considered community property and one cannot use it for selfish interest but only in line with community philosophy and regulations.[46]

---

39. Murphy sees in the sectarian literature the correlation between fellowship and the Holy Spirit. This correlation extends even to the New Testament (Rom 12:13; 15:26; 2 Cor 8:3–4; 9:12–13), where the holy ones demonstrate through partaking in the spirit as they give to the needy in Jerusalem. Murphy, *Wealth in the Dead Sea*, 158.

40. VanderKam and Flint, *Meaning of the Dead Sea Scrolls*, 347.

41. VanderKam, *Dead Sea Scrolls Today*.

42. Goff, "Review of *All the Glory*," 171.

43. This fact is confirmed by Collins who says "he could possibly do this by work rather than by drawing on private property of his own," Collins, *Beyond the Qumran Community*, 57.

44. Martinez and Tigchelaar, *Dead Sea Scrolls*, 87.

45. Martinez and Tigchelaar, 87.

46. Murphy, *Wealth in the Dead Sea*, 158.

In summary, the discussion of wealth among the sectaries reveals that the community was concerned about what one earned from one's work, either before or after one joined the community. The work of Murphy has demonstrated that wealth among the sectaries involves one's ability to make wealth – work is definitely entailed. The community required that individuals contribute to the many (1QS 6:20). The economic practices of the community were tied to their covenant obligations, as their religious obligations informed such a community economy. Even though we do not have evidence to suggest that anyone was denied membership for not bringing their wealth, all indications are that most did bring their wealth – for the community expected it. Also, the community considered one's work and productivity as part and parcel of its property, and failure to use it adequately attracted punishment. We can safely conclude that the community valued work since they have regulations to do with the results of work: wealth. Having considered wealth in the Qumran community, we are now in a position to discuss the place of work in the Qumran community.

3.3.2 Work and Community at Qumran

Having established that work relates to wealth at Qumran, now we are in a position to discuss more specifically the interplay of work and community in the Qumran community. The term מלאצה generally "describes a work, trade, vocation, or task" and in the sectarian writings "it is thus the term commonly used of what one must not do on the Sabbath."[47] The 1QS introduces three basic terms that aid our understanding of labour; they are מלאצה (work), עבודה (service), and הון (wealth).[48] Let us now consider the archaeological evidence. Since we are not only interested in the symbolic world envisioned by the text, it is important to look at the archaeological evidence to see if there is evidence of work done by the sectaries. Here we follow the lead of

---

47. Murphy, 156.

48. Murphy, 156; This evidence is corroborated by Josephus who reports concerning the Essenes that "After this every one of them are sent away by their curators, to exercise some of those arts wherein they are skilled, in which they labor with great diligence till the fifth hour." Josephus, Jewish War, 2:129 in Josephus, *Works of Josephus*, 605; After engaging in other activities, according to Josephus, they go back to their work until evening. Josephus, Jewish War, 2:129. This indicates that for Josephus, work played an essential role in the community life of the Essenes.

scholars who see a connection between the Qumran community and the Dead Sea Scrolls.

3.3.3 Work and Community: Archaeological Evidence

Before we can discuss the archaeological evidence that points to work done by the sectaries, it is essential to discuss what the Qumran settlement was, to justify the connection between the Dead Sea Scrolls and the Qumran community. Various views have been suggested by archaeologists going back to De Vaux who saw it as a settlement for the people behind the Dead Sea Scrolls. Other scholars like Pauline Donceel Voûte suggested that Qumran was a Villa, claiming that what De Vaux thought to be a scriptorium was, in fact, a dining room in which the diners ate while reclining (triclinium). Following Voûte, Yizhar Hirschfeld has suggested that it must have been a manor house.[49]

For Vanderkam, it seems unlikely for a wealthy individual to build a villa at such a place as Qumran considering the fact that Jericho is not very far.[50] Similarly, Jodi Magness denies the villa or fortress theory. For her, the existence of "animal bone deposits ritual baths (miqva'ot) would make Qumran anomalous site,"[51] such items would be inconsistent with a villa theory. She writes "Qumran provides a unique opportunity to use archaeological evidence combined with the information from ancient historical sources and scrolls to reconstruct and understand the life of the community."[52] As such, the connection between the Qumran scrolls and archaeological evidence is undeniable.[53] With this proposed connection between the Scrolls and the Qumran settlement, we are now in a position to see what has been unearthed by archaeologists that is critical for community work.

Even though we disagree with Hirschfeld on other points, we agree on the point that Qumran was a production centre of some sort.[54] Archaeological evidence has been found for, among other things, ritual baths, a refectory, a scriptorium, workshops, and a cemetery.[55] There was also a porter's workshop

---

49. Hirschfeld, *Qumran in Context*, 162.
50. VanderKam, *Dead Sea Scrolls Today*.
51. Magness, *Archaeology of Qumran*.
52. Magness, 13.
53. Magness, 13.
54. Hirschfeld, *Qumran in Context*, 129, 143.
55. Martínez, Barrera, and Watson, *People of the Dead Sea*, 9.

found in the ruins.[56] Further evidence for manual labour is seen in tools unearthed by the archaeologists, particularly at Ein Feshkha. These include weapons, a knife, blade tools of various kinds, and an iron pick.[57] The discovery of bronze fibulae used to mend togas, garments, and needles suggest that the community was involved in either manufacturing or mending clothes and leather.[58] For Hirschfeld, such activities were the prerogative of women, and this is consistent with the skeletons of women found in the nearby cemetery.[59]

The Dead Sea region saw an upsurge in economic activities during the late Hellenistic and early Roman periods. The coins found at Qumran provide evidence of the economic life of the community.[60] The Tyrian tetradrachms (which were used to pay half-sheqel temple tax) discovered at Qumran suggests that they may have paid the temple tax.[61] However, that they could have paid money to the temple does not mean they actually paid. They also considered the Jerusalem temple to be defiled; so the community set themselves up as an alternative to the temple. Magness allows that the community collected money meant for the temple even though they did not have temple contacts.[62] The people of Qumran did not pay temple tithe; as such, the money meant for tithe was diverted to community meals.[63] The community meals are only made possible by the proceeds of work done by the sectarians. Without such meals, the community would not be able to fulfil all it meant to be a community.

Qumran was also a pottery production centre. Marta Bala and Jan Gunneweg's archaeological research (done using Instrumental Neutron Activation Analysis [INAA]) confirms that there is such a thing as Qumran pottery distinct from Engedi and Masada.[64] It was not uncommon for people in the ancient world to make their pottery and also sell the surplus.[65]

---

56. See Magness, *Archaeology of Qumran*.
57. See Magness.
58. Hirschfeld, *Qumran in Context*, 149.
59. Hirschfeld, 149.
60. Hirschfeld, 129, 144.
61. See Magness, *Archaeology of Qumran*.
62. Magness, 193.
63. Stegemann, *Library of Qumran*, 185.
64. Balla and Gunneweg, "Was the Qumran Settlement," 39–61; Magness, *Archaeology of Qumran*, 14.
65. See Hirschfeld, *Qumran in Context*.

Furthermore, Jan Gunneweg has convincingly argued that the Qumran settlers made soap. Considering the concern for purity at Qumran, soap would have been a much-needed commodity.[66] If that is the case, then soap makers would have been in demand, and this is another area in which work would have been made available for the sectaries.

Archaeologists have discovered that the inhabitants of Qumran also had a date press and cultivated the dates at the springs at Ein Feshkha.[67] Magness asserts that it is possible that they grew other crops (like grain at Buqeia valley) and raised sheep, goats, and cattle. They could also have explored natural resources like bitumen and salt, which they then traded for what they did not have.[68] De Vaux noted concerning Ein Feshkha and Ein el Ghuweir that the apparatuses, buildings, and ceramic materials are similar to those at Qumran.[69] All evidence points to the fact that these settlements are related to Qumran. The settlement is situated on the springs of the Dead Sea about three kilometres south of Qumran.[70]

The oasis of Ein Feshkha is important for the activities that took place at Qumran. Hirschfeld is right when he says without "a consideration of its remains (Ein Feshkha) any reconstruction of Qumran . . . is simply inaccurate."[71] De Vaux considered Ein Feshkha "an agricultural and industrial establishment used to benefit the community of Qumran."[72] Agriculture was the backbone of the economy of Qumran as evidenced by the tools found at Qumran, which include hoes, knives, and sickles, and the same applies to the irrigation systems found in Ein Feshkha. It is also not far-fetched to assume that livestock played a critical role in the economy as well; animal bones point to this reality.[73] Freshwater and a good amount of sunlight made the land fertile and conducive for agriculture. In addition to agriculture, the people here also

---

66. Gunneweg, "Introduction," 163–69.
67. Magness, *Archaeology of Qumran*, 21.
68. Magness, 21.
69. Magness, 220.
70. Magness, 210.
71. Hirschfeld, *Qumran in Context*, 183.
72. Magness, *Archaeology of Qumran*.
73. Hirschfeld, *Qumran in Context*.

took advantage of what the Dead Sea had to offer; that is, bitumen and salt, which they used to both preserve and flavour food.[74]

Magness does not accept de Vaux's conclusion concerning the relationship between Qumran and Ein Feshkha. For her, Ein Feshkha does not have the unique features of Qumran – for instance, animal bone deposits, cemetery, miqva'ot. Since it lacks these "it is impossible to determine whether it was used or inhabited by a sectarian community."[75] We contend that if it was the industrial location for Qumran, then it did not need all that. This is where the sectarians worked, and Qumran is where they practised religion and communal life. Even Magness accepts that a sectarian community occupied Qumran.[76] Stegemann thinks that the construction plans of both Qumran and Ein Feshkha reveal that the production of scrolls was the main centre of interest. Leather was an essential ingredient in the manufacture of scrolls; hence, it is possible then that much of the work involved working with leather.[77]

The presence of a tannery and a late scriptorium is not surprising given that they made scrolls regularly. The scrolls that the community made were not only for their own consumption; other Essene communities scattered across the land of Israel needed them for the purpose of study.[78] As a result, the work of producing scrolls served to unify Essene groups across the board. However, this is not to say that everyone at Qumran produced scrolls; there were other men whose concern was the "administrative, commercial, agricultural, and culinary needs of the settlement."[79] Yet all members had to participate in the study of the scriptures and community rules.[80] There must have been a glass industry as indicated by the glassware found at the site. Hirschfeld puts commercial activities with industrial, which need not be the case.[81] The two are not mutually exclusive. The community could have engaged in religious activities and at the same time engaged in commercial activities, a fact to which the scrolls bear testimony.

---

74. Hirschfeld, 185.
75. Magness, *Archaeology of Qumran*, 221.
76. Magness, 221.
77. Stegemann, *Library of Qumran*, 54.
78. Stegemann, 52.
79. Stegemann, 52.
80. Stegemann, 52.
81. Hirschfeld, *Qumran in Context*, 129, 145.

Other products that could have come from the region include perfume (myrrh, frankincense, and nard), fruits, bitumen, and salt. Due to the constant demand for these products the Dead Sea Valley was connected with "international trade networks" such as Egypt and Rome.[82] For that reason, Hirschfeld rejects the assumption that Qumran was a "self-contained, isolated, and ascetic community," arguing that "Qumran, in fact, had an important place within the highly developed agriculture-based economy of the Dead Sea region."[83] Likewise, Martin Hengel suggests that the whole region around Qumran could have been a large estate which the members of the community cultivated. This could only have been possible with the "technical achievements and inventions of the Hellenistic age."[84]

In summary, the archaeological evidence suggests that the Qumran community was a community that made various products and grew agricultural products – all of which points to a range of work available for the sectaries. This community made its own food and much of what it needed for its continued existence. The tools with which they worked have been unearthed by the archaeologists. Vermes is right to say, "Work must have formed a necessary part of their existence."[85] Let us now turn to the Scrolls themselves to see what they have to say about work.

3.3.4 Work and Community in the Scrolls: Obligations for the Community Members

3.3.4.1 1Q28a; IQSa; 1Q Rule of the Congregation

Having considered the archaeological evidence for work at Qumran, we are now ready to look at what the Scrolls actually say about work. The community Rule 1Q28a Col. 1 speaks of the "work in the service of the congregation"[86] which is to be performed when one reaches the age of twenty-five (1Q28 1.13; 1QSa; 1QRule of the Congregation). There are similarities and differences between this text and Numbers 8. The age of service is the same: that is, twenty-five; however, in 1Q28 there is no age limit of service. In Numbers

---

82. Hirschfeld, 11.
83. Hirschfeld, 14.
84. Hengel, "Qumran and Hellenism," 47
85. Vermès, *Complete Dead Sea Scroll*, 27.
86. Vermès, 120.

those who have reached the age of fifty (retirement age) "assist their brothers in the tent of meeting" whereas in 1Q28, nothing is said about retirement, one is simply to "do his duty among his brothers" though when one is advanced in age, the assignment must match his strength.[87] The significant difference in 1Q28 is that one is to serve "in accordance with his intelligence and the perfection of his behaviour" and in Numbers no qualification is made on the service rendered.

Similarly, 1QSa i, 12–13 speaks of those who have gone through the ranks and graduate to "work in the service of the congregation."[88] Murphy sees here what she calls a "Levitically styled service" which in her opinion is related to the "service of the association" (עבודה החבר), which we find in CD XIV 12–17 which refers to "the redistribution of financial resources."[89] There may be similarities in terms of age limit with the Levites in Number 8:23–26; however, the kind of work for which the two communities are enlisted is different. The work in Numbers relates specifically to duties at the tent of meeting rather than the distribution of financial services in the CD. This "service" in question has to do with wealth in both the CD and the 1QS. What we see in this passage is a hierarchy of obligation, which goes beyond issues of wealth, starting with contribution, then redistribution, and finally settling issues concerning wealth.[90] Clearly here we do not have a situation in which one enjoys a free ride. To be a member of the community is to contribute to its well-being.

3.3.4.2 Community Rule

The community has individuals whose work is the internal life of community life. The priests, who are "the elite members of the community"[91] provided spiritual leadership to the community. They were also overseers of both the library and the scriptorium, led prayers, presided during the communal meals, and settled legal questions related to communal and private property (1QS ii.19–20; vi.8; vi.3–4; vi.5).[92] In addition, priests occupied themselves with

---

87. It has to be noted, however, that CD 14:7, 9; 10:6–10 prescribes a mandatory retirement for the המבקר of fifty years. Vermès and Goodman, *Essenes*, 8.
88. Vermès, *Complete Dead Sea Scrolls*, 10.
89. Murphy, *Wealth in the Dead Sea*, 214.
90. Murphy, 214–15.
91. Charlesworth, "Community Organization," 134.
92. Stegemann, *Library of Qumran*, 83.

scholarship on behalf of the community.⁹³ Since the priests were "the Sons of Aaron" they were tasked with judgement and property (1QS ix.7).⁹⁴ Due to their duties as administrators of the Essenes, this class of people could not practice a trade to provide for their daily needs, and the community seems to have used its communal resources to provide for them.⁹⁵

In addition to the priests, other officers had various responsibilities in the life of the community. These include the "Master" (משכיל), the "Examiner" (המבקר), and the "Overseer" (פקיד). The משכיל (master) was responsible for instructing the new members who were later examined by the המבקר (examiner) concerning their knowledge and purity (4Q298).⁹⁶ Trebolle Barrera wrongly equates the משכיל with the המבקר,⁹⁷ failing to recognize the fact that much more was required of the משכיל: he had to have "all understanding" (see1QS ix. 12–19). The "Overseer" (פקיד) was the second-ranked officer in the community. The roles of this individual seem to overlap with those of the המבקר (1QS VI. 14).⁹⁸ 1QS 1 11–15 reads "All those who submit freely to his truth will convey all their knowledge, their energies, and their riches (הון) to the Community of God in order to refine their knowledge in the truth of God's decrees."⁹⁹ In 1QS III.2 (4Q255 2; 4Q257 III; 4Q262 1) the triad of knowledge, energy, and wealth are not allowed to the entire community because of the wickedness of the owner. As such, the person in question will not be justified.

The passages cited above together indicate that nothing was to be withheld when one joined the community. A. R. C. Leaney comments "Their physical powers must be daily at the community's disposal, and so must their wealth."¹⁰⁰ Leaney further states that all that the members have (knowledge, power, and wealth) was to be contributed. The only way they could be purified was through counsel of the righteous ones.¹⁰¹ The presentation of knowledge

---

93. Stegemann, 83.
94. Charlesworth, "Community Organization," 134.
95. Stegemann, *Library of Qumran*, 185.
96. Charlesworth, "Community Organization," 133.
97. Martínez, Barrera, and Watson, *People of the Dead Sea*, 57.
98. Charlesworth, "Community Organization," 135.
99. Martínez, Barrera, and Watson, *People of the Dead Sea*, 71.
100. Leaney, *Rule of Qumran*, 122.
101. Leaney, 122.

results in refinement of one's knowledge, strength results in marshalling of energies in line with perfect paths, and wealth results in one's riches being used in accordance with just counsel (1QS 1. 11–13). Given that wealth includes one's ability to produce as opposed to just one's immovable assets, one's donation entailed a promise to give all that was to be earned in the course of life.[102] It can safely be concluded that the community required its members to work so as to produce.

Murphy sees here an echo of Deuteronomy 6:5. As such, heart, soul, and strength are equivalent to "knowledge, strength and wealth." From this perspective, the troika becomes a demonstration of covenant commitment for the novice initiate. Consequently, embodying these become demonstrations of "complete devotion to God."[103] In Deuteronomy, obedience shows love; it follows then that the sectaries are being called upon to "obey God with every aspect of and element of one's being."[104] As such, to come without one's wealth is to come incomplete. Considering that wealth includes one's ability to work, the one who comes without it, comes deficient before YHWH.

The deviant individuals are not allowed to enter into the community since they will contaminate the men of holiness, since such members of the community are not allowed to associate with such men in their "work or wealth" (1QS V:14). Not only are they forbidden from discussing "matters of Law or legal judgment" but they are not "to eat or drink what is theirs, nor yet to take anything from them." The only exception is that what they eat is paid for and not given free of charge (1QS V:15).[105] What is critical for our purpose is that the community is forbidden from living off other people who are not members of the community. The implication is that the community must live off its own resources generated by the internal economy, which they themselves participate in.

The first regulation of communal life is found in 1QS VI 22–25. For Murphy, the position of the rule shows the importance of wealth among sectaries; as such, it becomes "the most concrete symbol of covenant fidelity

---

102. Murphy, *Wealth in the Dead Sea*, 157.
103. Murphy, 120–30.
104. Merrill, *Deuteronomy*, 163.
105. Wise, Abegg, and Cook, *Dead Sea Scrolls*, 132–33. This regulation is in line with the Damascus Document provision for allowing commerce with Gentiles (CD 13:14–15; 12:9–11). Vermès and Goodman, *Essenes*, 9.

to the community."[106] The regulation states "If one is found among them] 3 [who has lied] knowingly [concerning mo]ney, he shall be [excluded from the pure food] 4 [of the Many for one year and shall be sentenced to a quar]ter of [his] bre[ad]."[107] This passage speaks of those who worked elsewhere, suggesting that the community had to rely on the worker to report their earnings truthfully. Those who failed to report their earnings truthfully had their rations reduced and were excluded from communal meals, which is one of the primary identity and boundary markers in the community.[108] From the perspective of the sectaries, this is the worst that could happen to an individual. Here we see the intimate connection between working and participating in communal meals. It is work and its results that guarantee participation at the table with fellow sectaries. This is reminiscent of the phrase "he who does not work should not eat" (2 Thess 3:10).

Food is one area of community life that reveals that the community worked. The Scrolls, especially 1QS (Col. vi), speak of the "pure Meal of the Congregation."[109] There are different views on the meal, as to whether it is a messianic banquet or a regular meal. Martinez, Barrera, and Watson see it as a community everyday meal.[110] Similarly, Lawrence Schiffman has suggested that the meals at Qumran were non-cultic, asserting that "These meals, conducted regularly as part of the present-age way of life of the sect, were re-enactments of the final messianic banquet with the sectarians expected in the soon to come end of days. Again, the life of the sect in this world mirrored its dreams for the age to come."[111] The community ate together and the text mentions that they had to prepare the table and the priest had to be present to bless the first fruits of the bread (1QS VI 2–6). For a meal to be considered a proper meal, ten members had to be present and a priest must be present. Per Bilder comments, "participation in the common meal is the primary expression of full membership in the community."[112]

---

106. Murphy, *Wealth in the Dead Sea*, 120–30.
107. Martínez and Tigchelaar, *Dead Sea Scrolls*, 541.
108. Mathews, *Riches, Poverty*, 110.
109. Vermès, *Complete Dead Sea Scrolls*, 78.
110. Martínez, Barrera, and Watson, *People of the Dead Sea*, 71.
111. Schiffman, *Eschatological Community*, 67.
112. Bilder, "Common Meal," 145–66.

Meals served to bring the individuals closer to each other. Murphy has noted that "Commensality, and particularly the shared meal of pure food, is a feature of communal intimacy."[113] Communal meals by their nature require someone to secure the food: as such this became the most important economic activity. It is this sphere that exposed them to outsiders, and the community documents seek to protect the covenanters against contamination.[114] Some forms of work were considered unclean but had to be done. The placing of the *miqver* in L31 near the workshops (potter's workshop) seems to serve the function of purification of workers. As such, workshops were mostly on the eastern side of the settlement, and this is consistent with Yadin's estimation that the rabbinic legislation outlawed workshops to the west of Jerusalem. This is also true of the cemetery (not only is it to the east but outside the settlement boundaries), which is considered to cause "the greatest degree of impurity."[115] Magness has further noted that the inhabitants of Qumran apparently conceived of their settlement as "a series of spaces with varying degrees of purity or impurity."[116]

3.3.4.3 *The Damascus Document (CD)*

In the Damascus Document, the "overseer" exercises pastoral authority over group members and admits new members (CD xiii.7–13).[117] In addition, he was also responsible for recording witness statements in capital offences (CD ix 16–22) and in case one sectary was getting married, his role was to confirm the moral standing of the bride (4Q271 3). The overseer had to be informed of any agreement related to buying and selling by community members.[118] The textual evidence seems to suggest that these individuals (master, examiner, and overseer) occupied themselves primarily with internal responsibilities and not with other economic activities and like priests the community met their needs.

---

113. Murphy, *Wealth in the Dead Sea*, 135; Similarly, Philo says "In no other community can we find the custom of sharing roof, life and board more firmly established in actual practice." Philo, *Omnis Probus*, 86.
114. Murphy, *Wealth in the Dead Sea*, 157.
115. Magness, *Archaeology of Qumran*, 127.
116. Magness, 127.
117. Knibb, "Community Organization," 136.
118. Knibb, 138.

Further evidence of work among the sectaries can be seen in the *Damascus Rule*[119] which instructs that the wages of two days every month be given to the examiner and the judges for the purpose of caring for the wounded, the poor, the destitute, the old, the afflicted, the foreigner, the virgin with no redeemer, the youth, and all this considered to be part of the service of the association (עבודה החבר) (CD XIV 12–19).[120] This command was serious enough for an infringement to warrant penance for six days (CD XIV 12–19). The reason the בית החבר is to do this is so that it may not be cut off, thus "to enable it to survive as a just society until the advent of the messiah."[121] This regulation reveals that the sectaries actually worked, were remunerated, and were required to give an account for what they earned, as Mark D. Matthews confirms (CD 14:20).[122] Clearly, this command relates to taking care of the most vulnerable of society. Murphy has noted that "the charitable donation was understood as an economic contract as well as a religious obligation."[123] However, it has to be noted that the *Serek* requires all of the property of its members which is not the case in the *Damascus Rule*,[124] for in the words of Albert Baumgarten the member "had sacrificed his personality to a greedy institution which demanded his sexual activity [and] his property."[125]

The use of the word "association" signifies that we are dealing here with "not only an alternative religious institution but to an alternative economic one as well."[126] In this sense, the community functions as a true covenant community which addresses the needs of those in distress.[127] Work and food

---

119. Collins sees the community behind it as "a family-based movement, but it is also an organized community that makes extensive demands on its members, and to a great degree undercuts the authority of the paterfamilias. It restricts relations with the outside world but has not withdrawn to anything resembling a monastic way of life. Marriage is the norm, although it is regulated and restricted" whereas the *Yahad* in the Rule of the Community is not. Collins, *Beyond the Qumran Community*, 51.

120. Murphy, "Disposition of Wealth," 122.

121. Murphy, 123.

122. Mathews, *Riches, Poverty*, 95.

123. Murphy, *Wealth in the Dead Sea*, 84.

124. See Collins who also notes "The demands of the *yahad* are stricter in the matter of property. The *Damascus Rule* required only the surrender of two days' wages. The *Serek* apparently envisions full community of property." Collins, *Beyond the Qumran Community*, 57–58.

125. Baumgarten, "Graeco-Roman Voluntary Associations," 98.

126. Murphy, *Wealth in the Dead Sea*, 85.

127. Murphy, 44.

became the boundary markers of the community in the Damascus Document, which sanctions that wealth is a tool to build community as opposed to elevating the individual at the expense of the group.[128] The community has strict guidelines on how they can trade with outsiders; much of their commerce is restricted to their fellow sectaries. As for the Damascus Document, the new sectarian is required to examine himself in light of the triad of strength, courage, and wealth, and in addition, the document adds his actions and intelligence. These become the basis upon which the candidates shall earn their place in line with the "inheritance in the lot of light" (CD A XIII).[129]

If one was not walking in holiness, that was grounds for not doing business with them – that is, in terms of money or work. The reason advanced is that the "Holy Ones of the Most High have cursed him" (CD–B Col. Xx. 7).[130] This reveals that the community was restricted to those whose walk was that of holiness and it is these that one could work with. One who does not walk in holiness cannot be consulted on matters of money and work. As such, those who join must understand that they have joined a community of "perfect holiness" and are called upon to do the duties of the upright. This clearly demonstrates the interplay of work and community at Qumran. 1QS Col. vi calls on the sectaries to walk/live together in their dwelling. In this text, obedience is required of the one of lesser rank to obey the "greater in matters of work and money. They shall eat in common and bless in common and deliberate in common."[131] These texts are essential for us because they connect community life with matters of money and work. What happens in the community affects matters of money and work and vice versa.

3.3.5 Synthesis – Dead Sea Scrolls on Work and Community

In summary, the 1QS speaks of the "work of the service of the congregation" (1Q28a Col. 1), which refers to work that mature community members are to do for the community. This is what each sectary looked forward to do. Also, 4Q258 Col. ii speak of consultation in terms of work and money; only one who walks in holiness can be consulted. Similarly, the one whose rank is

---

128. Murphy, 102.
129. Martinez and Tigchelaar, *Dead Sea Scrolls*, 573.
130. Vermès, *Complete Dead Sea Scrolls*, 104.
131. Vermès, 77.

higher should be obeyed in matters of work and money. The sectaries were required to come with all they had; their contributions were the triad of "knowledge, power, and wealth." Those who failed to report truthfully their earnings were excluded from the communal meals; this indicates that the results of work somehow earned one a place at the table with fellow sectaries. The communal meals brought the people closer together and much of their economic activities relate to these meals. The Qumran community upheld the concept of "oneness" (*yahad*) both in "law and possessions"[132] (1QS 5:2). As such they "held all things in common and were devoted in oneness to all responsibilities."[133] The CD differed from this slightly in that it required only the contribution of two day's salary a month.[134] This requirement fits the context of the people addressed who reside in towns and villages.

3.4 Conclusion on Dead Sea Scrolls and Qumran Community on Work and Community

We set out to see ways in which work and community intersect in the Qumran community. Our analysis revealed that the people behind the Dead Sea Scrolls were the sectarian community that domiciled at Qumran. Archaeological evidence revealed that the sectaries made scrolls, pottery, soap, cultivated dates and grain, and kept sheep, goats, and cattle. Agriculture played a significant role at Qumran and, as such, it provided most of the work the sectaries did. The community required its members to come with their wealth (what one owned as well as one's ability to earn through work). The community required that members contribute "knowledge, power, and wealth" (1QS 1 11–15). Wealth (holistically understood) was a prominent symbol of community unity.[135] By extension, work, which is what brings about wealth, was a way to bring the community together. In this sense, the community was

---

132. Collins, *Beyond the Qumran Community*, 144.

133. Charlesworth, "Community Organization," 133. Josephus writes "For it is a law that those entering the sect transfer their property to the order; consequently, among them all there appears neither abject poverty nor superabundance of wealth, but the possessions of each are mingled, and there is, as among brothers, one property common to all." Josephus, *Works of Josephus*, 2.122; cf *Antiquities*, 18.20; Philo, *Hypothetica* 10.4 and *Good Person* 77 (in Philo, *The Works of Philo*).

134. Collins, *Beyond the Qumran Community*, 144.

135. Murphy, *Wealth in the Dead Sea*, 154.

interested in the whole person and not part of the person. Our survey of the scrolls also revealed that the community has much to say about money and work. Regulations are provided as to when work is not to be done, that is, on Sabbath, and who to consult and obey in such matters of work and money. Also, the community punished those who failed to report their earnings truthfully; these were excluded from the communal meals. Participation at the community table is connected with working and earnings thereof.

Communal meals were a significant part of communal life among the sectaries. Much of their economic activities were tied to the provision of their communal life. In the Qumran community, one's work is demonstrated by reporting truthfully one's earnings, failure of which results in not eating. As such we can assume that the obedience in question relates to work. Obedience in matters of work requires the novice sectary to work and contribute to the lot of the community.[136] Also, the Qumran texts make it clear that only those who could not provide for themselves could expect the community to care for them (CD A VI. 20 =4Q266 3; 4Q267 2; 4Q269 ii; 6Q15 3, 4). It follows that the community would have had a problem with one who could provide for themselves and did not do so. As for the priests, even though they did not do work related to goods and services, what they did was considered work – production of scrolls and studying them.

---

136. Leaney, *Rule of Qumran*, 180. He further notes "It is almost certain that the group decided upon the use of money earned as wages by the members in their work in the world" (180).

CHAPTER 4

Work and Community in the Greco-Roman Perspectives

4.1 Introduction

In the previous chapter we examined the relationship between work and community in the DSS. This chapter will now look at the idea of work and community in Greco-Roman perspectives. First, we will consider the household; second, we will look at a particular philosophical school – the Epicurean school; and third, we will examine the voluntary associations. Our hypothesis, generated from the African context, shall be applied to these institutions. Various models have been suggested for the early Christian communities, including the household, voluntary associations, synagogues, and philosophical schools.[1] And much work has been done on the appropriateness of each model for early Christian communities.[2]

It is beyond the scope of this study to discuss the appropriateness of each model. Our focus will be on the household, a particular philosophical school, and the Greco-Roman associations, primarily because such associations encompass synagogues.[3] Ascough has demonstrated that there is paucity of

---

1. Ascough, "Voluntary Associations," 143–237; McCready, "*Ekklēsia* and Voluntary Associations," 101–19.

2. Meeks, *First Urban Christians*, 84; See Gager, *Kingdom and Community*; Smith, *Pauline Communities*.

3. McCready, "*Ekklēsia* and Voluntary Associations," 115. We are not arguing the early Christian communities were some form of associations, but they do provide a background for

evidence for the existence of synagogues in Macedonia and yet the same cannot be said of associations.[4] The household (as is the case in modern society) was the basic unit of society. Every individual's first interaction with work was within the household. The reason for our adoption of voluntary associations is that they involve a gathering of people who are not related to each other by blood as in the household or who only gather because of social, economic, or religious reasons as in the synagogue.[5] Associations drew their membership from household networks, geographic ethnic groups, occupational networks, religious networks, and neighbourhood or location networks[6] – as such they are broad enough compared to the synagogue or the household alone. The voluntary associations were a phenomenon that affected a cross-section of society. The philosophical schools on the other hand only attracted the elite of society who predominantly espouse a disdain for manual labour. The work that was often disparaged in philosophical writings is manual work often done by slaves, whereas the work of philosophers and rulers is praised. Individuals who ended up as philosophers (like Socrates) had to leave the trades for those who did not have what it takes to be philosophers.[7]

4.2 Work and Community in the Greco-Roman Household

There is no doubt that the οἶκος (household) was an essential institution in Greco-Roman society. The household has been rightly called the critical institution of the ancient world.[8] The household was "a model of ancient kinship structures and of the reciprocal relations typical of families."[9] It was much bigger than the modern western household in that it was a family group living off a landed estate that consisted of father, mother, children, and grandchildren.[10]

---

looking at the early Christian communities. In many ways, associations were different from the Christian communities.

    4. Ascough, "Voluntary Associations," 308.

    5. See Barclay, "Money and Meetings," 114, for reasons for considering Christ groups as associations.

    6. Harland, *Associations*, 28–53.

    7. Sellars, "Simon the Shoemaker," 210.

    8. Hubbard, *Christianity in the Greco-Roman World*, 179.

    9. Elliott, *What Is Social-Scientific*, 44.

    10. Hubbard, *Christianity in the Greco-Roman World*, 179–82.

In addition to members of the nuclear family, it encompassed slaves, hired workers, craftsmen, guests, and other visitors.[11] The number of people in a particular household varied from house to house, and the paterfamilias was in charge of the household. The largest household could achieve some level of independence, as Finley notes: "With their flocks and their labour force, with plentiful stone for building and with clay for pots, the great households could almost realise their ideal of absolute self-sufficiency."[12] The fact that the household was self-sufficient is significant for our purposes in that its very survival depended on the work of its members. Yet it is essential to note that it was by no means a closed community; the household connected with the outside world through "hospitality, gift-giving and gift exchange."[13] It was through goods and deeds that social relations are sustained and disputes are solved.[14]

The household was "the basic unit of production and consumption in antiquity."[15] As such, work was an important activity of the household, something in which everyone, regardless of rank, engaged. As Applebaum notes "There is evidence that all sectors of the society participate in work activities, noblemen and noblewomen, as well as commoners."[16] Everyone was required to contribute their fair share; in other words, everyone worked.[17] Women functioned as house managers especially when their husbands were absent.[18] Plutarch calls the woman of the house the "mistress of the household."[19] Musonius Rufus allows women to study philosophy so that they can be good managers, accountants, and rulers of the household slaves.[20]

---

11. See Applebaum, *Concept of Work*.
12. Finley, *Economy and Society*, 60–61.
13. Applebaum, *Concept of Work*, 4–5.
14. Applebaum, 5.
15. Saller, "Women, Slaves," 189.
16. Applebaum, *Concept of Work*, 5.
17. Geoghegan, *Attitude Towards Labor*, 3. In the Odyssey we learn that Penelope, Odysseus's wife worked and she even refers to her own household duties, his father Laertes worked on the vineyard, even Odysseus himself is said to have cut grass and ploughed. Homer, *Odyssey*, 18: 336–80.
18. Saller, "Women, Slaves," 190.
19. Plutarch, *Moralia. Advice to Bride and Groom*, 311.
20. Musonius Rufus, *Stoic Fragments*, 3:10.

The noblemen were not exempt from work: "they spent their time supervising, managing and directing the work in the field."[21] For Finley, the communal nature of work in Homeric society in undeniable. He observes, "With respect to work and wealth . . . the determinant was always the particular social grouping to which one belonged, not the skills, desires or enterprise of an individual."[22] The work done was always for the household in which one belonged. As such, an individual did not work for oneself but for their household. The head of the household then distributed the fruits of the collective labour.[23]

Labour was divided between work done in the household (women mostly did this kind of work) and the field (men mostly did this kind of work). The household work included spinning, weaving, grinding corn, baking bread, and cleaning beds and clothes, whereas men engaged in agricultural work which included ploughing, herding, building walls, and building fences.[24] Even in classical Greek society, the fact that women mostly worked in the household did not change. No wonder economics has its root in οἰκονομικός, which relate to the proper management of the household, a job done by women in an aristocratic household.[25]

Many men were able to perform various kinds of work.[26] It was not unusual, however, for men also to perform some kind of work in the household, as Applebaum asserts: "When the household is the productive and consumption unit combined, cooperation and reciprocity between men and women is decisive for the smooth function of the household."[27] The opposite is true as well; several women worked in jobs considered masculine as noted by Susan Treggiari who observes, "The frequency with which a woman is paired

---

21. Homer, *Iliad* 15: 556–57. Applebaum, *Concept of Work*, 10. Homer's descriptions of a rural setting on the Shield of Achilles has all the aspects of the communal nature of work in which both men and women, king and commoner, work and feasting, music and dance are present. *Iliad* 18: 366–76 See Applebaum, *Concept of Work*.

22. Finley, *Economy and Society*.

23. Applebaum, *Concept of Work*, 4.

24. Applebaum, 14.

25. Applebaum, 51.

26. Homer, *Iliad* 18: 543–75 Applebaum, *Concept of Work*, 14.

27. Applebaum, *Concept of Work*, 14.

with a man, usually a husband, in the same trade suggests that many of them worked alongside husbands."[28]

The household, for the most part, provided opportunities for child labour, particularly among the working families and, to a lesser extent, among the aristocratic families.[29] Margaret MacDonald has demonstrated that there was a huge gap between free and slave children.[30] Given that aristocratic families were among the minorities, the fact that working families required children to work is significant for this study. Writers such as Ulpian observe that children under five were not able to work properly, whereas at age seven their work was valued.[31] The rural economy provided opportunities for work in areas like herding, fodder gathering, trimming vines, and gathering vines for both free children and slave boys, whereas in urban environments children did various kinds of work including working as stonemasons, cobblers, jewellers, and bakers.[32] It was not unusual for slave children to attend a wedding in which they worked as servers, readers, and entertainers.[33] Children had three ways of learning various jobs: learning from workers in the household, being apprenticed, or training for the work they desired to do. Only a few could afford apprenticeships and training outside the home; consequently, the majority of children learned how to work from their parents at home.[34]

In classical Greek society even though the family remained an important institution, its former glory was usurped by the polis – that is, the city-states. Applebaum's estimation was "a community of citizens."[35] Aristotle saw the household as a microcosm of the city: which was true of the household was also true of the polis.[36] Specialization in the craft began in classical Greek society with Solon calling fathers to teach their sons trades.[37] It is the specialization of different trades that brought about the distinctions of one trade

---

28. Treggiari, "Lower Class Women," 76.
29. Bradley, *Discovering the Roman Family*.
30. MacDonald, *Work in the Field*.
31. *Dig.* 7.7.6.1; Saller, "Household and Gender," 108.
32. *Dig.* 7.7.6.1; Saller, 108.
33. Nepos, "Excerpt"; MacDonald, "Reading the New Testament," 380.
34. *Dig.* 7.7.6.1 Saller, "Household and Gender," 108.
35. Applebaum, *Concept of Work*, 24.
36. Meeks, *Origins of Christian Morality*.
37. Applebaum, *Concept of Work*, 27.

from another and the question of whether one worked for another person or not. Working for another was considered slavery and, as such, not fitting for a free man. Aristotle stated that "It is noble not to practice any sordid craft since it is a mark of a free man not to live at another's beck and call."[38] The demand for crafted items, fine clothes, and quality goods, which the household could not provide, necessitated the rise of the artisan class. Fathers often taught their trade to their sons who in turn would identify their work by mentioning their father's names. This is the case at Delphi where we encounter Agathon, his son Agasikrates and his son Agathokles all who happen to have practised the same craft.[39] Consequently, work was taken from the purview of the household and many artisans often operated alone as itinerant artisans. In a way the communal aspect of work was diminished. However, the need for community resulted in artisans coming together with other artisans to form artisan guilds.

It is clear from the preceding that work was an essential activity of the household. No one was exempt from work starting with the noblemen to the child of a slave. Men and women, slave and free, young and old, all had a part to play in either production or consumption of work in the household. The household then provided opportunities for work for every member of the household. We can safely say that a household is a community that was a working community. At the same time, slave members of the household were constrained to work. Even though some slaves loved their masters and worked without being forced, the majority were constrained. The work done by the aristocracy cannot be compared with the work done by the slaves who often did not have leisure. The existence of slave society inhibited the existence of genuine community in the household.

4.3 Work and Community in Epicurean Philosophical School

Having considered the work and community in the household, we now turn to the philosophical schools. These groups attempted to live together in communities in which the teachers (philosophers) gathered their students

---

38. Aristotle, *Art of Rhetoric*, 1:9, 1367a32.
39. Applebaum, *Concept of Work*, 45.

not only to learn their philosophical ideas but their way of life as well. The dominant voice concerning work among the philosophers is predominantly negative since most of them came from the upper class, and they represent the disdain for manual work that was common of Greek/Roman upper classes. However, this is not to say that all philosophers despised manual labour; some, like Socrates, Menedemus, Musonius Rufus, Simon the shoemaker, and Cleanthes combined the practice of philosophy and manual labour.[40] These working philosophers were often ridiculed, since it was considered not fitting for a philosopher to engage in a trade. Socrates, Cleanthes, Menedemus, and Simon the shoemaker, were all ridiculed for working.[41] Since we know more about Epicureans as a philosophical school, we are going to investigate them as a test case for our enquiry.

We are going to examine the relationship between work and community in the Epicurean school. Here the historical information about Epicurus and the garden is going to be important since it is the basis on which subsequent communities were based. Epicurus, the founder of Epicureanism, was born on the island of Samos, which is near Ephesus, around 341 BC.[42] His family was educated but poor, as his father was a school principal.[43] He is said to have learned philosophy under Nausiphanes, whom he disowned as his teacher later in life.[44] Epicurus is reported to have developed an independent mind and founded his own school, which he named after himself.[45] A garden, purchased at the cost of eighty minae, was the meeting place of the school.[46] He was able to convince his brothers (Neocles, Chaeredemus, and Aristobolus) and also his slave Mys to join the school.[47] It is possible that Mys may not have been the only slave; he was, however, prominent. Diogenes says Epicurus was gentle to his slaves as seen in his will and by the fact that they were members

---

40. Diogenes Laertius, *Lives of Eminent Philosophers*, 168–70.
41. Hock, *Working Apostle*, 29.
42. Diogenes Laertius, *Lives of Eminent Philosophers*, 10.14; De Witt, *Saint Paul and Epicurus*, 3.
43. De Witt, *Saint Paul and Epicurus*, 3.
44. Diogenes Laertius, *Lives of Eminent Philosophers*, 10.7–8.
45. Diogenes Laertius, 10.2. 529.
46. Zeller, *Stoics, Epicureans*, 406–7.
47. Diogenes Laertius, *Lives of Eminent Philosophers*, 10.3. 531.

of his school.⁴⁸ They studied while being slaves and were manumitted in his last testament.⁴⁹ It is possible that other members of the garden could have had slaves of their own, suggesting that work, if it was done, was outsourced to a certain extent. It is evident here that work did not play a significant role for some members of the school except for slaves.

The Epicurean belief in withdrawal from public life was for the sole reason of communion with fellow Epicureans.⁵⁰ In this school, we have a group that was founded for community. Epicurus would say, "Security from people, which is brought up to a point by a certain power to drive away [what threatens us], is achieved in the most abundant and unmixed way in the security which comes from quietness and withdrawal from the affairs of the majority."⁵¹ Diogenes Laertius apologetically suggests that the reason he did not enter public life is that he had respect for others. Those in view are those who came to his garden to seek guidance from him.⁵² In a way, from the perspective of the Epicureans, they withdrew so that they could congregate with like-minded people. Bertrand Russell believes Epicurean principles of pleasure informed Epicurus's withdrawal from public life since when a person attains power, those who seek to harm him also increase in number.⁵³

Withdrawal is not so that one can live a life of "solitude." One still needs friends.⁵⁴ Critics like Cicero and Plutarch considered this kind of abstinence from public life to be "parasitic" since the Epicurean community benefit from the public order and security that others bring about through their involvement in politics.⁵⁵ The typical Epicurean response to this was given by Diogenes of Oenoanda when he envisions what Sharpe calls an "Epicurean Millennium" in which the gods will give truth to human beings and justice

---

48. Diogenes Laertius, 10.10. 539.
49. Diogenes Laertius, 10.21. 549.
50. Sharples, *Stoics, Epicureans*, 118.
51. Epicurus, *Principal Doctrines*, 14.
52. Diogenes Laertius, *Lives of Eminent Philosophers*, 10.10. 539.
53. Russell, *History of Western Philosophy*, 267.
54. Madeira, "Cultural Meaning," 442.
55. Cicero, "De Re Publica," 1.1–11; Plutarch, *Moralia. Reply to Colotes*, 1127; Sharples, *Stoics, Epicureans*, 121.

and friendship will become a reality. When that happens, there shall not be any need for laws and possibly public service.[56]

Friendship is essential in Epicurean thought since those who withdrew did so to be with friends. Epicurus says "Friendship dances around the world, announcing to us that we should bestow ourselves for the enjoyment of happiness."[57] As such, the Epicurean garden can rightly be considered "a community of friends" and Epicurus would claim to practise his philosophy since he had love for all.[58] Yet the basis for such friendship was self-interest. For Epicurus, a friend must not always be seeking help, and one is also not a friend if they do not relate friendship with lending a hand[59] – even though in Epicurean thought "it is more pleasant to confer benefit than to receive it."[60] Nevertheless, "the friend's good is secondary, one's own pleasure is the ultimate aim."[61] All this fits with his understanding of pleasure as the "sole criterion of value."[62] For our purposes it is evident that even though the Epicureans seem interested in community, it was for the sake of self. Work and community cannot have a proper relationship if genuine community does not exist.

Friendship, according to Epicurus, is to be differentiated from love which he considered a "passion" or "instinct." Friendship is different in that it is "rational and reflective" and it is "freely formed and imposing no inalienable obligation, no binding impersonal law" and in it "man finds his true home."[63] In friendship, men are free for they impose on themselves duties voluntarily rather than those from the family or state. As such "the principle of community, rejected in its more stable forms, is accepted in its latest and most flexible shape, where it is maintained solely by participation in pleasures in common."[64]

---

56. Diogenes, *Thirteen New Fragments*, fr 56; Sharples, *Stoics, Epicureans*, 122.
57. Epicurus, *Sententiae Vaticanae*, Iii; Long, *Hellenistic Philosophy*, 72.
58. Diogenes Laertius, *Lives of Eminent Philosophers*, 10.10.539; Long, *Hellenistic Philosophy*, 72.
59. Epicurus, *Sententiae Vaticanae*, XXXIV; Long, *Hellenistic Philosophy*, 72.
60. Long, *Hellenistic Philosophy*, 72.
61. Sharples, *Stoics, Epicureans*, 120.
62. Long, *Hellenistic Philosophy*, 72.
63. Wallace, *Epicureanism*, 165.
64. Wallace, 165.

It was the Epicurean doctrine of friendship that became the basis for communal life. The common life of the garden had its foundation in their understanding of friendship.[65] As such, the learners were not students in the traditional sense but colleagues of the master not students in his lectures. They were shaped more by sharing life with their teacher than listening to his lectures.[66] A. A. Long has suggested that we should not think of Epicurean community as a college or research institution but as "a society of friends" who live together by following "common principles" having retreated from public life.[67] In this way, "those who committed themselves to Epicurus were not so much students 'reading for a course' as men and women dedicated to a certain style of life."[68]

The Epicureans maintained their private property because doing otherwise would betray the trust they were trying to build. Nevertheless, Epicurus required that members make their individual possessions available to the community.[69] Epicurus in his will stipulated that his house and garden become communal property.[70] He instructed Hermarchus (the trustee) to ensure that Nicanor (child of a disciple who had died)[71] is provided for since he has "rendered service to me in private life and have shown me kindness in every way and have chosen to grow old with me in the school should, so far as my means go, not lack the necessities of life."[72] Even though they did not have common property, members paid "a voluntary contribution" to the school chief and such contributions could continue even after death provided it was stated in their will.[73]

The community of the garden was maintained by contributions from friends who were requested to send "first fruits."[74] One friend in particular

---

65. Wallace, 59.

66. Wallace, 59.

67. Long, *Hellenistic Philosophy*, 15.

68. Long, 15.

69. Diogenes Laertius, *Lives of Eminent Philosophers*, 10.11; Baumgarten, "Graeco-Roman Voluntary Associations," 100.

70. Long, *Hellenistic Philosophy*, 15.

71. Wallace, *Epicureanism*, 47.

72. Diogenes Laertius, *Lives of Eminent Philosophers*, 10.20.549.

73. Wallace, *Epicureanism*, 62–63.

74. Plutarch, *Moralia. Reply to Colotes*, c.xviii. 3; Wallace, *Epicureanism*, 64; Russell, *History of Western Philosophy*, 265.

is Idomeneus, who is said to have been learned and wealthy, and who furnished Epicurus with "generous financial support" for a long time.[75] There is no evidence that the people living in the garden engaged in work/economic activities at the garden, but they seem to have had such activities in their home towns. Since membership of the school was not fixed, they came freely and spent time with their master.[76] There were exceptions; a mature member whom Epicurus mentions in his will was to be noticed by the trustees because he had left everything to pursue philosophy.[77]

These friends who were not at the garden could be called upon to procure corn or provide for the garden. It is friends who kept the garden supplied with provisions. Wallace has noted that "the members of the sect take a family human interest in the minutest concerns of each other."[78] This concern, however, had limits among the Epicureans, whose primary concern was themselves. The Epicureans had wealthy people or members of the nobility among their number: as such, members became benefactors for each other.[79] The existence of such individuals who had means meant that work did not become an essential part of community life among Epicureans.

Seneca seems to suggest that the Epicureans invited people to come to the garden without the need to pay. He attributes the words he cites to Epicurus himself.[80] He states

> "Stranger, here you will do well to tarry; here our highest good is pleasure." The caretaker of that abode, a kindly host, will be ready for you; he will welcome you with barley – meal and serve you water also in abundance, with these words: "Have you not been well entertained?" "This garden," he says, "does not whet your appetite; it quenches it. Nor does it make you more thirsty with every drink; it slakes the thirst by a natural cure, – a cure

---

75. De Witt, *Saint Paul and Epicurus*, 8.
76. Wallace, *Epicureanism*, 51.
77. Wallace, 51.
78. Wallace, 51.
79. Wallace, 64.
80. Seneca, *Epistles*, XXI:10. 147.

that demands no fee. This is the "pleasure" in which I have grown old.[81]

What is in view here is the learning one obtains from the garden; there is no need for payment. It is not clear if the meal in question in the motto (cited above) is metaphorical or if it is also referring to personal upkeep. However, if the group lived by the philosophy that says "We ought to look round for people to eat and drink with, before we look for something to eat and drink: to feed without a friend is the life of a lion and a wolf,"[82] they must have shared their food with each other. It is also not clear whether there were communal meals here except for their celebrations.

For Epicurus, the wise person "will make money, but only by his wisdom, if he should be in poverty, and he will pay court to a king if need be."[83] This suggests that the Epicureans did not consider it proper for a wise person to engage in commerce.[84] To a certain extent, Epicurus demonstrates the disdain for labour of the Greek upper class. This view is articulated by another Epicurean philosopher Philodemus, who once said "But the philosopher, properly speaking, does not work, nor, if he ever works, does he seem to put everything at risk so as [to need exhortation] not to do it."[85] Some Epicureans resorted to selling books as is the case with Marcus Pompilius Andronicus (native of Syria). Suetonius reports that he was not a good grammarian and could not make it in Rome, so he moved to Cumae where he "led a quiet life and wrote many books. But he was so poor and needy that he was forced to sell that admirable little work of his, 'Criticisms of the Annals of Ennius.'"[86]

The Epicureans were often criticized for being interested only in conviviality. Such accusation came even from the adherents of Epicurean thought like Horace, who is said to have been unaffiliated with any school. Horace writes "Even Metrodorus, intimate friend of Epicurus, is reported to have said that 'it is our business, not to seek crowns by saving the Greeks, but to enjoy

---

81. Seneca, XXI:10–11. 147.
82. Wallace, *Epicureanism*, 168.
83. Diogenes Laertius, *Lives of Eminent Philosophers*, 10.120. 647.
84. Wallace, *Epicureanism*, 168.
85. Tsouna, *Philodemus*, XI. 31.
86. Suetonius, "Lives of Illustrious Men," II:VIII, 393.

ourselves in good eating and drinking.'"[87] This, however, was far from what the Epicureans actually did. They lived a simple life with limited luxuries, and even critics like Philemon could say "This fellow [Epicurus] is bringing in a new philosophy; he preaches hunger, and disciples follow him. They get but a single roll, a dried fig to relish it, and water to wash it down."[88]

Seneca reports that Epicurus boasted that he "lived on less than a penny, but that Metrodous, whose progress was not yet so great, needed a whole penny."[89] Even though the rations were worse than those given to prisoners, according to Seneca one could still derive pleasure from it.[90] The simple life was in line with the Epicurean conception of pleasure as the removal of pain. Once pain is removed, pleasure cannot be enhanced.[91] As Wallace states "Costly fare only gives a character of variety and multiplicity to the enjoyment which it cannot increase."[92] Bertrand Russell believes that the Epicurean simplicity was both a matter of "principle and partly (no doubt) for lack of money."[93] Simplicity, as practiced by Epicureans, was a result of their belief about wealth and financial gain, which was perceived to result in unhappiness.[94]

The individual ethics are determined by the individual in question and not by the interests of the community. As such the individual has only a duty to make their own life enjoyable.[95] In short "The rights of the individual are in a sense paramount over those of the community."[96] In this sense, Epicureanism is in many respects "practical, realistic and modern."[97] In Epicurean thought "Man the individual is the only *real* unit of social life: all other unities are so far *ideal* and fictitious, and are due to the combined effort of individual wills."[98] In this community, the focus is on self rather than on the community.

---

87. Horace, *Satires*, i. 1:14, 1926H.
88. Clement of Alexandria, *Stromata*, II 493; Wallace, *Epicureanism*, 50.
89. Seneca, *Epistles*, XVIII:10, 121.
90. Seneca, XVIII:11, 123.
91. Wallace, *Epicureanism*, 51.
92. Wallace, 52.
93. Durant, *Story of Philosophy*, 264–65.
94. O'Keefe, "Epicureans on Happiness," 51.
95. Wallace, *Epicureanism*, 157.
96. Wallace, 159–60.
97. Wallace, 160.
98. Wallace, 160.

Whatever one does has its focus on the individual concerned and not on the community.

In summary, even though the Epicureans had a strong emphasis in community, their community had nothing to do with the larger society from which they withdrew. The charge of being "parasitic" cannot be ignored since the Epicureans lived off others who had the means either within or without their community. In this community, it is inevitable that here, the relationship between work and community is not clearly evident. There is no evidence to suggest that there was a work that took place in this community. Members of the community seem to have relied on wealthy benefactors who in turn expected the philosopher to become a resident philosopher. This Epicurean community is not a working community but rather a learning community. Let us now turn to the voluntary associations to determine the relationship between work and community.

4.4 Work and Community in Greco-Roman Associations

This section explores how work relates to community building in Greco-Roman associations. We shall consider the financial obligations in associations, responsibilities within the associations, and exemption from service or work and regulations of certain trades within the associations. Our discussion shall focus on financial obligations and responsibilities within the associations. We offer these as evidence that association members had to work as a means to support their obligation within the society. Before we look at these issues, we need to define associations and highlight their purpose and membership criteria.

4.4.1 Definition, Purpose, and Membership of Associations

Here we shall attempt to define and briefly discuss the purpose for which associations were formed and the kind of people they attracted. The social situation of members is crucial in helping to ascertain whether these people worked or not. It can be said that associations are those groups that bridged the gap between the family and the polis in the Greco-Roman world.[99] Colin

---

99. Kloppenborg, Ascough, and Harland, *Greco-Roman Associations*.

Roberts, Theodore Skeat, and Arthur Nock defined them as groups "which a man joins of his own free will, and which accepts him of its free will, and this mutual acceptance creates certain obligations on both parties."[100] Lloyd Gaston has defined them as coherent groups "which could be recognised as such by outsiders, with its own rules for membership, leadership and association with one another."[101] However, it should be noted that a group does not need recognition by outsiders for it to function as a group. Jinyu Liu enumerates the characteristics of a *collegium* noting that the minimum size was three people; a club needed to have a name, its own by-laws, regulations, common treasury, and a patron or patrons.[102]

These clubs started appearing around the third century BC, primarily to protect the interests of their members.[103] It is the Hellenistic period where we see an upsurge of epigraphical evidence for associations of different persuasions. Yet it was not until the imperial period that we have evidence for the activities and organization of numerous associations.[104] At times the restrictions on their (private associations) formation were sometimes enforced; yet this did not seem to affect their proliferation and at times some associations served as apparatus of government.[105] Different terminology is used for associations including: ὀργεῶνες; θίασος (Rome); ἔρανος; ἔφηβοι; (νεώτεροι); ἐκκλησία (Athens); συναγωγή, σύνοδος (Delos); and κοινόν (Berytian). Some of these terms like ἐκκλησία and συναγωγή were also used by the Christian ἐκκλησία and Jewish groups respectively.[106] Stephen G. Wilson, while acknowledging that terminological similarity could be coincidental, asserts that associations were "part of a broad social phenomenon."[107] The Roman associations were known as *collegia*, with other Latin terms like *sodalitas*, *factio*, *curia*, and *fratres*. John S. Kloppenborg finds this broad range of terms

---

100. Roberts, Skeat, and Nock, *Gild of Zeus*, 1936; Meeks, *First Urban Christians*.

101. Gaston, "Pharisaic Problems."

102. Liu, "Pompeii and *Collegia*," 53–69. However, it must be acknowledged that clubs did not always practice common activities, Last, *Pauline Church*.

103. Goodman and Sherwood, *Roman World*, 191. These interests include providing burial for the members and even bailing each other when in debt.

104. Ascough, "Voluntary Associations," 245–46.

105. Ascough, 245–46.

106. Kloppenborg and Wilson, *Voluntary Associations*, 18.

107. Wilson, "Voluntary Associations," 23–42.

makes it difficult to differentiate various types of associations.[108] Regardless, the most commonly used term in association records is κοινόν, especially in Greek associations.

Scholars often divide associations into three major divisions based on their primary purpose: first, occupational; second, cultic; and third, burial.[109] The majority of associations were funeral ones;[110] however, funerary associations also existed for social reasons. Because they were legally permitted, some associations used this route to satisfy the social needs of the group.[111] The opposite is also true: some groups started for other purposes could end up existing as burial societies. Waltzing affirms that "many private associations, originally founded to honor a divinity, ended up regarding religion as an accessory and the funeral as their principal aim."[112] The drawback with studying associations based on purpose is that it does not take cognizance of the multiplicity of functions within associations.[113] The reason for this is that most associations catered for a variety of "interrelated purposes."[114]

These professional associations or guilds were able to put together considerations for the trade, religion and/or faith, and social concerns in a way not seen before. In some of these guilds, people were brought together by a craft, which was practised by all the members.[115] The guilds provided various professions with a sense of community and a way in which proper appreciation was rendered for work they offered.[116] Work is the primary reason different people are brought together in the guilds; such people would not commune under any other circumstance.[117]

Members had obligations to the association, which included regular attendance at the society meetings, payment of fees, service duties, and donations

---

108. Kloppenborg and Wilson, *Voluntary Associations*, 18.
109. Harland, *Associations*, 44.
110. Harland, 28.
111. Ascough, "Voluntary Associations," 236–47.
112. Harland, *Associations*.
113. Frenz Poland is right to note that "every association is in some sense a cult association." Cited in Harland, *Associations*, 29.
114. Harland, *Associations*, 29. Last, *Pauline Church*, 23.
115. Geoghegan, *Attitude Towards Labor*, 54–55.
116. Goodman and Sherwood, *Roman World*, 191.
117. Jones, *Associations of Classical Athens*, 46.

towards banquet meals.[118] The meals were an essential part of the communal life of associations,[119] and in some associations attendance was mandatory. Given then that the majority of private associations were composed of the poor of the society,[120] the only way that they could earn their living was, in the words of Lynn H. Cohick, "through hard work and bit of luck."[121] Those who joined voluntary associations were "freedmen, slaves, peregrini and resident aliens."[122] Similarly, Moyer V. Hubbard sees association membership as predominantly from the lower social class: that is, "freedmen, shopkeepers, working class, artisans, slaves."[123] If members of the upper stratum took part in associations, they did so as patrons of the groups.[124] If this is the composition of associations, the question of disposable income becomes pertinent. Keith Bradley in reference to manumission has pointed out that slaves could make money from "profit obtained by chance, or by the kindness or generosity of a friend, or by the slaves' carrying a charge to his own account, or giving an undertaking, or accepting a liability or the obligation to pay a debt."[125] It was not uncommon for slaves to work as wet nurses and *paidagogus* (guardian) and some were compensated for their services.[126] Rural slaves according to Varro reared livestock as a way to complement their food rations, so that they could live comfortably and possibly be more diligent.[127] Slaves based in the city tended kitchen gardens where they grew a variety of vegetables for their consumption and sold the surplus for cash.[128]

In summary, associations were social groups that brought together people with common characteristics for mutual benefit. Those at the lower social level found them useful in meeting the needs which the polis did not address. Given that those who joined associations were from the lower strata of society,

---

118. Ascough, "Paul and Associations," 68–89.

119. Öhler, "Cultic Meals," 475–502.

120. Scheidel and Friesen, "Size of the Economy," 61; Meggitt, *Paul, Poverty*; Longenecker, *Remember the Poor*; Friesen, "Poverty in Pauline Studies," 323–61.

121. Cohick, *Women in the World*, 225.

122. Kloppenborg, "Collegia and Thiasoi," 43, 53.

123. Hubbard, *Christianity in the Greco-Roman World*.

124. Stegemann and Stegemann, *Jesus Movement*, 280.

125. Bradley, *Slavery and Society*.

126. Saller, "Slavery and the Roman Family," 82–110.

127. See Varro, *On Agriculture*.

128. Pliny, *Natural History*; Jashemski, *Gardens of Pompeii*; Bradley, *Slavery and Society*.

they had to work in order to provide for themselves as well as keep up with membership obligations, as we shall see below. Let us now discuss more specifically the interplay of work and community in Greco-Roman associations.

4.4.2 Financial Obligations in Association

This section will look at the need for contributions of membership fees in associations. Did people pay in order to be members? And were there any other financial obligations apart from fees? There is a paucity of evidence of associations which did not require membership fees; only one seems to have solely depended on benefactors; Aesculapius Hygla of Rome.[129] Given the benefits or advantage associations provided, those who joined were willing to pay – hence the term voluntary associations. The need for contributions presupposes that members had to have a source of income to participate in these associations.[130]

The Bacchic society required its members to pay an entrance fee of fifty denarii and a libation for those whose fathers were not members. Failure to pay the entrance fee resulted in one being evicted from the banquet until they paid what they owed. The members of the associations were required to pay for banquets since attendance was mandatory. Fines were charged to those who failed to attend and on those who broke community rules during meetings.[131] Each member "shall speak and act and be zealous for the Association, contributing to the fixed monthly dues for wine. If he does not fulfil these obligations, he shall be shut out of the gathering (*stibas*)."[132]

The society had an opportunity for further revenue when members were disorderly, fought, or failed to attend the meeting of the society, or when they took the issue of the society to public courts, or sang without permission.[133] The requirements for payment presuppose that the members of the society have a source of income. It is logical to conclude that if a person was without a source of income, they could not afford to be a member of the community.

---

129. *CIL* VI 0234; Kloppenborg, "Collegia and Thiasoi," 51.

130. Last cites C. C. Edgar who once said, "The club was, of course, kept up by subscription," 115. The associations often took about 10 percent of the income of their members, and their very survival depended on these subscriptions. Last, *Pauline Church*.

131. Ascough, "Forms of Commensality," 36.

132. *IG* II² 1368, 13–16.

133. *IG* II² 1368, 13–16.

In Karanis (Egypt) Epiodoros, a member of the association, decided to resign from being a member, citing the fact that he was impoverished and hence was unable to keep up with contributions to the common fund.[134] These payments reveal that one could not sustain membership in an association if they did not have a source of income.

Similarly, the inscription of the *collegium* of worshippers of Diana and Antinous states that "we must all agree to contribute faithfully so that our association many be able to continue in existence a long time."[135] The very existence of the society requires that contributions be taken, failing which the society will cease to exist. In this society, the members take turns to provide dinners and members who fail to comply were to pay thirty sesterces to the Treasury and the one next in line will provide in his place. The dinners are the glue of the society's existence, and if they are not offered, the society ceases to be a society.[136] John M. G. Barclay has observed the close relationship between membership and giving and receiving money, concluding that "all such financial transactions served to solidify the social identity of the group, and clarify the boundaries between insiders and outsiders."[137] Given the social profile we have painted thus far of association members as mostly drawn from the lower echelons of society, it follows, then, that financial resources could only have been generated through work. Patrons supported the associations but by no means did they take care of all the expenses.

The Bacchic society minutes assume that the members of the society are working. It prescribes that if one receives a legacy, honour, appointment, or promotion in their work, they are to make a libation equivalent to what they have received. Examples of such promotions include rod bearer, council member, president of games, member of the elder council, member of the lawgivers, magistrate, the sacrificer, police chief, and sacred victor. The society itself is served by the treasurer and the secretary (the latter being chosen by

---

134. *PMich* IX 575, 173.

135. *CIL* XIV 2112, 195.

136. *CIL* XIV 2112, 197. For people to eat someone has to pay, and for one to pay, they must have work. Barclay addresses the financial sources of the associations when he says "The 'associations' only came into existence by the donation of money-whether from a single benefactor (living or dead), by the subscription of a number of founder-members, or by the collection of membership-dues from those who made up the 'associations.'" See Barclay, "Money and Meetings."

137. Barclay, "Money and Meetings," 116.

the treasurer). The treasurer's responsibility is keeping track of the property of the society and providing oil for all meetings of the association. In addition to the work of the society, the treasurer has to have a way to earn an income so that they can meet their obligations to the society. In some associations the treasurer was exempted from paying membership fees for two years.[138] It is also true, however, that some individuals inherited money from their forebears and did not have to work for it.

Stephanos, of the society of Aphrodite, is identified as a breastplate maker and later became a supervisor (*epimelētēs*) of the association affairs, and performer of sacrifices. He is honoured "on account of the ambition and the nobility of character that he has exhibited toward the association of the society members."[139] As a reward for his diligence, the society resolved to crown him with an olive wreath and to pay him twenty drachmas. This society desires that others within the association or outside see that "the society members know how to return appropriate χάριτας (thanks)."[140] Likewise, the society of Tynaros decided to honour the supervisors for having "faithfully and ambitiously executed their responsibilities, both regarding the sacrifices and all other affairs of the association (*koinon*)." For this reason, the society resolved to honour them with olive wreaths and a plaque worth twenty drachmas.[141]

Among the Dionysiasts, Dionysios emerges as the epitome of true benefaction in a society. His beneficence was shown both to the society and individual members and was for the common good. The epitaph states that he was a "benefactor (*philantrōpōs*) at all times."[142] He served the society both as a priest and a treasurer. As treasurer, he contributed "one thousand silver drachmas from his own resources."[143] Dionysios also offered a place for conducting sacrifice to the god. The Dionysiasts honoured him and crowned him so that he would be remembered even after he was dead. Dionysios's son Agathokles inherited the office of treasurer from his father, and the society made him a priest for life. He too devoted himself, "wishing to demonstrate his goodwill

---

138. *IG* II² 1368, 13–16.
139. *IG* II² 1261, 23.
140. *IG* II² 1261, 23.
141. *IG* II² 1262, 24.
142. *IG* II² 1356, 30.
143. *IG* II² 1356, 30.

and beneficence to all of the Dionysiasts."¹⁴⁴ Even those who inherited the office from their fathers had to prove themselves by their contribution as Agathokles son of Dionysios did.

Apart from the elite benefactors like Dionysios, there were also what Richard Last has called "peer benefactors."¹⁴⁵ The group of *Thiosotai* in Scythia Minor provide us with an example of peer benefaction. Elite patrons could provide tremendous gifts such as meeting places whereas peer benefactors are those who were content with administrative functions and make contributions to societal activities. Also, they could go beyond the requirement of membership fees. They could be anyone ranging from "officers, ordinary members, socially strong, or socially weak."¹⁴⁶ Individuals which the honorific rewards targeted and this kind of contribution brought in more to the association than membership fees.¹⁴⁷

In summary, the societies required money to run their affairs. These funds came in the form of membership fees, fines, and benefaction. It is impossible to find a society that completely exempted members from paying subscription fees. Apart from fees, societies required members to hold leadership positions such as secretary and treasurer. To do that these people needed to finance their offices from their personal resources. We can safely say that these societies were a gathering of working people or at least people who could afford the membership fees. Since the associations did not pay anyone (except appropriate honours), their members had to work to earn money required to maintain their membership and earn the honours that societies could give to those who contributed to their affairs. We will now turn to the responsibilities inside and outside associations.

4.4.3 Responsibilities Inside and Outside Associations

We have established that associations required membership fees and other forms of benefaction; now we will look at the responsibilities required of either officers or regular members of societies. Societies appeared to be interested in industrious people. The Association of Banqueters of Sparta

---

144. *IG* II² 1356, 31.
145. Last, *Pauline Church*, 166.
146. Last, 151.
147. Last, 151.

(Peloponnesos) identifies its members in the membership list by the responsibilities they have inside and outside the association. These responsibilities include being supervisors, priests and priestesses, officers of the youth, elders, overseers, heralds, flute players, master builders, carvers, guilders, spinners, paean singers, dyers, secretaries, readers, bakers, butchers, and many others.[148] It is possible that they contributed to the association with what they had and the skills they possessed. There were professional associations for fuller, linen-workers, purple dyers, silversmiths, and many others. Kloppenborg has noted that the membership of these associations would have been people who were part of that trade and resided in the location where the association met. He states that since the trades were mostly located in populated streets, the association of silversmith "might include non-silversmiths who happened to live on the same street."[149] Consequently, the various classifications of associations should not be overemphasized.

Similarly, in the association in Amphipolis (Macedonia), Marcus Caecilius Sotas was known as the coppersmith.[150] In Thrace, Flavius, a member of the society, is recognized as the manufacturer of hats, and Herakleianos as the baker of white bread.[151] Camillus Polynices of the Association of Carpenters is branded as a goldsmith (*aurifex*). The society is said to be a (*corpus*) body of carpenters (*fabri tignuarii*) "who discharged all of their offices (*honores*)."[152] This inscription is as much about the association as it is about Camillus Polynices and his son, who was also of the same association.[153] According to Michael Peachin, it was not unusual for children to follow their parents in the family trade and at times they could surpass their parents in the practice of the trade.[154]

A society in Kallatis (Scythia Minor) decided to construct a temple for their god. The society members are called upon to contribute towards this construction project. Various honours are promised for the members who contribute. Three men are to ensure the temple is constructed "magnificently

---

148. *IG* V, 1 209, 35.
149. Kloppenborg, "Membership Practices," 192.
150. *SIG*² 773, 37.
151. SEG 39 (1989), 53.
152. *ILS* 7687, 217–18.
153. *ILS* 7687, 217–18.
154. See Peachin, *Oxford Handbook*.

and quickly."¹⁵⁵ More honours are guaranteed for those who oversee the construction work. The rest of the epigraph lists members who contributed, first those who contribute gold coins and then those who gave thirty silver drachmas, followed by those who provided workers starting with thirty, fifteen, and then ten workers.¹⁵⁶ This is a classic case of a society coming together for a common cause and working to ensure that the temple is built.

Over a lifetime someone could hold many responsibilities. For instance, in Hierapolis, Gaius Ageleius Apollonides was honoured for having been a "member of the virtuous councillors, commander of the city, market overseer, member of the Board of Ten, leader of the association (*conventus*) of the Romans, provider of the oil, auditor of public accounts, director of public works" and he is also said to have been "useful in meeting imperial needs."¹⁵⁷ Likewise, the M. Ulpius Domesticus of the Synod of Athletes in Rome, is said to have been "head of the athletes for life and high priest of the whole athletic meeting, incredible victor in all the important games, officer in charge of the Augustan baths, their own patron and ambassador who requested the sanctuary for the whole athletic meeting."¹⁵⁸

It is clear that those honoured were quite industrious, and the societies honoured members in the hope that the others might be inspired to follow suit. They clearly did not condone idleness but praised hard work and even honoured it. That societies gave honours to individuals is a testimony to how they valued contributions in kind and cash. Since the Greco-Roman society hungered for honours, societies capitalized on such desire. In conclusion, Greco-Roman associations are communities that appreciated work, provided opportunities for people to contribute to the well-being of the society, and honoured those who did so.

4.4.4 Summary of Work and Community in Associations

The above discussion has established that within voluntary associations members had financial obligations; they had responsibilities in and outside the association; the work they did resulted in exemption from further service;

---

155. *IGLSkythia* III 35, 58.
156. *IGLSkythia* III 35, 58.
157. *IHierapJ* 32, 97.
158. *IGUR* 237, 211.

and the association records include regulations of professions. The associations also honoured those who worked hard and provided regulations for how specific trades were to be done. All these reveal that associations were working communities who at times came together simply because their members already worked together. Even when they got together, there was work to be done so that the society's affairs could go on unhindered. The societies required various positions to be filled and those who filled them were required to finance their offices from their own resources. Associations were keen on dispensing honours to those who either served or provided benefaction for the group. These honours were ways to solicit more service and beneficence from those who required honour.

4.5 Conclusion – Work and Community in Greco-Roman Perspectives

This chapter sought to establish how work was perceived in aspects of the Greco-Roman world and the relationship between work and community. We looked at three institutions – the household, a philosophical school, and the voluntary associations. The household offered opportunities for work for all its members, both old and young and free and slave. The Epicurean school members withdrew from society to fellowship with fellow Epicureans. Since many of them had benefactors, the school did not integrate work as part of their community life. Among the Epicureans we did not find positive relationship between work and community. The associations, in contrast, were seen to be crucial in that here we have communities (guilds) which were founded by people who worked in the same trade. It is actually in associations where the connection between work and community building comes to the fore. As we proceed with our enquiry, we can safely say that the Greco-Roman society built community around work, there is a positive relationship between work and community (the philosophical schools not withstanding). We will now turn in chapter 5 to investigate 1 Thessalonians using the rubric of work and community.

CHAPTER 5

Work and Community in First Thessalonians

5.1 Introduction

Having set up this thesis with an African cultural analysis of the relationship between work and community, we then considered the Second Temple period Jewish and Greco-Roman background in previous chapters and have found that work and community have a positive relationship. We are now ready to investigate the Thessalonian correspondence using the same approach. This chapter analyzes 1 Thessalonians; the texts we shall look at include 1 Thessalonians 2:9; 4:9–12; and 5:12–14. Chapter 6 will look at 2 Thessalonians 3:6–15. These texts are critical for our investigation because they actually discuss the subject of work. In these texts, Paul either talks about his own work or the work of the community members done for the community and in some cases, he offers himself and his co-workers as examples. Our goal is to determine the extent to which these texts confirm our hypothesis of a positive relationship between work and community formation and therefore offer a different perspective on Paul's sayings. African parallels between the Thessalonian texts and the African worldview will be highlighted in order to demonstrate how these texts can be understood in an African setting.

5.2 The Work of the Apostles and the Beginning of Community Life at Thessalonica in 1 Thessalonians 2:8-9

5.2.1 Introduction

This section will demonstrate that the physical work of the apostles was critical during the commencement of community life for the church in Thessalonica. This work occupied the apostles constantly and served various communal purposes. The workshop did not only provide the platform from which the gospel was preached but also the gospel audience. The apostles' work enabled them not to be burdensome. As such, the work proved to be consistent with the gospel Paul preached.

Paul speaks about his work to the Corinthians and Thessalonians (1 Cor 4:12; 9:4-18; 1 Thess 2:9; 2 Thess 3:8). Luke also provides further evidence that manual work was important to Paul (Acts 20:34). In 1 Thessalonians 2:9 Paul teaches the Thessalonians by means of painting a picture of the kind of people they (Paul and his co-workers) proved to be while in town. Older commentaries held that the wider section of 1 Thessalonians 2:1-12 is an *apologia* of Paul and his co-workers' life and labours.[1] For instance, Hiebert argued that Paul was deeply aware that the very advancement of the gospel depended on the personal integrity of those who proclaimed it. For that reason, he reveals his inner life, not to show how great he was, but to vindicate the message that he preached.[2] More recently this view has been defended by Jeffrey Weima who points to the appeal to God as witness (2:5, 10); Paul's approval by God for his ministry (2:5) and the antithetical statements in 2:1-12 (not x but y) as evidence.[3]

The purpose of this letter is instructive to the function of 1 Thessalonians 2:1-16. Paul wrote this letter to encourage and give instruction to the Thessalonians.[4] Nijay K. Gupta is right that "Paul did not write 1 Thessalonians as his deposition in view of an apostolic trial."[5] We do not have evidence in 1 Thessalonians that Paul is dealing with opponents. As such, Paul's intent

---

1. Hiebert, *Thessalonian Epistles*, 77; Moffatt, "First and Second Epistle," 4: 26, 29; Schmithals, *Paul & the Gnostics*, 125.
2. Hiebert, *Thessalonian Epistles*, 78.
3. Weima, *1-2 Thessalonians*, 123-24.
4. Weima, 123-24.
5. Gupta, *1-2 Thessalonians*, 52.

is to be a model for the Thessalonians, rather than to offer an apology. Some scholars who see this passage as an apology use 2 Corinthians 12:11-19 where Paul is being defensive – this clearly is collapsing two different contexts into one.[6] George Lyons has made a convincing argument that Pauline autobiographical accounts function not to prove Paul's authority but instead his ethos; they are not for the purpose of defence but instruction. Lyons writes "The autobiographical remarks in 1 Thessalonians function paraenetically to remind Paul's converts of the Christian ethical values they share, as embodied in the ethos of their typos. They are his imitators, but they, too, are examples."[7] Our text then is understood here not as apology but as Paul's instruction to the community concerning his conduct which included working for their upkeep.

5.2.2 Work as Sharing Community Life: "*Mgeni siku mbili, ya tatu mpe jembe*"

The Swahili proverb *Mgeni siku mbili, ya tatu mpe jembe* literally translates "a guest for two days, the third day give him/her a hoe." The proverb discourages guests from overstaying as guests. If they are to overstay, then they are to be treated like every other member of the community. In African fashion, when Paul and his associates came to Thessalonica they did not wait to be given a hoe. Instead, they took a hoe on their own and became one with their hosts in work. After Paul talks about sharing life (v. 8), he follows immediately by discussing how the apostles worked (v. 9). Apparently, Paul understands that μεταδοῦναι (to share) life is to partake in work as well.[8] There is no better way to share life together than to work together.[9] Teaching or preaching the gospel was not only talk but was accompanied by action. The image of a working apostle would have been a memorable lesson to the Thessalonians, even creating "cognitive dissonance."[10] As Best remarks "Paul not only gives what he has, the gospel, but what he is, himself."[11]

---

6. Gupta, 51.

7. Lyons, *Pauline Autobiography*, 185–221. Lyons's problem with the apology reading of Paul's autobiography is its methodology which is basically "mirror reading" which says that Paul is saying the opposite of what his opponents are saying. Lyons states "Just because a statement may be intelligently reversed is not evidence that this must have taken place," (Lyons, 184).

8. Miquez, *Practice of Hope*, 66.

9. Rigaux, *Saint Paul*; Green, *Letters to the Thessalonians*, 129.

10. Shogren, *1 and 2 Thessalonians*, 185.

11. Best, *First and Second Epistles*, 102; Byron, *1 and 2 Thessalonians*, 75.

Paul's self-description of his own and his fellow workers manual work as "toil and hardship" (κόπον and μόχθον) seems to match the picture of artisans.[12] The word toil has its roots in a verb which connotes "striking" or "beating."[13] When used of work it suggests "work that produces tiredness, wearisome toil."[14] The second term μόχθος, conveys "pain, effort, fatigue, suffering, and grief."[15] It could be that κόπος "stresses the fatigue associated with labour" and μόχθος "conveys the painfulness of work."[16] Paul further describes his labour with a plural pronoun ἡμῶν perhaps indicating that the labour and toil is that of his co-workers and himself together. Every member of the missionary team was involved in working for their sustenance so that they would not be a burden. Working was a team effort, not one working to support the rest. In some way, the community of missionaries modelled a community living together and working together.

Paul further clarifies what he means by "labour and toil" when he says "we worked" ἐργαζόμενοι. This word comes from the root ἐργάζομαι, defined as "to work at, make, build; to do, perform, accomplish."[17] The ἐργά group of words are used six times in the Thessalonian Correspondence (1 Thess 2:9; 4:11; 2 Thess 3:8, 10, 11, 12). All uses convey the idea of accomplishing something through the exertion of energy. The work was indeed hard and laborious. Through hard work, Paul was able to accomplish something of importance. The work the apostles did provided for their sustenance and, as we will see, also relieved the community of the need to provide for the missionaries.

What Paul says is consistent with what we know about the workday of artisans, who often worked from early morning to sunset; some, like miners, worked up to ten-hour shifts.[18] G. W. Peterman has noted that Paul being a free artisan had to travel extensively and that his job made him financially unstable most of the time.[19] Paul's manual work is "an act of self-giving"

---

12. Richard, *First and Second Thessalonians*, 102.
13. κόπον, *TBDAG*: 1159.
14. Morris, *Epistles of Paul*, 73.
15. μόχθος, *TBDAG*: 1366.
16. μόχθος, *TBDAG*: 1366.
17. ἐργάζομαι, *LSJ*: 311.
18. Applebaum, *Concept of Work*, 49.
19. Peterman, *Paul's Gift*, 7.

which demonstrates how Paul shared his life with the Thessalonians.[20] As such, Paul demonstrates his love for his converts by sharing with them his very self and working to provide for himself so as not to make demands on his followers.[21] As Peterman observes "The model of selflessness, the willingness to give up one's own status and share another's troubles is the ultimate sign of true friendship."[22] Paul was clearly disregarding status in that "he was stepping down the social ladder for the sake of Christ."[23] Unlike the nobleman of Aristotle who does all he does to gain virtue, Paul's example of selflessness is Jesus who already had a higher status or virtue but relinquished it so that he may be of service to others.[24] The aspect of following Christ has been well articulated by G. Dautzenberg:

> Paul understands his work and his suffering as an expression of his apostolic existence, as part of a special relationship with the suffering of Christ. And just as the suffering of Christ is an expression of his redeeming love for people, so the work of the apostle or his renunciation of maintenance by the congregations is an expression of the love of the apostle for his congregations, for whose salvation he is responsible according to God's plan of salvation.[25]

Dautzenberg goes beyond the evidence in the text since the Thessalonian letters do not make a connection between Paul's work and the suffering of Christ. However, there is a connection between work as an expression of love for others within the community.

The present tense of ἐργαζόμενοι signals that work was done continually – the entire duration. However, day and night does not mean they worked constantly. The phrase demonstrates how demanding and tedious the labour of

---

20. Malherbe, *Letters to the Thessalonians*, 160.

21. Weima, *1–2 Thessalonians*, 149.

22. Peterman, *Paul's Gift*, 115. Aristotle says "To a nobleman there applies the true saying that he does all for the sake of his friends . . . if need be, even to the point of death." Aristotle, *Nicomachean Ethics*, 1169a.

23. Witherington III, *1 and 2 Thessalonians*, 54; Jon A. Weatherly says "Paul took a voluntary step down the social ladder by engaging in such work," (Weatherly, *1 & 2 Thessalonians*, 71).

24. Peterman, *Paul's Gift*, 117.

25. Dautzenberg, "Der Verzicht Aufdas Apostolische Unterhaltsrecht," 212–32. Author's own translation.

the artisan was for Paul and his co-workers.[26] Hock explains this phrase when he says that it means working from before dawn till sunset.[27] The majority of the Thessalonians would have identified with this kind of work life, given that this was normal for them.[28] Hill has identified an important implication of Paul's working hours: his contact with the elite of Thessalonica would have been limited if he spent his time primarily in the workshop.[29] This supports our characterization of the church as predominantly working people. If the gospel was going to be preached, then it had to be preached while working. Paul connects the fact of his working with the preaching of the gospel. On one hand, through work, people contribute to others legitimate needs; on the other hand, they give witness to the gospel of Christ.[30]

Paul reveals the purpose of his working when he says, "that we might not burden (μὴ ἐπιβαρῆσαί) any of you" (1 Thess 2:9). The word ἐπιβαρῆσαί has its roots in ἐπιβαρέω which has the meaning "to weigh down, overload, depress" and in the passive voice it connotes "to be weighed down or oppressed."[31] Paul understands the situation of the Thessalonians: adding three mouths to feed who did not contribute financially/materially meant that these people would probably not be able to cater for all their needs. These artisans did not make much from their work and as such their meagre income would have been thinly stretched. It is evident that Paul has communal concerns as his motivation for working. His practice of κοινωνία would preclude being a burden to others for one's advantage. The idea of κοινωνία is central to Paul's thought and is properly understood as the context for "the giving and receiving of gifts of all kinds."[32] The idea of partnership is crucial for the Messiah's people.[33] Paul

---

26. Richard, *First and Second Thessalonians*, 102.
27. Hock, *Social Context of Paul's Ministry*, 13.
28. Hill, "Establishing the Church," 251.
29. Hill, 253.
30. Paige, *1 & 2 Thessalonians*, 263.
31. ἐπιβαρέω, TBDAG: 756.
32. Horrell, Hunt, and Southgate, *Greening Paul*, 210.
33. Wright, *Paul and the Faithfulness*, 11; Christopher J. H. Wright says

> A study of the root koinon- in the New Testament reveals that a substantial number of the occurrences of words formed or compounded from it either signify or are in contexts which relate to, actual social and economic relationships between Christians. They denote a practical, often costly, sharing, which is a far cry from that watery "togetherness" which commonly passes as "fellowship."

Wright, *Living as the People of God*, 97.

perceived eating food without paying for it as inconsistent with the gospel he proclaims. As such, proclamation of the gospel of God ἐκηρύξαμεν cannot be used as an excuse for being a burden.

5.2.3 The Workshop as Platform for Paul's Preaching

As we noted in chapter 2, work is an occasion for social interaction among Africans. As is the case within the age sets, members get together to work and interact with one another as they perform their various tasks. At the end of the day the work is done, and the social needs have been accomplished. Paul integrated his work with the proclamation of the gospel: as such, he understood that more gets accomplished while working. We could think of Paul in the workshop with his age set. Recent scholarship has noted the importance of Paul's work to his apostolic calling.[34] Not only did the workshop provide the apostles with their sustenance, but it also provided them with the forum for preaching the gospel.[35] Malherbe has noted that Paul was "a tentmaker preaching to his fellow workers while cutting and stitching."[36] Similarly, Hock says Paul like Socrates in Simon the shoemaker's workshop was "busy at tent making and busy at preaching the gospel."[37] He further notes that,

> It is difficult to imagine Paul not bringing up the subject of the gospel during the discussions with fellow workers, customers and others who entered the shop – given the relative quiet of a leather working shop, given the many hours Paul spent at work, given the utter commitment of Paul to gain converts for Christ, and given the sympathy that Paul showed in other ways for Cynic traditions.[38]

---

34. Hock, *Social Context of Paul's Ministry*, 62.
35. Richard, *First and Second Thessalonians*; Gorman, *Cruciformity*, 183; Wanamaker, *Epistle to the Thessalonians*, 104; Malherbe, *Letters to the Thessalonians*, 259.
36. Malherbe, *Letters to the Thessalonians*, 163; Weima shares the same idea in *1–2 Thessalonians*, 151.
37. Hock, "Workshop," 450.
38. Hock, *Social Context of Paul's Ministry*, 41.

Paul characterized his life with both work and preaching the gospel.³⁹ In so doing Paul is one with the workers in an artisan community as he works alongside his converts.⁴⁰

The type of work Paul did has also received considerable attention from scholars.⁴¹ Being an artisan meant that his income was limited, and he belonged to the lower class of society. The kind of work he undertook could not provide sufficient income and as a result Paul experienced deprivation in spite of his abilities (Phil 4:12; 1 Cor 4:11; 2 Cor 6:5, 10; 11:27).⁴² Acts 18:3 reveals that Paul, Aquila, and Priscilla were "tentmakers" (σκηνοποιοὶ). Given that tents in antiquity were made of leather, Paul was apparently a "leather-worker" who could make and possibly repair various types of leather goods.⁴³

Herbert Applebaum has demonstrated that leather work was often done within the confines of the οἶκος.⁴⁴ The artisans could move the workshop from one place to another by taking their workers and tools where their new base was located, provided they could find raw materials, which were usually supplied by the customer. Both manufacturing and sales took place in the workshop.⁴⁵ This allowed Paul the mobility he needed to work as an itinerant missionary. Paul entered communities by means of his work as an artisan. Yet, work was not just a bait, as even after getting converts he still saw the need to work.

There has been debate as to whether Paul's working was informed by the Jewish rabbi's practice of working to support themselves or the practice of Hellenistic philosophers like Musonius Rufus.⁴⁶ It is indeed true that the Jewish rabbinic sources are much later than Paul and have to be used carefully. However, Paul was a Jew who lived in the Greco-Roman world and both

---

39. Byron, *1 and 2 Thessalonians*, 76.

40. Bridges, *1 & 2 Thessalonians*, 51.

41. Witherington III, *Acts of the Apostles*; Hock, *Social Context of Paul's Ministry*; See Witherington, *1 and 2 Thessalonians*.

42. Green, *Letters to the Thessalonians*, 130.

43. Wilhelm Michaelis, "Σκηνή, Σκῆνος," *TDNT* 7. 393–94; Weima, *1–2 Thessalonians*, 150; Hill, "Establishing the Church," 80.

44. Applebaum, *Concept of Work*, 19.

45. Applebaum, 47–48.

46. Hock, *Social Context of Paul's Ministry*, 22–49; Wanamaker, *Epistle to the Thessalonians*, 104; Holmes, *1 and 2 Thessalonians*, 66; Malherbe, *Letters to the Thessalonians*, 160–61.

worlds had an impact on him.⁴⁷ As such, there is no need to pit one world against the other. We simply need to be aware of each background and what it can contribute to our understanding of Paul and his working ministry.

The literary remains of the upper-class Greek and Roman society reveal that they had utter disdain for manual labour,⁴⁸ particularly work which was done for another person. Paul being an educated person (Roman citizen, according to Acts) came from this class, and the fact that he worked demonstrated self-enslavement and status abdication.⁴⁹ The only work Greeks and Romans could do without losing respect was that of a farmer, who was "the antithesis of the artisan on his workbench."⁵⁰ The problem with artisan work, for the Greeks, was that it was done on behalf of other people, namely, the end users of the product. The artisan then did not live for himself but for the one for whom they made the product. Since the artisan was considered not free, then their work was seen as a form of slavery. Aristotle and Plato held that the one who used a product knew the product more than the one who made it.⁵¹

Knowledge of this perception of artisans leads us to conclude that Paul is renouncing his rights. It is also evident that he accommodated himself to people to whom he was ministering. Even his adaptability reveals his imitation of Christ. In this Paul expressed his love for those to whom he sought to present the gospel.⁵² The master (Jesus), whom Paul follows, instead of choosing a life of wealth, chose poverty and toil and took as his home that of a manual worker.⁵³ It must, however, be noted that whereas Jesus did not do his public ministry alongside manual work, Paul did exactly that.⁵⁴ The gospel, which Paul proclaimed, was "based on love and the self-sacrifice of Jesus

---

47. Ronald Hock argues that Paul is heavily influenced by the working philosophers and not Jewish rabbis. He critiques those who claim rabbinic background to Paul's working. Hock, *Social Context of Paul's Ministry*.

48. See chapter 4 section 4.1. Xenophon, *Whole Works of Xenophon*, 650.

49. Applebaum, *Concept of Work*, xiii; Gorman, *Cruciformity*, 183; Paige, *1 & 2 Thessalonians*, 81; Malherbe, *Letters to the Thessalonians*, 161; Green, *Letters to the Thessalonians*, 130; Banks, *Paul's Idea of Community*, 150.

50. Applebaum, *Concept of Work*, xiii, 31.

51. Applebaum, 31.

52. Gorman, *Cruciformity*, 183–91.

53. There is no reason to believe that Jesus did not work as a carpenter; the Gospel of Mark reveals people knew Jesus not just as a son of a carpenter but as a carpenter in his own right (Mark 6:3) Geoghegan, *Attitude Towards Labor*, 94–95.

54. Geoghegan, *Attitude Towards Labor*, 94–95.

[so] was incompatible with missionaries who sought their own self-interest and financial gain at the expense of their converts."[55]

Paul's exhortations on work in the Thessalonian correspondence reveal that Paul's working was not out of necessity, as has been suggested by Green; it is not because the donations from Philippi were not enough.[56] The donations must have come much later after Paul's ministry at Thessalonica had commenced. Paul was more concerned about the example that he was setting for his converts and how the gospel should be applied in their lives. Paul was aware of options for earning support/sustenance that existed for itinerant preachers. Hock claims that four options were open to philosophers: "charging fees, entering the households of the rich and powerful, begging, and working."[57]

Various philosophers and sophists chose among these options as their means of support. Aristotle is a good example of a philosopher who entered a house of a king (Philip of Macedon) to teach his son (Alexander).[58] The Cynics took the option of begging so that they could avoid greed.[59] The Epicureans, as this study has found out, did not work as part of their communal life: their benefactors provided their needs. The fourth option, that of working to earn one's support, is taken by Paul. Hock notes that some Cynics chose work; the concern for Cynics like Musonius was not to be dependent on anyone, and also they saw the pedagogical value of working.[60] For Musonius the question of support for a philosopher was not just a theoretical question, it was intensely practical, as he actually worked to support himself and his students during his exile by Nero to Gyara.[61] Others who stand in this tradition include Simon the shoemaker who did philosophy while working.[62] Although Paul fits with philosophers who saw working as a legitimate way to meet their needs, he had theological reasons, including, arguably, community-related

---

55. Wanamaker, *Epistle to the Thessalonians*, 103; Malherbe, *Letters to the Thessalonians*, 162.
56. Green, *Letters to the Thessalonians*, 130.
57. Hock, *Social Context of Paul's Ministry*, 52; See also Peterman, *Paul's Gift from Philippi*, 209.
58. Verbrugge, *Paul & Money*.
59. Hock, *Social Context of Paul's Ministry*, 55–56.
60. Musonius Rufus, *Stoic Fragments*.
61. Hock, *Social Context of Paul's Ministry*, 40.
62. Hock, 39–40; Verbrugge, *Paul & Money*, 56.

reasons, for taking up a trade. The benefits of work were different for Paul than for Musonius.

Even though Paul would support the right for the worker to receive a wage (1 Cor 9:3–7) and though he did receive support from Philippi during his mission at Thessalonica (Phil 4:15–16), he did not want such support to stand in the way of the gospel. As Lenski states "These were gifts of love, which for that reason Paul could not refuse; they were not pay, wages, support, not a violation of Paul's principle to preach the gospel gratis."[63] Richard captures Paul's desire when he writes "He wished to avoid the impression that the missionaries acted for financial gain (2:5) or that the appeal for financial support should hinder the freedom of potential converts."[64] Paul did not want the church to appear like one of the Greco-Roman associations where membership fees were required for one to continue enjoying privileges.[65] However, he expected that if one was going to participate in communal meals, they needed to contribute their labour.

Paul's *modus operandum* was not to receive support from where he was currently doing mission work but to expect it from communities that he initiated but had left. This way the missionaries could operate with pure motives and speak the gospel boldly (ἐπαρρησιασάμεθα).[66] Working "proved that the missionaries were motivated by an unselfish consideration for their flock."[67] Richard contends Paul in 1 Thessalonians 2:9 is "intent on presenting the apostle's manner of labor and conduct as a model for the new converts to emulate, a model based on a philosophical ideal of the day."[68] As such, Paul's working functioned as non-verbal communication to his converts.[69]

It should also be remembered that Paul and his co-workers worked together. The use of plural pronouns is the characteristic way in which Paul recalled his working. Murray J. Smith, has reminded us to bear in mind that even the letters were written by the trio (Paul, Silas, and Timothy) and not

---

63. Lenski, *Interpretation*, 249.
64. Richard, *First and Second Thessalonians*, 104.
65. Paige, *1 & 2 Thessalonians*, 82.
66. Richard, *First and Second Thessalonians*, 104; Wanamaker, *Epistle to the Thessalonians*, 103; Peterman, *Paul's Gift from Philippi*, 150.
67. Hiebert, *Thessalonian Epistles*, 99.
68. Richard, *First and Second Thessalonians*, 103.
69. Hill, "Establishing the Church," 80–83.

just the apostle Paul on his own.[70] The same way they proclaimed the gospel together, they also worked, established the church, and offered comfort to the Thessalonians.[71] The desire of scholars like E. Randolph Richards to diminish the role of co-workers in the writing process is based on anachronistic assumptions from the modern world. His is not a strong argument against a collaborative effort.[72] If the communal approach to mission and writing is acknowledged, so should the communal approach to work. Paul certainly did not consider himself above his fellow apostles; he participated in all that needed to be done, including working with his own hands.

The placement of verse 9 between the metaphors of a nurse/mother (v. 8) and exhorting father (v. 11) shows that Paul presents himself as a good parent, who in both the Jewish and Greco-Roman perspective would be expected to take care of children, rather than the other way around.[73] Even the syntax of 2:9 demonstrates a relationship with 2:7b–8, particularly the use of the particle γάρ.[74] Paul understands that good parents should not be a burden to their children. Likewise, the missionaries, regardless of their economic situation, did not want to be a burden to the Thessalonians. They entered the ministry not to enrich themselves but through hard work they proclaimed the gospel in Thessalonica.[75]

In summary, 1 Thessalonians 2:1–12 Paul is teaching the gospel through his ηθος. Verse 9 fits in that context in which Paul is teaching through his example. The apostles' labour was hard, and it constantly occupied them. The gospel was preached while working in the workshop, just like Africans do social interactions while working. Paul worked out of communal considerations; he and his company did not want to be a burden to the Thessalonians. The gospel Paul proclaimed was not for sale. Hence, it had to be preached without cost to its audience. Sharing life for Paul meant getting into the workshop, becoming one with the artisans and doing what they do. Paul's work provided

---

70. Smith, "Thessalonian Correspondence," 277.

71. Smith, 277.

72. Richards, *Secretary in the Letters*, 153–58. Richards states that the co-authors were "not full contributors on an equal level with Paul . . . [their] role is subordinate and does not extend to the point of writing sections on his own. His input is probably filtered through Paul." (Richards, 154–55).

73. Roberts, "Images of Paul," 145; Burke, *Family Matters*, 46–47.

74. Verbrugge, *Paul & Money*, 207.

75. Green, *Letters to the Thessalonians*, 131.

him with an audience for his gospel message. For Paul, work played a crucial role in starting community life at Thessalonica.

5.3 Brotherly/Sisterly Love, Work, and Community in 1 Thessalonians 4:9–12

5.3.1 Introduction

This section will demonstrate how the exhortations on love and work relate to each other. It is argued here that love is most demonstrated in acts of service to others, as the Thessalonians did in Macedonia, and also in living quietly, sticking to one's affairs and working. It will be shown here also that φιλαδελφία is related to Paul's ethical exhortations to "live quietly, attend to one's affairs and work with one's hands." It is also asserted here that love is foundational to communal life and work in Paul's teaching. In the African setting members of the same clan care for each other like family. It is not uncommon to refer to each other as brother and sister. Within the clan system if one is in need their needs are met by members of the clan and the clan itself functions like an economic system with division of labour between families.

Before moving to the main discussion, we need to say a word about the literary relationships in this passage. Some take "now concerning" to imply that Paul is referring to a letter from the Thessalonians.[76] For others, it refers to oral questions asked through Timothy.[77] However, the majority hold that it is simply commencing a new topic,[78] the adversative δέ seeming to point to a new subject.[79] It is possible that Paul has the two aspects in mind; he is certainly writing in response to issues raised and at the same time he is commencing a new topic.[80] The relationship between verses 9–10a and 10b–12 has generated some debate. Martin Dibelius did not see verse 10b as related

---

76. Bruce, *1 & 2 Thessalonians*, 80; Green, *Letters to the Thessalonians*, 202; Malherbe, *Letters to the Thessalonians*, 243.

77. Wanamaker, *Epistle to the Thessalonians*, 159; Richard, *First and Second Thessalonians*, 213.

78. Mitchell, "Concerning peri de," 229; Paige, *1 & 2 Thessalonians*, 132; Witherington, *1 and 2 Thessalonians*, 118; Best, *First and Second Epistles*, 171.

79. Ellingworth and Nida, *Handbook on Paul's Letters*, 88; Witherington, *1 and 2 Thessalonians*; Weima, *1-2 Thessalonians*, 285.

80. Walton, *Leadership and Lifestyle*, 148–50.

to verses 9–10a, insinuating that the proximity is coincidental.[81] Ronald Hock in an influential study on the significance of Paul's work on his apostleship does not relate love to Paul's exhortations in 4:11–12. But his analysis ignores the context in which the exhortations are situated and instead situates them in philosophical writings.[82] It is our assertion that the subject of brotherly/sisterly love relates specifically to the paraenesis of verses 11–12.[83] It can be asserted that verses 11–12 are grammatically related to vers 10.[84] Paul has already connected the issue of working with self-giving love in 1 Thessalonians 2:8–9.[85] The main verb παρακαλοῦμεν "we exhort" is related to the four infinitives which follow in verses 10b–11, clearly indicating that φιλαδελφία has to do with Paul's exhortations on work.[86]

5.3.2 Φιλαδελφία and Community Life

Φιλαδελφία was known among blood siblings, and early Christians like Paul adopted it for love among believers (Rom 12:10; Heb 13:1; 1 Pet 1:22; 2 Pet 1:7). The term had never previously been used of love among members of a religious group.[87] Christians were to relate with one another not simply as friends, but intimately as family. For instance, in 2 Macc. 15:14, Jeremiah is said to be "a man who loves the family [φιλάδελφος] of Israel." In Maccabees, Jeremiah does not only love those of his family but the entire nation of Israel.[88] The identity of Christians as αδελφοι is the reason they can practice φιλάδελφος. This identity is rooted in the Christian story, what David G. Horrell terms the "Christian myth." As such, all are brothers and sisters,

---

81. Dibelius, *An die Thessalonicher I-II* (1937), 23.

82. Hock, *Social Context of Paul's Ministry*, 43; Agrell, *Work, Toil and Sustenance*, 98–99; Helen-Ann M. Hartley on her part acknowledges the connection between brotherly love and work but does not express the nuance in which this relationship subsists. Her strength lies in situating the exhortations not only in love but in holiness. Hartley, "We Worked Night," 178.

83. Contra Calvin, *1, 2 Thessalonians*, 361; Frame, *Critical and Exegetical Commentary*, 157–63; Hiebert, *Thessalonian Epistles*, 180.

84. Weatherly, *1 & 2 Thessalonians*, 143.

85. Malherbe, *Letters to the Thessalonians*, 242.

86. Wanamaker, *Epistle to the Thessalonians*, 162; Burke, *Family Matters*, 46–47; Witherington, *1 and 2 Thessalonians*, 118.

87. Hans Freiherr von Soden, "Ἀδελφός, Ἀδελφή," *TDNT* 1.144–46.

88. Shogren, *1 and 2 Thessalonians*, 168; Paige, *1 & 2 Thessalonians*, 135; Milligan, *St. Paul's Epistles*, 52; Witherington, *1 and 2 Thessalonians*, 119; Fee, *First and Second Letters*, 159.

precisely because they have been adopted into the family of God through the redemption made available by Christ, our brother in the family.[89]

Paul utilizes a paralipsis – that is pretending to gloss over a subject only to proceed to give it a comprehensive treatment[90] – to inform the Thessalonians that they do not need to be taught about filial love. He wants to "stress continuity with prior instruction" and make his audience ready for a broad application of love.[91] Paul speaks of the Thessalonians as "brothers/sisters" eighteen times. The brotherhood/sisterhood of the Thessalonians is one that has its basis in φιλαδελφία (1 Thess 4:9–12). Collins describes it as "the love for one another within the brotherhood, i.e., specifically the members of the church of the Thessalonians."[92] Yet their love is not limited to those within the house church; as Richard asserts, "the non-Christian outsiders provide a context for the community's life of holiness and are beneficiaries of that community's loving behavior."[93] Paul understands the house church at Thessalonica as a distinct brotherhood/sisterhood. This designation speaks of the togetherness of the Thessalonians which has an outward focus. Considering that siblings in Greco-Roman society had responsibilities to each other, work can be understood as a demonstration of one's contribution to the members of the household.[94] The love for the brothers and sisters is one that is "God taught" (θεοδίδακτοί hapax legomenon), and the object of the adjective is "to love one another" (τὸ ἀγαπᾶν ἀλλήλους) (1 Thess 4:9). In a sense love for one another is the foundation for contribution to the community through work.

When scholars try to understand θεοδίδακτοί they often do so by contrasting it with αυτοδίδακτος. It is claimed that one is either God taught or self-taught. Epicurus is often cited as a chief example.[95] Even De Witt who subscribes to this position affirms that Epicurus was no atheist. He states that Epicurus "maintained the belief in the existence of gods to be innate in the mind of man and to exist there in advance of all religious

---

89. Horrell, *Solidarity and Difference*, 113.
90. Richard, *First and Second Thessalonians*, 210; Malherbe, *Letters to the Thessalonians*, 243.
91. Richard, *First and Second Thessalonians*, 210; Malherbe, *Letters to the Thessalonians*, 243.
92. Collins, *Studies on the First*, 297.
93. Richard, *First and Second Thessalonians*, 3; Collins, *Studies on the First*, 296.
94. Plutarch, *Brotherly Love*; Burke, *Family Matters*, 218.
95. De Witt, *Saint Paul and Epicurus*, 5.

experience."⁹⁶ However, it has to be noted that even with Epicurus the issue is not whether one is God-taught or self-taught but he is a polemic against his teacher, Nausiphanes, from whom he and his students worked hard to distance themselves.⁹⁷ The closest parallel to our *hapax legomena* comes from Nonnos in Dionysiaca where the αυτοδιδακτος is preceded by θεος that is θεος αυτοδιδακτος and translated by W. H. D. Rouse as "God untaught" which clearly is not a correct translation. Had it been Paul writing here, he would have dropped σιγμα and αυτο. The philosophy that Nonnos was taught is not what one teaches themselves through human teachers but the philosophy one learns without a human mediator, leaving God as the teacher.⁹⁸ Since Paul is a human instrument in the hands of God and is the one who taught the Thessalonians the gospel, he certainly does not wish to contrast God-taught with self-taught.

The phrase "God taught" (θεοδίδακτος) is indeed a *hapax legomena*,⁹⁹ appearing for the first time in Greek literature in this passage. It is likely that it is a term Paul has coined.¹⁰⁰ "Taught by God" echoes Isaiah 54:13: "'And I will cause all your sons to be taught by God [διδακτους θεου]' (ESV) where Isaiah is describing a time when God will be among his people in a unique way so that they do not need a human teacher."¹⁰¹ Israel's prophets including Jeremiah and Ezekiel spoke of the eschatological blessing which God will bring about. Jesus cites Isaiah 54:13 in John 6:45, saying "all will be taught by God [διδακτοι θεου]."¹⁰²

If Paul is applying this eschatological blessing to the Gentile converts at Thessalonica, it means that they are part of the new people of God.¹⁰³ Since the eschatological promises are ushered through the coming of Jesus, there is no

---

96. De Witt, 5.

97. Sextus Empiricus, *Against the Professors*.

98. Aelius Aristides, *Dionysiaca*, 193: 43; Aelius Aristides, *Orations*, 92: 401; Homer, *Odyssey*, 22:340, 371; Philo of Alexandria, *Flight and Finding*, 167; *On the Creation*, 148, 116–17; Dionysius of Halicarnassus, *Roman Antiquities*, 13:1, 41; Plutarch, *Moralia, Volume VIII*, 216g, 397; Galen, *Thrasybulus*, 895k, 365; Achilles Tatius, *Leucippe*, 1:10, 33.

99. Abraham J Malherbe, *Paul and the Thessalonians: The Philosophic Tradition of Pastoral Care* (Philadelphia: Fortress Press, 1987), 105.

100. Malherbe, *Letters to the Thessalonians*, 244; Weima, *1–2 Thessalonians*, 286.

101. Weima, *1–2 Thessalonians*, 288.

102. Weima, 288.

103. Weima, 289; Byron, *1 and 2 Thessalonians*, 144–45.

doubt that Paul sees in Jesus how God demonstrates love. The story of Jesus is for Paul one big lesson about love and is the one which makes the command "love your neighbour as yourself" possible. Given that God is a worker who creates (works) out of love and the Thessalonians are "God taught," could it be that one of the lessons they are taught is that of working as an expression of love? The answer to this question is definitely yes.

Dionysius of Halicarnassus speaks of Sabine Valerius, whom he commends for being worth of praise for living an ascetic lifestyle. Valerius is said to have been self-taught (αὐτοδίδακτος) philosophy.[104] It is the manner of life which reveals that this person has learned philosophy. Likewise, the Thessalonians have demonstrated they have been taught through their manner of life. However, unlike philosophers who claim to be self-taught, Paul claims that they are God taught.[105] Paul may not necessarily be making a connection between what he says and what philosophers say but making the point that this love that the Thessalonians have springs from God, not themselves. Natural love is only for natural siblings, not strangers. But the Thessalonians have been God taught to love all people, not just those to whom they are related by blood.

The question then is what does it mean to be God taught? Richard explains that it is "to have one's heart inundated by a God-given, Spirit-inspired love that is open to all."[106] Similarly, for Beale: "In short, Jesus taught the love command during his earthly ministry and then sent the Spirit to continue to teach it to his people and to empower them to fulfil it."[107] To be God taught then is not so much "divine communication" as it is "divine relationship" between God and his people,[108] which becomes the basis for mutual love. The method of God's teaching should not derail us; what should concern us is that God not only teaches but enables love. God's presence in the community through the Spirit continues to empower the community to love as they are doing to all the saints in Macedonia.

---

104. See Dionysius of Halicarnassus, *Roman Antiquities*.

105. Malherbe, *Letters to the Thessalonians*, 244; Paige, *1 & 2 Thessalonians*, 135.

106. Richard, *First and Second Thessalonians*, 216; Weima, *1–2 Thessalonians*, 218; Marshall, *1 and 2 Thessalonians*, 115.

107. Beale, *1–2 Thessalonians*, 125; Aasgard, *My Beloved*, 159–60.

108. Rogers and Rogers, *New Linguistic*, 478.

Given that the Christian community had people of various social backgrounds, it makes sense that Paul would exhort them to love one another since naturally they would not love each other. Those who were socially superior would have desired to set themselves apart from social inferiors in different ways.[109] As such, Best notes that "To the Christian, brother is not merely a metaphor but a reality; since the natural ties of kinship had often been broken at conversion they appreciate more firmly the ties of spiritual kinship."[110] Similarly, Wanamaker notes "Paul's emphasis on mutual love for fellow Christians was intended to create a new sense of identity and commitment among people who had no basis for a mutual relation prior to their conversion to Christ."[111] As such Paul's communities were not just isolated ghettos but communities tied together by their common faith and love. Paul had already called on the Thessalonians to "abound in love for one another and for all" (1 Thess 3:12) meaning that this love is not just one to be shared with outsiders alone, but it is manifested in their internal communal life.[112] In this sense, "Paul is concerned that love not have an exclusively inward direction, despite his great interest in community dynamics and boundaries."[113]

The Thessalonian epistles as a whole reveal that there were people in the community who were not working to support themselves. As a result, they became dependent on the well-to-do members. Certainly, the well-off might have felt obligated to provide for their fellow religionists in obedience to Paul's command to love one another.[114] Paul upholds brotherly/sisterly love but explains what love looks like on both sides of the divide. Christians are to "work with your own hands" primarily because they love others. The implication is that failure to work is tantamount to a lack of love for others.[115] Members of the Christian community were then to be fruitful contributors to their community, ensuring its shalom.[116] In the second century, we see the

---

109. Witherington, *1 and 2 Thessalonians*, 120; Green, *Letters to the Thessalonians*, 203.
110. Best, *First and Second Epistles*, 172.
111. Wanamaker, *Epistles to the Thessalonians*, 160.
112. Furnish, *1 Thessalonians*, 97.
113. Richard, *First and Second Thessalonians*, 215.
114. Wanamaker, *Epistles to the Thessalonians*, 160.
115. Richard, *First and Second Thessalonians*, 220; Bruce, *1 & 2 Thessalonians*, 91.
116. Richard, *First and Second Thessalonians*, 223; Geoghegan, *Attitude Towards Labour*, 129; Burke, *Family Matters*, 221; Meggitt, *Paul, Poverty*, 162.

same idea being advanced in the Didache; the community has the obligation of securing work for the itinerant evangelist who stays longer than two or three days.[117] Paul is not proposing withdrawal from community as a way to avoid conflict but doing meaningful work and contributing to the wellness of the community from within.[118] As such "the community's love cannot be separated from its work."[119] For Paul there is labour that belongs to love (1 Thess 1:3); love is not just a "mere feeling" but is expressed in "concrete acts of service." Such a kind of love does not concern itself with reciprocation as in patron-client relations.[120]

The Thessalonian love is already manifest not only with "one another" but to "all the brothers of the whole of Macedonia." Their love is not just for those in their internal community but those far and wide. These people understood that they were part of a worldwide companionship or in the words of Meeks "a worldwide people."[121] The question then is how did the Thessalonians love all the believers in Macedonia? Social relationships in the ancient world had an economic element, and economic relationships were not devoid of the social element.[122] It follows then that if the Thessalonians loved the Macedonians, they must have had social relations with them and that this relationship included economic exchange. Gifts were critical in the establishment of friendships; to refuse a gift was tantamount to insult.[123] Barclay, contra Derrida,[124] has recently argued against the modern concepts of a "pure" gift or "altruism" in which gifts are given with no strings attached asserting that "benefits were generally intended to foster mutuality, by creating

---

117. Didache 12:1–4 reads

> ²If the comer is a traveller, assist him, so far as ye are able; but he shall not stay with you more than two or three days, if it be necessary. ³But if he wishes to settle with you, being a craftsman, let him work for and eat his bread. ⁴But if he has no craft, according to your wisdom provide how he shall live as a Christian among you, ⁵but not in idleness. If he will not do this, he is trafficking upon Christ. Beware of such men.

Cited in Lightfoot, *Apostolic Fathers*, 234; Geoghegan, *Attitude Towards Labour*.

118. Witherington, *1 and 2 Thessalonians*, 221.
119. Malherbe, *Letters to the Thessalonians*, 249.
120. Banks, *Paul's Idea of Community*, 54.
121. Meeks, *First Urban Christians*, 107.
122. Donlan, "Reciprocities," 139; Peterman, *Paul's Gift*, 15.
123. Plutarch, *Lives*, 18:1–4; Peterman, *Paul's Gift*, 5; Banks, *Paul's Idea of Community*, 87.
124. Derrida, "Time of the King," 121–47.

or maintaining social bonds."¹²⁵ As such the Thessalonian church must have been included in the Macedonian churches that contributed to the Jerusalem collection for the saints.¹²⁶ Scholars have long noted that the congregation's love was demonstrated in their financial support to missionaries and the hospitality offered to fellow believers passing through the commercial metropolis of Thessalonica.¹²⁷ Their offering of hospitality to Christian travellers becomes more significant when we consider the location of Thessalonica on the Via Egnatia.¹²⁸ Paul also commends the Macedonians (Thessalonians included) for being generous beyond their means (2 Cor 8:1–2).

5.3.3 Φιλαδελφία Demonstrated

In 1 Thessalonians 4:11 Paul lines up four infinitives after each other: "to aspire to live quietly, to mind your own affairs, and to work with your hands" (φιλοτιμεῖσθαι ἡσυχάζειν καὶ πράσσειν τὰ ἴδια καὶ ἐργάζεσθαι). The word φιλοτιμεῖσθαι has its roots in φιλότιμος which is translated as "loving or seeking after honour."¹²⁹ It can also be translated "ambitious"¹³⁰ and in the infinitive, it is translated as "strive eagerly to do a thing, endeavor earnestly, aspire."¹³¹ Rigaux sees in φιλοτιμεῖσθαι an oxymoron with an irony since Paul is saying "make it your ambition to have no ambition."¹³² The ambition or striving for which they are not to have has three objects, namely ἡσυχάζειν καὶ πράσσειν

---

125. Barclay, *Paul and the Gift*, 562.
126. Downs, *Offering of the Gentiles*, 54.
127. Richard, *First and Second Thessalonians*, 217; Paige, *1 & 2 Thessalonians*, 136; Wanamaker, *Epistles to the Thessalonians*, 161; Malherbe, *Letters to the Thessalonians*, 245.
128. Burke, *Family Matters*, 211.
129. φιλότιμος, *LSJ*: 1940.
130. φιλότιμος, *TBDAG*: 2287.
131. φιλότιμος, *LSJ*: 1940.
132. Author's own translation. He says

> Si I on conserve à Φιλοτιμεῖσθαι ce sens de «faites-vous un point d'honneur à vivre dans le calme», on obtient cette figure que les rhèteurs appellent un oxymoron où il y a une pointe d'ironie. C'est comme si Paul disait appellent un oxymoron où il y a une pointe cl'ironie ayez pour ambition de ne point en avoir, faites-vous remarquer par votre silence. Si Macèdoniens qu'ils soient, les Thessaloniciens sont devenus Grecs et les honneurs ne les trouvent pas msensibles.

Rigaux, *Saint Paul*, 521.

τὰ ἴδια καὶ ἐργάζεσθαι.¹³³ Gaventa has noted that all three phrases find parallels in philosophical writings of the ancient world.¹³⁴

The first of the three objects of φιλοτιμεῖσθαι is ἡσυχάζειν which comes from Ἡσυχάζω which can be translated as "to be calm or peaceful, keep quiet or still, remain fixed or motionless."¹³⁵ Since it has so many variations of meaning, the context helps to decide the appropriate meaning for each use. In our passage, it certainly does not mean inactivity since in the same sentence Paul talks about working with one's hands.¹³⁶ Questions have been raised about the background of the call to "live quietly." The issue of preaching has been raised as what Paul has in mind when he says they must "live a quiet life." It is suggested that those Paul is instructing are incessantly sharing their faith and becoming a public nuisance.¹³⁷ This, however, seems unlikely as these people's faith seems shaken by afflictions to the extent that Paul has to send Timothy to strengthen them (3:1–5).¹³⁸ Others have suggested a political interpretation, claiming the believers were citizens of the city who played a political role as members of the demos. These new converts are said to have disrupted the demos meeting by means of their preaching and protests over their mistreatment.¹³⁹ Paul's remarks are understood as suggesting that they should renounce their citizenship and live as if they were non-citizens.¹⁴⁰ This view is certainly inconsistent with the picture we have painted so far of the Thessalonians as working artisans.

Other exegetes have suggested that the context of patron-client relationship gives a better explanation of the phrase "to live a quiet life." Given that clients had obligations to their patrons to advance their cause in the citizen assembly, it is claimed Paul considers this meddling.¹⁴¹ Paul then is seen as telling the clients to stay out of political affairs related to patron-client

---

133. Weatherly, *1 & 2 Thessalonians*, 145.
134. Gaventa, *First and Second Thessalonians*.
135. Ἡσυχάζω, TBDAG: 2287.
136. Ἡσυχάζω, TLNT: 1. 1.181.
137. Barclay, "Conflict in Thessalonica," 522–23; Still, *Conflict at Thessalonica*, 245–50; Furnish, *1 Thessalonians*, 98.
138. Weima, *1–2 Thessalonians*, 295; Gorman, *Becoming the Gospel*, 75.
139. De Vos, *Church and Community*, 160–70.
140. Weima, *1–2 Thessalonians*, 295.
141. Winter, "If a Man Does," 313; Green, *Letters to the Thessalonians*, 210–11.

relationships.¹⁴² Such a move would allow the Christians to maintain "a low profile in the public arena" and not draw unnecessary attention to themselves.¹⁴³ This view has been challenged by Weima who claims that the work which clients did for their patrons would not be considered idleness.¹⁴⁴ Certainly, Paul does challenge the entire system of patronage; the system itself is opposed to the gospel. However, we do not have sufficient evidence to adopt it as the explanation for the call to "be quiet."

The word has also been taken to mean someone who withdraws from the public arena, something that in the late Roman republic and early empire was attractive to those who sought the life of philosophy.¹⁴⁵ The Epicureans attempted to live a quiet life as a community, and they were one of the few communities that sought the quiet life as a group.¹⁴⁶ As such "Epicureans believed that their security or happiness (*eudaemonia*) derived from a quiet life (*hēsychia*) and retirement from the world (*lathe biōsas*), and they therefore freed themselves from their prison of public life and politics."¹⁴⁷ Even though the Epicureans did not necessarily withdraw into individualism (as noted by Meeks, who sees the Garden as not only an "alternative community" but a "counter-cultural community, an antipolis"),¹⁴⁸ it must be noted that one joined the community not for its sake but for one's own sake. As Malherbe observes "while the philosophers' retirement was to be filled with contemplation and cultivation of personal growth, the Thessalonians were to spend their time in manual labour."¹⁴⁹

Paul's remarks then are considered appropriate since he is dealing with labourers who are prone to not live a quiet life by interfering in other people's affairs.¹⁵⁰ Paul's focus seems to be on economic and social relationships rather than political affairs like the philosophers, something Malherbe recognizes.¹⁵¹

---

142. Weima, *1–2 Thessalonians*, 295.
143. Weima, 295.
144. Weima, 295.
145. See Malherbe, *Paul and the Thessalonians*.
146. Malherbe, 102.
147. Malherbe, 102.
148. Meeks, *Origins of Christian Morality*, 38.
149. Malherbe, *Paul and the Thessalonians*, 98.
150. Malherbe, 106.
151. Malherbe, 98.

If this is the case, one wonders whether being called to pursue "quietism" would not have the unintended effect of causing these people to cease their responsibilities to the community and withdraw to themselves. It rather shifts attention from the community to the individual whereas Paul wants the community to be the focus. Rather than the withdrawal or "the Apatheia" recommended by some philosophers (Epicureans, Stoics), Paul advocated for active Christian input in the public life and provision of necessities of life for those in the household of faith and fellow human beings.[152]

It has been suggested that attending civic festivities that were dedicated to pagan gods presented opportunities for rest from labours. Miguez has suggested that it is not a withdrawal from the public as if to say politics is bad. Rather a rejection of public policies offered by the imperial ideology and the gods, which are barren in terms of offering quietness and tranquillity needed by the artisan.[153] It is indeed true that the festivities offered most people the only opportunity to be away from their work. However, the context in which this phrase appears does not support such an interpretation. Miguez's interpretation is in keeping with his agenda of reading Paul's letter to the Thessalonians from a political perspective; it certainly fits his agenda but not the context of the text. If Paul wanted the Thessalonians to stop attending the civic festivities, he would have said it outright.[154]

It is Philo of Alexandria who offers us help in understanding ἡσυχάζειν "to be quiet."[155] Philo provides us with contrast between the honourable person and the vulgar person, whom he describes as one who

> runs about through the market-place, and theatres, and courts of justice, and council halls, and assemblies, and every meeting and collection of men whatever, like one who lives with and for curiosity, letting loose his tongue in immoderate, and interminable, and indiscriminate conversation, confusing and disturbing everything, mixing up what is true and what is false, what is unspeakable with what is public, private with public things,

---

152. ΚΑΡΑΒΙΔΟΠΟΥΛΟΥ ΙΩΑΝΝΗ, "Φιλαδελφία»," 194–96.

153. Miquez, *Practice of Hope*.

154. Peter Oakes has asserted following Harrison that cult participation was never obligatory. He further points to the corporate nature of imperial cult which would allow Christians to attend the cult meetings in passivity. Oakes, "Re-Mapping the Universe," 312–15.

155. ἡσυχία, *TLNT*,1. 1.181.

> things profane with things sacred, what is ridiculous with what is excellent, from never having been instructed in what is the most excellent thing in season, namely silence (hēsychian). (21) And pricking up his ears, because of the abundance of his leisure, and his superfluous curiosity, and love of interference, he is eager to make himself acquainted with the business of other people.[156]

Indeed, the person Philo describes is a person who does not know what must be done when. The person goes to the right places but while there does the wrong things, and, in addition, this person is fruitless. There is also a sense in which the person mixes things that are important with things that are not important, and as such does not know when to speak and when to remain quiet. Paul then has in mind some people in the community who do not know what they must do and when they must do it. Fee is right when he notes that "quiet in this case has to do with some of them not being disruptive regarding the lives of others."[157] As a result, these people are fruitless, and they are a nuisance to others in the community and outsiders as well.

The second infinitive Paul makes use of is πράσσειν from πράσσω, and its meaning ranges from travelling on a voyage, turning out a certain way in business, having a certain income, making payment, and being busy or occupied with, being interested in, or attending to one's own affairs.[158] Its use in the Pauline corpus reveals that Paul favours "doing or practicing" something when he uses it (Rom 1:32; 2:1; 7:15; 1 Cor 5:2; Gal 5:2; Phil 4:9). For instance, Paul says "Keep on doing the things [ταῦτα πράσσετε] that you have learned and received and heard and seen in me, and the God of peace will be with you" (Phil 4:9). The ASV seems to capture what Paul has in mind: "do your own business."

Plato speaks of how he was stirred up with a desire of taking up πράττειν τὰ κοινὰ καὶ πολιτικὰ "public and political affairs."[159] In Georgias, he speaks of πράττειν τὰ πολιτικὰ (the affairs of the state).[160] What is consistent between the two uses is that service is rendered to the community. Plato serves the κοινὰ

---

156. Philo of Alexandria, *Abraham*, 20 in *Works of Philo*, 412.
157. Fee, *First and Second Letters*, 162.
158. πράσσω, TBDAG: 1735–36.
159. Plato, *Epistles*, VII: 484.
160. Plato, *Lysis*.

directly whereas Paul's audience does τὰ ἴδια with the purpose of not being dependent but contributing members of the community. This fits with the meaning of "living quietly" we have adopted above. It is also Plato who writes "The philosopher lives quietly and tends to his own affairs" (λαβὼν ἡσυχίαν καὶ τὰ αὑτοῦ πράττειν).[161] As such the virtuous person is one who practices "this principle of doing one's own business."[162] Also, there was a popular saying attributed to Plato: "to do one's own business [τὰ αὑτοῦ πράττειν] and not be a busybody is justice [dikaiosyne]."[163] It is also Plato who espouses the idea that each trade (craftsmen and carpenters) contributes to the smooth running of the state.[164] The state then is one big community, and various people contribute to its overall well-being. Paul certainly has this sense in mind: the affairs one engages in are not just one's own but are done with the community in mind.

The last infinitive used in this passage is ἐργάζεσθαι from ἐργάζομαι: "to work, do, labour, accomplish."[165] In the LXX this word translates two Hebrew words for work, namely פעל "to make or to accomplish,"[166] and עבד "to serve, to till, to work."[167] It has been suggested that Paul in saying "work with your own hands" is making use of a "scriptural idiom"; that is "work of one's hands" as opposed to insisting on the manual aspect of work and its role in meeting the individual and community needs which in Paul's opinion is commended by outsiders.[168] Hence the issue is not that Paul is contrasting manual work and other kinds of work but generally depicting work as a way to provide for personal and communal needs.[169] Paul is by no means calling the wealthy members of the community to take up manual labour, but each individual to do meaningful work and contribute to the community.[170] Be that as it may,

---

161. Plato, *Republic*, 6:496D.
162. Plato, 6:496D.
163. Plato, 6:496D.
164. Plato, 6:496D; Dio Cassius, *Roman History*.
165. ἐργάζομαι, *LSJ*: 681.
166. פעל, *HALOT*: 295.
167. Wenham, *Genesis 1–15*, 67.
168. Richard, *First and Second Thessalonians*, 220; Witherington, *1 and 2 Thessalonians*, 123. The following scripture passages can be cited in support of this interpretation Deut 2:7–8; Job 1:10; Ps 89:17; Isa 2:8–9; Jer 1:16–17; Testament of Judah 2; Acts 7:41; Heb 1:10; 2:7; Rev 9:20.
169. Richard, *First and Second Thessalonians*, 220.
170. Martin, *1, 2 Thessalonians*, 138.

we have to recognize that "work with your hands" fits well with the profile of the majority of Paul's audience as working artisans. Paul's audience is not the leisured class who can afford not to work but those who belong to the working class; that is, "the non-slave men and women," those whose primary asset for work is their hands.[171] Paul is saying that work (of any kind) is needed to ensure the prosperity of the community.[172] Members of the Thessalonian community happen to serve their community through the work of their hands.

Paul with these verbs does not address the "ostentatious philanthropist" whose concern is honour and who obtained their resources through inheritance or the work of others.[173] If members of the community "aspire to live quietly, tending to one's affairs, engage in manual labour" they will actually make the community thrive in acts of love for those in the church and those outside.[174] For Johnson, when that happens it would be "*a reconfiguration of public life in cruciform, and therefore, holy, terms, not a withdrawal into the sphere of the private.*"[175] Bridges has captured the communal context of 4:11 when she says:

> The artisans worship together. They are dependent upon one another for their income. One person's work influences another person's work. If one person becomes lazy, the entire community suffers. If one person becomes less productive, interfering in the affairs of another's work and forgetting his own job, then chaos results.[176]

There were people in Paul's day who were tempted to leave the trades for an easy life as philosophers. Lucian castigates such philosophers when he says

> You shall see what will happen presently. All the men in the workshops will spring to their feet and leave their trades deserted when they see that by toiling from morning till night, doubled over their tasks, they merely eke out a bare existence from such wage earning, while idle frauds live in unlimited

---

171. Hill, "Establishing the Church," 227–29.
172. Best, *First and Second Epistles*, 176; Martin, *1, 2 Thessalonians*, 138.
173. Shogren, *1 and 2 Thessalonians*, 171.
174. Johnson, *1 and 2 Thessalonians*, 120.
175. Johnson, 120. Emphasis in original.
176. Bridges, *1 & 2 Thessalonians*, 107.

plenty, asking for things in a lordly way, getting them without effort, acting indignant if they do not, and bestowing no praise even if they do.[177]

The people Lucian describes were motivated by laziness to adopt the "philosophic" life.[178] In light of the possibility for abandoning the trades, Paul's injunctions make sense. As Malherbe remarks "It is possible, however, that experience had taught him that his converts might abandon their employment as some converts to Cynicism did . . . and that his practice was also prophylactic."[179] He uses philosophical language to challenge philosophical ideals. For Paul, Christians must distance themselves from "the socially irresponsible Cynics."[180]

Living quietly, attending to one's own affairs, and working with one's hands is what the Thessalonians converts are to aspire to. Paul is not calling these people to withdraw into individualism but rather to contribute to the well-being of the community through their work. Becoming members of the Christian community is not to escape work but to engage in it with a renewed sense of purpose. These exhortations come after the discussion on how they already love all people throughout Macedonia. These are ways in which they can continue to love more and more (1 Thess 4:10). This is not new information; Paul had already commanded them (παρηγγείλαμεν). Let us now consider the implications of these instructions to all of humanity.

5.3.4 The Implication of Proper Behaviour to All Humanity

Paul's communal concern is even more evident when he states the purpose for doing what he has commanded: "so that you may behave/walk properly toward outsiders" (περιπατῆτε εὐσχημόνως πρὸς τοὺς ἔξω) (1 Thess 4:12). With the use of the present subjunctive περιπατῆτε, Paul's concern is their conduct; in other words, their way of life. The present subjunctive informs us that Paul wishes "to stress the linearity of the verbal action."[181] Paul intends

---

177. Lucian, *Runaways*.
178. See Malherbe, *Paul and the Thessalonians*, 100.
179. Malherbe, *Letters to the Thessalonians*, 257.
180. Malherbe, *Paul and the Thessalonians*, 101.
181. Thorley, "Subjunctive Aktionsart," 208.

to say "continue walking" or we can say continue living.[182] All the NT uses of εὐσχημόνως are in the Pauline corpus (Rom 13:13; 1 Cor 14:14; 1 Thess 4:12) – the meaning varies from order, proper, to honourable. It can also be translated as "to behave with decorum" or "show of goodness."[183] For Paul, one is to behave in the manner that is consistent with goodness. Such goodness is demonstrated by actions rather than merely by words.

Carrying out the things prescribed in 1 Thessalonians 4:11 is part of what it means to behave honourably. This is to be done towards the outsiders (πρὸς τοὺς ἔξω); they are the beneficiaries of the good done by the believers.[184] For Paul, "Christians should work and conduct themselves in the community in such a way that they receive the 'respect' and not the censure of 'outsiders.'"[185] The believers in the rest of Macedonia are insiders on Paul's map; those who do not belong to the house church in Thessalonica constitute what Paul calls τοὺς ἔξω. They nevertheless are not to be excluded; they are part of the larger community of humanity whom the Thessalonians are to serve. Paul is not specifically talking about preaching to outsiders but the use of good Christian conduct as an evangelistic tool.[186] Since outsiders are watching, Christians should provide gospel witness through their lives, including how they work.[187] In this case, working with one's own hands and meeting one's needs is not only loving but wins the respect of outsiders. Yet as noted by Meeks that is not the only motive since Christians were to "seek the welfare of their city by having the wherewithal to do good to others" which entailed distribution of the results of their labour.[188] It is clear then that Paul sees "self-sufficient work as a boundary marker that sets the church apart from outsiders."[189] Work is not a preserve of the Christian community, even though for Paul the Christian community is a working community.

Opinions are divided as to whether Paul means dependent on "anybody" or no need of "anything," as μηδενὸς can either be masculine or neuter: if

---

182. Hanna, *Grammatical Aid*.
183. εὐσχημόνως, *LSJ*: 734.
184. Richard, *First and Second Thessalonians*, 3; Collins, *Studies on the First*, 296.
185. Green, *Letters to the Thessalonians*, 212.
186. Malherbe, *Letters to the Thessalonians*, 260.
187. Witherington, *Work*, 44.
188. Winter, *Seek the Welfare*, 58.
189. Weima, *1–2 Thessalonians*, 300.

masculine then "dependent on anybody"; if neuter then "having no need of anything." A section of commentators accept "so that you will not be dependent on anybody" as the correct reading of the text.¹⁹⁰ For instance, Fee remarks "At issue is not the 'needs' of the slackers theselves [sic], but their quite unnecessary imposition on the generosity of others."¹⁹¹ Among these scholars, some prefer to see the Stoic idea of self-sufficiency (αὐταρκεία), arguing that Paul in Stoic fashion does not want to be dependent on anybody.¹⁹² Yet others prefer "not need anything" and affirm that "'need' (χρείαν) is usually followed by a thing, not a person."¹⁹³

Could it be that Paul chose ambiguity because he wants both meanings? Paul does not want them to be dependent on anybody, and he also does not want them to be in need of anything. Witherington is right to note "if a person lacks for nothing essential then there is no reason to be economically dependent on another."¹⁹⁴ However, Paul's αὐταρκεία is not that of the Stoic, but it is self-sufficiency that has a place for mutual dependence and allows for one who is self-sufficient to contribute to the needs of others.¹⁹⁵ For Paul, self-sufficiency does not end with self, it actually ends with others. In the words of Hartley "Paul stresses that the Christian αὐτός should not be in isolation; true αὐταρκεία arises when the ἄλλος has a share in it."¹⁹⁶ Likewise, Meggitt sees in 1 Thessalonians 4:9–12 what he calls "inter-community mutual ethic."¹⁹⁷ Similarly for David E. Briones: Paul's αὐτάρκεια is "self-sufficiency within the confines of divine-dependence."¹⁹⁸ God is a chief participant in Paul's αὐτάρκεια, yet the community's mediation should not be overlooked; something which Briones sees in Philippians. Paul is self-sufficient because of the Philippians acting on behalf of God to provide for his needs.¹⁹⁹

---

190. Jewett, *Paul the Apostle*, 75.

191. Fee, *First and Second Letters*, 163; Marshall, *1 and 2 Thessalonians*, 117.

192. Witherington, *1 and 2 Thessalonians*, 124.

193. Williams, *1 & 2 Thessalonians*, 78; Richard, *First and Second Thessalonians*, 221; χρεία, *BAGD*: 884–85.

194. Witherington, *1 and 2 Thessalonians*, 124.

195. Malherbe, *Letters to the Thessalonians*, 252; Peterman, *Paul's Gift*, 141.

196. Hartley, "We Worked Night," 178.

197. Meggitt, *Paul, Poverty*, 161.

198. Briones, *Paul's Financial Policy*, 112.

199. Briones, 112.

These exhortations fit the context of Paul's discussion of φιλαδελφία. For Paul "Brotherly love demanded sober and industrious habits."[200] Love for others is then the impetus for one not to be a parasite and continue in detrimental unequal relationships.[201] Horrell has noted that "Paul focused on the relationships ἐν ἐκκλησία, and the merit or otherwise of one's actions is to be determined by the degree to which they promote κοινωνία and do good to the community of faith."[202] As Michael Holmes says "The proper exercise of Philadelphia includes working to support one's needs and not taking financial advantage of one's brother or sister in Christ."[203] Burke has rightly observed how Paul reflects family ideals where members of the family had responsibilities to the οἶκος and were required to work for its good.[204]

Plutarch in his essay "On Brotherly Love" speaks of how brothers like twins should "contrive together to assist each other."[205] The expectation among siblings was that they would "love one another . . . and show each other tolerance and be generous towards each other . . . and forgiving."[206] Aasgaard points to what he sees in the use of αδελφοι which he interprets to be what he calls a "role ethics" or more precisely a *"sibling ethic."*[207] Relationships and expectations are formed in a way that each sibling is to perform certain role-designation.[208] The important values that the family was to uphold were those of harmony within the family and preservation of the honour of the family.[209] The fictive family[210] language serves to call the community to an "other-regarding" morality, which gives consideration for the "weaker sibling." Such concern for others in the community is due to the fact that members

---

200. Bruce, *1 & 2 Thessalonians*, 91.

201. Witherington, *1 and 2 Thessalonians*, 123; Bruce, *1 & 2 Thessalonians*, 91; Weima, *1–2 Thessalonians*, 300; Best, *First and Second Epistles*, 179.

202. Horrell, Hunt, and Southgate, *Greening Paul*.

203. Holmes, *1 and 2 Thessalonians*, 139.

204. Burke, *Family Matters*, 218.

205. Plutarch, *Brotherly Love*; Burke, *Family Matters*, 218.

206. Aasgaard, *My Beloved*, 519.

207. Aasgaard, "'Role Ethics,'" 530.

208. Aasgaard, *My Beloved*, 513–15; Horrell, *Solidarity and Difference*, 113.

209. Aasgaard, *My Beloved*, 519; Horrell, *Solidarity and Difference*, 113.

210. Fictive kinship is metaphorical language used to denote siblings who are not really siblings "socio-biologically speaking." Yet those who are not siblings are addressed as if they are. Aasgaard, "'Role Ethics,'" 515; See Lakoff, *Metaphors We Live By*.

of the house church belong to the same family which is characterized by φιλαδελφία (Rom 12.10; 1 Thess 4.9).[211] Since family obligations extend to "the realm of material goods,"[212] there is no way in which the church can genuinely love others if the church is in need; it certainly will be hindered from meeting those in need and hence cannot help them.[213]

In summary, Paul's discussion of what φιλαδελφία entails is related to his ethical exhortations on "living quietly, attending to one's own affairs and working with one's hands." These for Paul are the expressions of what it means to love another person as if they were one's brother or sister. Depending on other people for survival falls short of the kind of life Paul envisions. Yet meeting one's needs is just the beginning, as φιλαδελφία requires that one also meets the needs of others. This, the Thessalonians did to the Macedonians, and Paul was asking them to do it again and again. It can then be said that work is a critical part of community life for Paul. One does not escape it by joining the Christian community; in fact, one is enlisted for further service when joining the community. Work is for Paul an expression of love. The fact that work is an expression of love is also part of the African setting. Africans, in traditional setting, rarely say "I love you": love is demonstrated by one's actions. Members of the community express their love for each other through acts of kindness, such as participating in work parties, as we demonstrated in chapter 2. The only drawback is that this is intra-community love: according to Paul, the love which is taught by God is for all people, including outsiders. Here is where Paul's message challenges African way of doing things – even outsiders should be treated as members of one's community.

5.4 Work in Service of the Community in 1 Thessalonians 5:12–14

5.4.1 Introduction

We shall demonstrate in this section that in 1 Thessalonians 5:12–14 Paul is calling for recognition for those who serve the community. We shall argue that those who serve are not necessarily official leaders of the community, for

---

211. Horrell, *Solidarity and Difference*, 115.
212. Horrell, 115.
213. Martin, *1, 2 Thessalonians*, 140.

the community does not have leaders yet. These individuals are involved in the management of the affairs of the house church, and their work involves manual labour. It will be shown that such service is critical for community life and Paul desires that everyone participate in service to the community.

5.4.2 Are the Injunctions General or Specific?

Some scholars consider the injunctions in 1 Thessalonians 5 general in nature and unrelated to the Thessalonian situation.[214] Best has argued in this direction, asserting that "vv.14(15)–22, is very general and is derived probably from traditional material, and this may be so for the first portion also."[215] Wanamaker on his part notes that "On the whole the information in 5:12–22 has greater value for determining general characteristics of community life and personal relations within the Pauline mission than the specific situation prevailing at Thessalonica."[216]

If we grant that Paul is using traditional material, his use of the same elsewhere reveals that he usually tailors the traditional material to the specific situation of the letter – Philippians 2:5–11 is a case in point.[217] The comparison of 1 Thessalonians 5:12–22 and Romans 12:3–18 is usually cited as evidence that we are dealing with general instructions Paul gave to the community.[218] This need not be, for Paul's exhortations here are certainly related to the situation at Thessalonica. The differences with Romans 12:3–18 reveal that Paul is addressing specific community concerns.[219] The exhortation to "hold fast to the good" relates specifically to the issue of testing of prophecy: however, "hate what is evil" and "cling to the good" in Romans 12:9 refer generally to human conduct.[220] The similarities should not overshadow the clear differences between 1 Thessalonians 5 and Romans 12. As Weima has noted "the

---

214. Moore, *1 and 2 Thessalonians*.
215. Best, *First and Second Epistles*, 223.
216. Wanamaker, *Epistles to the Thessalonians*, 146.
217. Burke, *Family Matters*, 226. However, not everyone agrees that Phil 2:5–11 is traditional.
218. Marshall, *1 and 2 Thessalonians*, 145–46.
219. We do not need to rehearse the differences here, they have been demonstrated especially by Weima. Byron, *1 and 2 Thessalonians*, 183; Marshall, *1 and 2 Thessalonians*, 145–46; Wanamaker, *Epistles to the Thessalonians*, 190–91; Richard, *First and Second Thessalonians*, 272–74; Weima, *1–2 Thessalonians*, 378.
220. Weima, *1–2 Thessalonians*, 378–79.

subjects of respecting congregational leaders (vv. 12–13b); ministering to the rebellious idlers, the fainthearted, and the spiritually weak (v. 14); and testing prophecy (vv. 19–22) – these have no parallels in Rom. 12."[221]

5.4.3 Recognition of Community Workers

It is critical that these remarks be understood from the perspective of family relations. Paul, as suggested by Burke, is primarily concerned about relations between ἀδελφοί (vv. 12a, 14a).[222] As such, his desire through his teaching in 5:12–15 is to strengthen community boundaries through fostering internal unity.[223] Paul probably makes use of Ἐρωτῶμεν instead of the usual παρακαλοῦμεν because of παρακαλεῖτε in 5:11.[224] Since παρακαλοῦμεν is used in 5:14 its omission from 5:11 is not significant. Paul requests that they εἰδέναι (recognize): the word has to do with "knowing the worth of a person such that they are shown 'respect, honor.'"[225] Such use of εἰδέναι is supported by the use of οἴδατε in 1 Corinthians 16:15 and ἐπιγινώσκετε in 1 Corinthians 16:18 where those who are to be known are also to be respected or honoured.[226]

Paul utilizes three participles – κοπιῶντας, προϊσταμένους, νουθετοῦντας – all connected by καί. He has in mind "one group of individuals in terms of three aspects of their activity."[227] The first κοπιῶντας comes from κοπιάω "to work hard, grow weary."[228] It is significant to note that the word used for hard work is the same word Paul uses to talk about his labour and toil (κοπιάω) (1 Cor 4:12; 2 Cor 6:5; 11:23, 27; 1 Thess 2:9; 2 Thess 3:8).[229] The verb has the sense of toiling hard to meet the needs of the community, and their toiling is done "among you." The labour Paul has in mind includes preaching and teaching (1 Tim 5:17, "those who work hard in the word and teaching" [TLV]) and taking care of the poor.[230]

---

221. Weima, 378–79.
222. Burke, *Family Matters*, 227.
223. De Vos, *Church and Community*, 174.
224. Weima, *1–2 Thessalonians*, 382.
225. εἰδέναι, BDAG: 694; Weima, *1–2 Thessalonians*, 383.
226. Weima, *1–2 Thessalonians*, 383.
227. Frame, *Critical and Exegetical*, 192; Wanamaker, *Epistles to the Thessalonians*; Weima, *1–2 Thessalonians*, 183.
228. κοπιάω, TLNT: 1.1.322.
229. Beale, *1–2 Thessalonians*, 161; Hartley, "We Worked Night," 171.
230. Weima, *1–2 Thessalonians*, 384.

As if cautioning those who would stress the spiritual aspect of Paul's labour, Bridges asserts, "labour means physical, manual labour"; in other words, "the kind of labour that is done with one's hands, intensive labour that uses muscle and energy."[231] For Bridges these people could be "master craftsmen" whose work is the training of young apprentices.[232] The reason for the use of the same term is that Paul does manual labour so that he may preach the gospel.[233] In this case, we can conclude that Paul means physical work done for the service of the gospel. For Johnson "Paul's use of it connotes activity requiring the kind of exertion and hardship that has a cruciform character."[234]

The second word that describes the people Paul has in mind is προϊστάμενος: "be at the head of," "lead or rule," "stand before so as to guard," "protector," or "care for or be concerned about."[235] Apollonius of Tyana uses προϊσταμένος to speak of those who "truly represent philosophy" (προϊστάμενος φιλοσοφίας).[236] In some sense, the προϊστάμενος is one who has embodied the philosophy of a particular way of life in its entirety. Many of the other ancient authors translate προϊστάμενος as leader usually in the context of secular leadership and not religious settings.[237] Josephus says of Abimelech that he showed "bitter animosity against the champions of justice" (πρὸς τοὺς τοῦ δικαίου προϊσταμένους ἐκπικραινόμενος).[238] All these uses reveal that the people described do more than lead in a religious way; they are servants of the communities.

The use of προϊστάμενος in the Bible is mostly in the Pastoral Epistles where it is used primarily of bishops and deacons whose qualification is that they must be able to manage their household (1 Tim 3:4; 3:5; 3:12). Most interpreters usually focus on the title of those it refers to and fail to notice what they do, which is the management of their households, not their work in leading the community. Its use in Romans 16 is also of interest; we have the noun προστάτις used by Paul of Phoebe, who is said to be a "benefactor"

---

231. Bridges, *1 & 2 Thessalonians*, 157.
232. Bridges, 157.
233. Best, *First and Second Epistles*, 224.
234. Johnson, *1 and 2 Thessalonians*, 149.
235. προϊσταμένους, BDAG: 707; προϊσταμένους, LSJ, 1482–83.
236. Philostratus, *Apollonius of Tyana*, 47.
237. Strabo, *Geography*; Plutarch, *Lives*.
238. Flavius Josephus, *Jewish Antiquities*, V: 267.

(Rom 16:1–2).²³⁹ There has been discussion on how the word προστάτις used of Phoebe in Romans 16:1–2 should be understood. Some scholars like Philip Payne take it to mean "leader, ruler."²⁴⁰ Edwin D. Freed takes the same interpretation suggesting that Phoebe was "responsible for guiding or presiding over the affairs of an assembly."²⁴¹ This translation is criticized, since Paul says Phoebe has been a προστάτις "of many others and myself also." Critics say Paul could certainly not have been under someone in a church he founded; Freed's response is that Paul believes in submission of one to another (Eph 5:21). Verbrugge makes a very important point: "Paul does not write that Phoebe is a προστάτις of the ἐκκλησία of Cenchreae, but of many (πολλῶν) individuals. He is not referring to her official role in the church but to the way in which she treated *many individuals* in Cenchreae, including Paul."²⁴²

The other view is that προστάτις means "patron or benefactor."²⁴³ Esther Yue L. Ng writes "She is envisioned as offering monetary support procuring political advantage, serving as legal representative for individuals, opening her house to receive visitors or provide meeting grounds, etc."²⁴⁴ The implication of this is that Phoebe becomes Paul's patroness, and Osiek suggests that Paul intends that to be the case; Phoebe will appear as Paul's patron to the Roman church, and in turn, Phoebe will make Paul look good to the Romans.²⁴⁵ Now that she is going to Rome, Phoebe is going to need hospitality in the same way she assisted previously those in need like Paul.²⁴⁶ We agree with both Osiek and Ng that Phoebe assisted Paul with hospitality; we do not, however, consider what she did to be patronage. The call to do good, as noted by Winter, was universalized among early Christians. All were now required "to do good" not just those who traditionally went with the title of patron and even not just "the rich Christians."²⁴⁷ It follows then that Phoebe

---

239. Witherington, *1 and 2 Thessalonians*, 160; Wanamaker, *Epistles to the Thessalonians*, 193; Fiorenza, *Memory of Her*, 181.

240. Payne, *Man and Woman*, 62.

241. Freed, *Morality of Paul's Converts*, 63.

242. Verbrugge, *Paul & Money*, 95.

243. Ng, "Phoebe as Prostatis," 6.

244. Ng, 6.

245. Osiek, "Politics of Patronage," 150.

246. Ng, "Phoebe as Prostatis," 10.

247. Winter, *Seek the Welfare*, 42.

cannot be used as a way to argue for an understanding of προϊστάμενος as a leadership role, since its use elsewhere is that of a patron.

Coming back to our passage, some scholars mistakenly think Paul is talking about the office of an elder, suggesting he has leaders in mind.[248] The participle does not suggest offices in the Thessalonian church, but generally people who "work or labour" in the community, or those who provide the material needs of the community.[249] As Bruce states "προϊσταμένους is plainly not an official designation."[250] In reality, what we see in Paul is a renunciation of offices along with titles and honours that went with the offices; his modus operandi was radically different from attitudes in religious organizations of the first century. In other words, Paul is renouncing official positions in favour of special functions within the community.[251]

The evidence proposed for conceiving these people as leaders includes their similarity to office bearers at Philippi (Phil 1:1), the idea that churches often followed synagogues in their organization, and that Paul appointed leaders in his churches before his mission at Thessalonica (Acts 14:23).[252] However, it is possible, as suggested by Best, that Luke might be "reading back into Paul's time the procedure of a later period."[253] Be that as it may, Paul never mentions bishops and deacons at Thessalonica and it is possible that he left town before he was able to appoint leaders at Thessalonica.

Weima even cites a second-century BC inscription (OGIS 728.4) which speaks of Marcus Annius as ruling.[254] However, as we have noted already, association leaders had functions beyond their assigned duties, which included providing resources for the association. It is used in a general sense in that the leaders do more than preside but serve as "patrons/caregivers/ protectors."[255]

---

248. Beale, *1–2 Thessalonians*, 161; Stott, *Message of 1 & 2 Thessalonians*, 191.

249. Richard, *First and Second Thessalonians*, 268; Wanamaker, *Epistles to the Thessalonians*, 160.

250. Bruce, *1 & 2 Thessalonians*, 118; Weima, *1–2 Thessalonians*, 385; Banks, *Paul's Idea of Community*, 141.

251. Banks, *Paul's Idea of Community*, 131, 142.

252. Weima, *1–2 Thessalonians*, 387; Shogren, *1 and 2 Thessalonians*, 219–20.

253. Best, *First and Second Epistles*, 226–27; Banks, *Paul's Idea of Community*, 146; Porter, *Paul of Acts*, 206. (The use of different genres [narrative vs. letter] and different literary purposes could be behind the differences.)

254. Weima, *1–2 Thessalonians*, 387–90.

255. Witherington, *1 and 2 Thessalonians*, 160; Bruce, *1 & 2 Thessalonians*, 119; Fee, *First and Second Letters*, 205; Meeks, *First Urban Christians*, 134.

Witherington emphasizes that these people are patrons of the Christian community.[256] Similarly, Wayne Meeks perceives these leaders as wealthy patrons who offer support materially to members of the Christian community.[257] L. Michael White remarks "We should thus think of the reference in 1 Thess 5:12 as referring to the 'presidents and patrons' of the house churches, that is the pater or mater familias who owned the house and opened it for hospitality to the churches."[258] For White, this is in keeping with tradition with regard to social expectations concerning pater/materfamilias who offer hospitality. Paul himself honours the labours of such individuals.[259] This reconstruction is at odds with what we have established concerning the social make-up of the Pauline church at Thessalonica. Those who are to be recognized should be understood as people within the community who have the ability to meet needs of others but not necessarily to function as patrons.[260] Besides, Paul is too critical of patron-client relationships for him to be sanctioning them here.[261] It is actually the honour and status culture which the Christian community met and was to "unlearn . . . and to learn what it means to exist as an exclusive alternative community."[262] The people may have done something that was traditionally done by the patrons, but they do not do all that patrons do; neither do the clients do what clients usually do since their doing is "in the Lord." Meeks is probably right when he observes that "a position of authority grows out of the benefits that persons of relatively higher wealth and status could confer on the community."[263] Doing so should not, however, make them patrons, nor should it entail that leadership is based on material resources.

Trevor Burke has argued based on the familial metaphors that Pauline communities were hierarchical.[264] He is captivated by the paternal metaphors in 1 Thessalonians 2:12 and disregards the fact that Paul calls himself an

---

256. Witherington, *1 and 2 Thessalonians*, 160.
257. Meeks, *First Urban Christians*, 134.
258. White, "Paul and the *Pater Familias*," 467–68.
259. White, 467–68.
260. Elias, *1 and 2 Thessalonians*, 217.
261. Winter, *Seek the Welfare*, 60; Downs, "God Paul's Patron," 153; Briones, *Paul's Financial Policy*, 21.
262. Gorman, *Cruciformity*, 356.
263. Cited in Wanamaker, *Epistles to the Thessalonians*.
264. Burke, "Paul's New Family," 269–87.

infant.²⁶⁵ He mistakes structure for hierarchy. Yet it is possible to have a structure in a community and still be egalitarian.²⁶⁶ Burke even suggests that what we have are "ordinary/led brothers:" in other words a "hierarchy of brothers."²⁶⁷ He has allowed the ancient sources he is reading to define what Paul is saying rather than allowing Paul to speak on his own. His conclusions concerning hierarchy in the household reflect Plutarch whom he is reading rather than Paul.²⁶⁸ For the household could no longer belong to the paterfamilias after it has been constituted as εκκλησιά. It becomes in the words of Stanley E. Porter "the household of God" and not only is this a "theological statement" but an "ethical one" as well.²⁶⁹

The communities Paul founded then cannot be said to be "hierarchical in structure," as authority was not vested in certain individuals.²⁷⁰ Banks considers Paul's communities "theocratic in structure." All are to participate in communal activities using gifts distributed by the Spirit who dispenses them unequally: as such, some are required to contribute more than others.²⁷¹ This is the reason why those mentioned are able to provide admonition to the rest of the community.²⁷² Paul's desire then is that the Thessalonians "respect and acknowledge their authority, leadership, and work."²⁷³ Bruce observed that "leaders did not do the appropriate work because they had been appointed as leaders; they were recognized as leaders because they were seen to be doing the work."²⁷⁴ The "hard work" of the προϊσταμένους is one and the same with the "labour of love" in 1 Thessalonians 1:3.²⁷⁵

---

265. *nēpioi* is supported by the majority of manuscripts which include P65 S B D G whereas *ēpioi* has fewer which include A K 33 *pm sy sa*. Recent scholars have revisited this textual problem and recognized the fact that "babes" is a difficult reading and therefore should be preferred. Fee, *First and Second Letters*, 73.

266. Burke, "Paul's New Family," 269–87.

267. Burke, *Family Matters*, 234.

268. Burke, 234.

269. Porter, "Paul, Virtues, Vices," 369–90.

270. Banks, *Paul's Idea of Community*, 148.

271. Banks, 148.

272. Wanamaker, *Epistles to the Thessalonians*.

273. Witherington, *1 and 2 Thessalonians*, 160.

274. Bruce, *1 & 2 Thessalonians*, 120.

275. Bruce, 120.

For Paul, those who labour through their generosity, or by exhortation and admonition (νουθετοῦντας), are to be honoured as ministers in the Lord. The word used has its roots in νουθετέω defined as to "admonish, warn, rebuke . . . advise concerning."[276] They admonish the community regarding their doctrine and morals.[277] Admonishing entails warning the audience concerning the consequences of their behaviour, and its aim is a change in behaviour.[278] The admonishing is not simply talk. Their very lives of service are a rebuke to those who do not contribute to the community. Here we see parallels with Greco-Roman associations where people were honoured for the work they did, and the honours seem to be a way to solicit more contributions to the community. The difference, however, is that any form of contribution is welcome in the Christian community and it should be recognized.

The honours were certainly different from the ones given in the associations – the epigraphs which were bequeathed.[279] Paul does not even use the word φιλοτίμος which was the word for loving honour, but instead uses εἰδέναι, which can mean "to know" or "to recognize."[280] Versions that translate εἰδέναι "respect" (ESV) or "appreciate" (NASB) are interpreting rather than translating. The NIV's "acknowledge" is closer to the original. Christians do not seem to have been concerned themselves with such kinds of honours, and Paul does not seem to be concerned with φιλοτιμως. Although early Christian communities seem to mimic the associations of the Greco-Roman world, they also maintained their distinctiveness; to the outsider they looked like one of the groups, but they were quite different internally.[281]

The other word phrase that is used of these individuals is ἡγεῖσθαι αὐτοὺς ὑπερεκπερισσοῦ, often translated "esteem them very highly," or "hold them in the highest" (NIV). The word comes from ἡγέομαι, translated as "to guide, lead, go before," and also as "regard, hold, think."[282] Some scholars conclude that the people in question are leaders based on an aspect of the meaning of

---

276. νουθετέω, *LSJ*: 1182.

277. Green, *Letters to the Thessalonians*, 250.

278. Best, *First and Second Epistles*, 226; Byron, *1 and 2 Thessalonians*, 185.

279. Kloppenborg, "Civic Identity," 121; Kloppenborg, Ascough, and Harland, *Greco-Roman Associations*; Nijf, *Civic World*, 121.

280. Heinrich Seesemann, "Οἶδα," *TDNT* 5. 116–19.

281. Kloppenborg, "Civic Identity," 115.

282. ἡγέομαι, *TBDAG*: 901–2.

ἡγέομαι. In the Pauline corpus this word appears often, with five occurrences in Philippians (2:3; 5; 25; 7; 3:8) where the meaning is either "regard or consider." In Philippians 2:3 Paul calls on the Philippians to consider (ἡγούμενοι) others as better; in 2:6 it is used of Christ who "did not consider [ἡγήσατο] equality with God something to be grasped" (NASB).

In 2 Thessalonians 3:15 Paul uses it to say, "do not regard him as an enemy" (ESV) (μὴ ὡς ἐχθρὸν ἡγεῖσθε). It follows that Paul's use of this word in 1 Thessalonians 5:13 is closer to "regard" or "consider" rather than "esteem." The community is then called upon to "regard highly" those who work for the community. These people should not regard themselves highly, since that will be counter to their cruciform identity. To be cruciform is to disregard what one is and operate as if that status does not matter. Service takes greater precedence than one's position or status. This is to be done ἐν ἀγάπῃ. Given then that their service is offered ἐν κυρίῳ, it follows that their consideration must also be in love.

These individuals are to be recognized εἰδέναι by other believers because of the work (ἔργον) they do.[283] Instead of the word κόπον, Paul now makes use of ἔργον, probably because he is trying to capture all that the three participles (v. 12) convey in term of the responsibilities of those who serve the church. It should be noted that the reason they are to be regarded is primarily διὰ τὸ ἔργον αὐτῶν: "because of their work,"[284] and not "because of their social position" and their status in the city.[285] Green writes:

> In the Thessalonian church, those who were distinguished by their labours for the church, their leadership and provision, and their moral influence over others were those who should be recognized as the true leaders in the church. Neither their status nor their title but rather their service among the believers is what separated them for this ministry. True Christian leadership is not show but substance, not self-serving but self-sacrificial.[286]

---

283. Richard, *First and Second Thessalonians*, 276.

284. Bruce, *1 & 2 Thessalonians*, 119.

285. Bruce, 119. The following are in agreement Bruce, *1 and 2 Thessalonians*, 119; Witherington, *1 and 2 Thessalonians*, 161; Fee, *First and Second Thessalonians*, 207; Weima, *1 and 2 Thessalonians*, 388; Green, *1 and 2 Thessalonians*, 248; Johnson, *1 and 2 Thessalonians*, 150.

286. Green, *Letters to the Thessalonians*, 250.

No doubt "their work is done for the sake of the community and its members."[287] The reason for this was that "in Christian ministry generally status depends on function and not vice versa."[288]

The economically well-to-do members demonstrated their love by taking the responsibility of caring for the less well-off through supplying their material needs.[289] In turn, the members of the community were to respect their leaders, and this respect was demonstrated in love.[290] What is emerging here then is a cycle of love: the προϊστάμενος demonstrate their love through their labours (κοπιῶντας) and in return the recipients return love though their respect for those who serve them. They are to reciprocate in the same manner with self-giving love for those who have already worked for them.[291] Such reciprocity is "grace-enabled" and is what defines life in the community of Christ, who gave himself up in sacrificial love.[292] As Green asserts "Their great regard for their leaders is not mere submission to a person of higher rank but is rather part of a relationship that is characterized by love."[293] This love becomes the basis for the peace which they are called upon to embrace: "Live in peace with each other." Consequently "Both the exercise of authority and submission to it were to be done in the context of mutual recognition of Jesus as Lord and their love for one another."[294]

The textual issue in verse 13 is critical for interpretation. Some manuscripts substitute ἐν ἑαυτοῖς "among yourselves" (A, B, D2) with αυτοις (with them) (P30 ℵ D). The evidence favours "among yourselves" (ἐν ἑαυτοῖς).[295] In addition, ἐν ἑαυτοῖς also fits with the context of the passage. The remark is not addressed to a particular group in the church, but the entire community, and peace is to be cultivated among all people in the group. The question

---

287. Wanamaker, *Epistles to the Thessalonians*.

288. Bruce, *1 & 2 Thessalonians*, 119. The following are in agreement Wanamaker, *1 and 2 Thessalonians*, 193; Malherbe, *Paul and the Thessalonians*, 88–90.

289. Wanamaker, *Epistles to the Thessalonians*, 194.

290. Green, *Letters to the Thessalonians*, 251.

291. As Horrell notes, "it is the Christological paradigm of self-giving for the sake of other that forms a central moral norm in Pauline ethics." Horrell, Hunt, and Southgate, *Greening Paul*, 193.

292. Johnson, *1 and 2 Thessalonians*, 150.

293. Green, *Letters to the Thessalonians*, 251.

294. Byron, *1 and 2 Thessalonians*, 187.

295. Marshall, *1 and 2 Thessalonians*, 149.

that follows is whether this remark requires conflict between people in the church or whether Paul is simply instructing the church on what they must do. Some have suggested that it is possible that tension may have arisen as a result of the "ruling over" and "admonishing."[296]

The situation of the ἄτακτοι is taken as what is bringing about the tensions.[297] Some scholars also claim that it is no coincidence that the call for peace is followed by a command to admonish the ἀτάκτους (1 Thess 5:14). The word admonish appears in both 5:12 and 5:14 and in 2 Thess 3:6–15 the discussion of the ἄτακτοι is followed by a peace benediction (2 Thess 3:16).[298] Some have seen this as coming from a lack of proper recognition for those who work for the community.[299] However, there is no evidence for this conclusion. It does not seem as if those who were serving the community through their work had complained about it. Paul simply is giving recognition of the work that is done and censoring those who are not contributing to community life. It is not certain the issue of the ἀτάκτους had deteriorated to the extent of causing conflict. Had Paul wanted to address conflict related to this issue he would have been emphatic. We now turn to the issue of the τοὺς ἀτάκτους.

5.4.4 Censoring of οἱ ἄτακτοι

It is significant that a section on honouring those who labour is followed by an exhortation to "admonish the idle." Could Paul be calling on each member to contribute their fair share to community life? Chrysostom takes 1 Thessalonians 5:14 as a reference to the leaders and not the entire congregation.[300] Gary Shogren agrees.[301] It follows according to this interpretation that the leaders are those who are tasked with admonishing the idle. However, such an interpretation is inconsistent with Paul's address to the "brothers and sisters" in the congregation. When Paul is referring to a particular group of people, he usually identifies them (2 Thess 3:6–15). There is every indication

---

296. Weima, *1–2 Thessalonians*, 389.

297. Marxsen, *Der erste Brief an die Thessalonicher*, 62; Marshall, *1 and 2 Thessalonians*, 149–50; Jewett, *Thessalonian Correspondence*, 102–5; Green, *Letters to the Thessalonians*, 252; Beale, *1–2 Thessalonians*, 162.

298. Weima, *1–2 Thessalonians*, 390.

299. Weima, 389.

300. Saint Chrysostom, *On the Priesthood*.

301. Shogren, *1 and 2 Thessalonians*, 221.

that Paul is addressing the whole church and not just the προϊσταμένους. The issue Paul is addressing is a community issue; what is done or not done by a section within the church will affect every member of the church.[302]

If some people are not working, then the community has to sustain them, and the community's reputation is at stake if some people are walking out of line.[303] Paul has already spoken about what he would want to see everyone doing, and now he is asking everyone to get involved in offering service to the community. The community cannot only be served by a select group of people; anyone can, in fact, labour for the community.[304] The phrase "admonish" entails confrontation, and Paul is calling on the church to confront the idlers with their mistaken lifestyle.[305]

The question that remains to be answered is the problem of the οἱ ἀτάκτους – what problem are they causing? The word ἀτάκτους comes from ἄτακτος: ἄτακτος can be defined as "out of order, out of place . . . frequently of soldiers not keeping rank or an army in disarray."[306] Ceslas Spicq has demonstrated that the meaning of the term is going against the order of nature or of God and that the word was often used in military contexts of someone who was out of step and did not follow procedures.[307] As such he labels this group as "refractaires," the "obstinate" or "insubordinate."[308] These people are "disorderly," "unruly," or "insubordinate."[309] The emphasis is not so much on being idle but on the rebellious attitude to the requirement of work.[310]

---

302. Glad, *Paul and Philodemus*, 203; Glad says of 1 Thess 5:14 that Paul exhorts the Thessalonians to admonish the disorderly, this is the evidence we have of mutual correction in the Thessalonian correspondence. The ἀδελφοί are the ones who are addressed to admonish. The Thessalonians in general are to respect those who admonish others. Glad, *Paul and Philodemus*, 207–8. This practice is what he calls psychagogic practice which Glad sees in both the Epicurean and early Christian communities. For Glad Psychagogic practice is "mutual participation by members in exhortation, edification, and correction." Glad, *Paul and Philodemus*, 8.

303. Bruce, *1 & 2 Thessalonians*, 119; Green, *Letters to the Thessalonians*, 252; Marshall, *1 and 2 Thessalonians*, 94.

304. Byron, *1 and 2 Thessalonians*, 187.

305. Martin, *1, 2 Thessalonians*, 177.

306. ἄτακτος, *GLNT*: 67.

307. ἄτακτος, *TLNT*: 1.223; Menken, *2 Thessalonians*, 130.

308. Jewett, *Thessalonian Correspondence*, 104; Marshall, *1 and 2 Thessalonians*, 150; Rigaux, *Saint Paul*, 582.

309. ἄτακτος, *BDAG*: 148.

310. Gerhard Delling, "Τάσσω, Τάγμα," *TDNT* 8. 48; Weima, *1–2 Thessalonians*, 392. Contra old commentators who saw the ἀτάκτους as idlers or loafers: Milligan, *St. Paul's Epistles*,

This interpretation is supported by the Greek root of ἄτακτ which has the meaning of "disruptive or antisocial behavior."³¹¹ The Greek infinitive τασσειν which has the connotation of "to order" is the origin of the word ἄτακτος, "disorderly," and this word is attested to in Jewish and Christian literature where it speaks of order instituted by God right from the creation of the world (Gen 3:17–19).³¹² It then follows that the order that is at stake is the order prescribed in Genesis 2:15 rather than Genesis 3:17–19 as suggested by Menken.³¹³ The order of Genesis 3:17–19 is the fallen order and Genesis 2:15 is the creation order. Martin asserts "In an active sense such a person is unruly or insubordinate. In a passive sense, such persons are not doing what they ought and thus are lazy or idle."³¹⁴ Failure to adhere to the proper order is not only "insubordination to God" but equally importantly "a disruption to the covenant community."³¹⁵

At the same time, there is no need to pit this passage against 2 Thessalonians 3:6–15 as Gaventa does.³¹⁶ We certainly cannot separate the use of ἄτακτος here and those in 2 Thessalonians, considering there is no context in 1 Thessalonians to aid our investigation. We shall, however, make our conclusions concerning the identity of the ἄτακτος and the kind of disruption they caused in the community when we investigate 2 Thessalonians 3:6–15, which provides context to inform our conclusions.

In summary, in 1 Thessalonians 5:12–14a Paul calls on the members of the community to "recognize" those who labour, manage communal affairs, and admonish those who do not work. There is no indication that they hold officially recognized offices, but they have committed themselves to serve the community in various ways. The reason they are to be "recognized" is "because of their work" (διὰ τὸ ἔργον αὐτῶν). Recognition for Paul comes as a result of work done on behalf of the community. Paul understands that there cannot be a community without those who give of themselves to serve the

---

152–54; Frame, *Critical and Exegetical Commentary*, 197; Best, *First and Second Epistles*, 229; Marshall, *1 and 2 Thessalonians*, 150–51.

311. Wilson-Reitz and McGinn, "2 Thessalonians," 200.
312. Menken, *2 Thessalonians*, 131.
313. Menken, 131.
314. Martin, *1, 2 Thessalonians*, 177.
315. Beale, *1–2 Thessalonians*, 165.
316. Gaventa, *First and Second Thessalonians*, 82.

community in various ways – within the African setting everyone is meant to contribute to the well-being of the community. Since Paul raises the issue of the ἄτακτος, we can conclude that he wants everyone in the community to follow the example of those who currently work for the community. Communal life for Paul requires that every person contributes something for the good of the community. As Volf has noted, "To do good to the community was to do good to oneself, and to harm the community was to harm oneself."[317] It can then be said that "work" in its various forms is integral to community life in Paul's perspective.

5.5 Conclusion

Chapter 5 has investigated 1 Thessalonians 2:9; 4:9–12; and 5:12–14a. All the texts confirm our hypothesis that Paul's exhortations on work are aimed at communal formation. Paul's ministry in Thessalonica showed us that his work was done in a workshop where he also had the audience for the gospel. The reason he worked was out of consideration for others in the community – not to be a burden (1 Thess 2:9). Our second text (1 Thess 4:9–12) demonstrated that there is a connection between love and work. Work is a demonstration of love for others in the community – both internal and external. The third text revealed that individuals within the community offered themselves to serve the community through their varied acts of service. They were then to be recognized for the work they do, and those who were living disorderly were required to follow the example of the community servants. Community life would be unimaginable without people who work for the community. It is also evident that these texts are reflected in the African setting. The idea of mixing work and social interactions, acts of service as demonstration of love, and recognition of community workers all find parallels within the African worldview. We can conclude then that 1 Thessalonians demonstrates a relationship between work and community. Let us now turn to chapter 6 where we shall test whether this is the case in 2 Thessalonians.

---

317. Volf, *Work in the Spirit*, 187.

CHAPTER 6

Working, Eating, and Community Life in 2 Thessalonians 3:6–15

6.1 Introduction

This chapter will investigate 2 Thessalonians 3:6–15 and demonstrate that Paul's exhortations are aimed at community formation. The rubric of work and community we are going to use stems from the African worldview – where they saw the two are intertwined. The passage is about work and the lack thereof: our task, then, is to see in what ways community (*Ubuntu*) is apparent. We shall argue that the ἀτάκτοι are disrupting communal life by failing to work to earn their daily bread. It will be shown that their way of life is contrary to the paradigm that Paul and his co-workers provided while in Thessalonica. Since the ἀτάκτοι are not contributing sufficiently to the community, their participation must also be limited; meaning, they should not take part in communal meals. Those following Paul's paradigm must continue to do so and those who refuse to obey must not experience community life with all its privileges.

We shall argue that for Paul work advances communal life and the lack of it destroys the community. The chapter shall consider the problem of ἀτάκτοι mentioned throughout the pericope and try to ascertain who they are in the community. We shall also look at Paul's example, which forms an inclusion in between verses 7 and 9. After that we shall look at Paul's teaching concerning work and eating (2 Thess 3:10); and then reconsider Paul's paradigm and its application in the community (2 Thess 3: 11–12). The chapter shall conclude with a look at discipline for the ἀτάκτως who refuse to heed Paul's instructions (2 Thess 3:13–15).

6.2 Literary Context of 2 Thessalonians 3:6–15

The section 2 Thessalonians 3:6–15 is related to the previous section 2 Thessalonians 3:1–5, as suggested by some interpreters.[1] In 2 Thessalonians 3:1–5 (v. 1) Paul is addressing the brothers and sisters whom he asked for prayer. In verse 6 he commands the same "brothers and sisters" to keep away from any "brother or sister" who is walking disorderly – they are to be treated as a "brother and sister" and not as an enemy. In both passages, Paul writes to his brothers and sisters and instructs them on what they must do. In verse 4 we find another lexical link in the verb "command" (παραγγέλλομεν), which Paul brings back in verses 6, 10, and 12. Paul has confidence that the Thessalonians will "do the things we command" (v. 4): these things include what he is about to command them concerning how to deal with the disorderly.[2]

Some have observed how Paul uses "command" here instead of the softer verb "appeal"; for instance, Gordon D. Fee considers the shift "unexpected."[3] Given the subject matter "disorderly idlers" (1 Thess 4:11; 5:14; 2 Thess 3:6, 10), these people who are mentioned three times, since it seems to have become worse it should not be surprising that Paul uses a harsher term.[4] Hans Urs von Balthasar captures the reason for stronger language when he says "After the exhortations in the first letter, Paul resorted to a more drastic commandment because the community was probably in question."[5] It should be observed that the commands are given "in the name of the Lord Jesus Christ," implying that there is a theological sanction to the instruction. The community should pay attention to the Lord Jesus himself as their origin.[6] Some interpreters delineate this passage as ending at 3:16 and read verses

---

1. Marshall, *1 and 2 Thessalonians*, 218.
2. Weima, *1–2 Thessalonians*, 602.
3. Fee, *First and Second Letters*, 327.
4. Weima, *1–2 Thessalonians*, 603; Bassin, *Epîtres de Paul*, 265.
5. Balthasar, *Thessalonicher*, 9. Author's own translation.
6. Wanamaker, *Epistles to the Thessalonians*, 281.

17 and 18 on their own.[7] However, the majority of scholars tend to consider verse 16 with verses 17 and 18; this seems to be incorrect since verse 16 makes sense as a benediction. Peace is not only needed for what Paul is discussing in 3:6–15 but for all that he has said in the letter.

6.3 The Problem of Walking in Idleness

In the African setting one who belongs to an age set and does not participate in work parties is often shunned and looked down upon. Such people, who do not assist others or take part in communal work, are the equivalent of the ἄτακτος. Paul begins this passage with the central issue of concern – the ἄτακτοι. It is evident that verse 6 and verse 14 form an *inclusio* around the paraenetic section of chapter 3, since both verses talk about keeping away or avoiding and not associating with the disorderly one.[8] The verb στέλλεσθαι (2 Thess 3:6) can be translated "to keep one's distance, keep away, stand aloof."[9] The only other place where it is used in the New Testament is in the Pauline corpus – that is, 2 Corinthians 8:20, where Paul speaks about having people travel with him as he delivers the gift to Jerusalem so as to "avoid" (στελλόμενοι) blame. In this case, the one to be avoided is every brother (or sister) who is living ἀτάκτως (in a disorderly manner).[10]

The use of "brother or sister" here reveals that Paul is addressing "an intracommunity issue" rather than the general Greco-Roman society at large. These commands are for those in the community of faith; they may apply to those outside, but their primary concern is the people of God.[11] As Ascough notes "The *exhortation* is framed as a community concern. Paul appeals to his authority to 'command' the Thessalonians, and invokes fictive kinship language (ἀδελφοί) to address a community problem – adherents who are ἀτάκτως περιπατοῦντος."[12] In other words, there is a way of "living" (περιπατοῦντες) that does not condone living in a disorderly manner.

---

7. Furnish, *1 Thessalonians*, 181.
8. Richard, *First and Second Thessalonians*, 379.
9. στέλλω, *BDAG*: 942.
10. ἄτακτος, *LSJ*, 267; Weima, *1–2 Thessalonians*, 604.
11. Johnson, *1 and 2 Thessalonians*, 217.
12. Ascough, "Of Memories and Meals," 58–59.

The verb ἀτακτέω generally speaks of one who is "undisciplined," "neglects one's duty," or "fail to discharge obligation."[13] The word appears in classical writers including Xenophon,[14] Plato, and Plutarch. Plato broadens the meaning when he speaks about disorderly people in the sense of "irregular living of any kind."[15] Plato speaks in Timaeus of things being in a state of disorder (ἀτάκτως) at the time when God gave them a potential for harmony and proportion. In the same text, Plato speaks of God giving offsprings the task of executing the structure of mortal things.[16] There is a sense in which things can be disorderly, and people can be disorderly if they do not attend to the task of bringing order to creation. The same is true in Plutarch who rebukes those who have abandoned the "sane and well-ordered life" and who end up in "disorderly and brutal pleasures."[17]

In Jewish writings the only usage of the term is found in 3 Macc. 1:9, which states "Those women who had recently been arrayed for marriage abandoned the bridal chambers prepared for wedded union, and, neglecting proper modesty, in a disorderly [ἄτακτον] rush together in the city." The context of this passage is that of Jewish resistance to Ptolemy. Priests are said to have prostrated themselves before God, young women and their mothers to have sprinkled their hair with dust as they lament, mothers and nurses to have neglected their new-born children everywhere in response to the profanation planned by Ptolemy. The verse, then, describes what brides did as a protest to what the king (Ptolemy) planned to do. This was not a negative reaction; it was positive, since all the people in the city were doing something about the events that were to unfold. This usage is clearly different from Paul's usage of ἀτάκτως. Paul describes a situation in which some in the community are neglecting what they ought to be doing without good cause. As such, unlike the brides in 3 Maccabees, it is a negative thing to be out of order without good cause. By walking in a disorderly manner, the people concerned are failing to render service to the community that is critically needed.[18]

---

13. ἄτακτος, *LSJ*: 267.
14. Xenophon, *Oeconomicus*, VIII:3.
15. Plato, *Commentatio ad Legg*, ii. 660b, cf vii. 860c.
16. Plato, *Timaeus*, 179.
17. Milligan, *St. Paul's Epistles*, 152.
18. Denney, *Epistles to the Thessalonians*, 378.

The censoring of the individual is to be undertaken by the community rather than just by the leaders.[19] The community taking action against an individual spells doom for the person in question.[20] It is the plural ἀδελφοί who are to "keep away" from singular ἀδελφός. Living in idleness is tantamount to living contrary to the "tradition that they received from us" (παράδοσιν ἣν παρελάβοσαν). Regarding it as content παράδοσιν refers to the "instruction that has been handed down."[21] The tradition Paul speaks of has to do with the gospel he preached to them either by word or deed. All that they have learned from Paul forms part of the tradition he handed to them. Paul's way of life among the Thessalonians is also part of that tradition, and through it Paul calls them to follow his example.

In summary, the ἄτακτοι are those who are not living according to the proper order of working for one's upkeep. These people concern themselves with things that should not be their concern, rather than productive work. The community is then to keep away from those who are not following the tradition and the example of the missionaries. The disorderly are living in a manner contrary to the example laid down by the missionaries, and it is to that example that we now turn.

6.4 Paul as the Paradigm for the Community 2 Thessalonians 3:7–9

The idea of imitating the elders is common in the African setting. Not only are Africans to follow living elders but also those who have gone – the ancestors. One becomes a deviant when they chart their own way rather than following the elders and the ancestors. The fact that Paul, an elder of the community of the Thessalonians, calls the Thessalonians to imitate him is very much consistent with the African worldview. Scholars have long noted that Paul stands in a long tradition of philosophers who saw the value in offering one's life as an example when teaching. It was Quintilian who noted that "what

---

19. In such a collectivist culture, the individual found their identity in the group which they belonged as it is in the African concept of Ubuntu. John Mbiti captures this philosophy when he says "I am because we are and since we are therefore I am." Mbiti, *African Religions*, 141.

20. Green, *Letters to the Thessalonians*, 345.

21. παράδοσις, BDAG: 763.

really carries greatest weight in deliberative speeches is the authority of the speaker."[22] Seneca in his epistles has this to say:

> Cherish some man of high character, and keep him ever before your eyes, living as if he were watching you, and ordering all your actions as if he beheld them ... Happy is the man who can make others better, not merely when he is in their company, but even when he is in their thoughts! One who can so revere another will soon be himself worthy of reverence. Choose therefore a Cato; or, if Cato seems too severe a model, choose some Laelius, a gentler spirit. Choose a master whose life, conversation, and soul-expressing face have satisfied you; picture him always to yourself as your protector and your pattern. For we must indeed have someone according to whom we may regulate our characters; you can never straighten that which is crooked unless you use a ruler.[23]

Seneca further exhorts his readers

> Let us choose ... from among the living, not men who pour forth their words with the greatest glibness, turning out commonplaces ... but men who teach us by their lives, men who teach us what we ought to do and then prove it by their practice, who show us what we should avoid, and then are never caught doing that which they have ordered us to avoid.[24]

Seneca believed the great philosophers such as Socrates and Epicurus did not form their students through their lectures but by living together under the same roof.[25]

In using himself as an example, Paul was following the widespread practice in the first century; he was aware that failure to use himself as an example would open room for accusations that he was not a good teacher.[26] It was a widespread practice that "Teachers of the day were expected to instruct

---

22. Quintilian, *Institutio Oratoria*, 3.8.12.
23. Seneca, *Epistles*, XI.8–10: 63–5; see also 25:6; 53.8; 94.40–41.
24. Seneca, *Epistles*; Malherbe, *Letters to the Thessalonians*, 83.
25. Seneca, *Epistles*, VI.6: 29.
26. Weima, *1–2 Thessalonians*, 607.

their disciples both with their words (*logos*) and with their manner of life (*ethos*)."[27] As such, the students were expected to learn not just the wisdom of their masters but imitate their behaviour as well.[28] Weima remarks "it is an axiom in education that verbal instruction must be supplemented, if not preceded, with a model of the desired behaviour or skill. By presenting himself as a model to be imitated, therefore, Paul is enacting an effective teaching strategy."[29] Witherington acknowledges that imitation works best in societies where there is great respect for authority – the elders who have gone through it all.[30] The African idea of looking up to the ancestors as models and living in imitation of them so that one day, one can graduate and become an ancestor is at home here.[31]

Elizabeth A. Castelli's reading of mimesis as "a hierarchical relationship of power" between Paul and his converts does not take into consideration these ancient sources and how mimesis functioned as a form of pedagogy.[32] She claims that mimesis cannot succeed because of "its fixation on the privileged and normative status of the model."[33] Yet, Paul was different from philosophers in that he stresses the power of God at work in his own life and that of his converts.[34] That Paul's communities have to imitate him is evident in 1 Corinthians 4:16; 11:1; Philippians 3:17; 1 Thessalonians 1:6. The communities Paul founded imitate Christ through imitating Paul since he imitates Christ (1 Cor 11:1; 1 Thess 1:6).[35] The idea of imitation with the object as Christ, Paul, or a community is present in all Pauline letters (including deutero-Pauline), with the exception of Romans.[36] In 2 Thessalonians imitation of Paul is in a specific manner; namely, "the fact that he did not live at the expense of others, but that he supported himself."[37] Paul calls on

---

27. Martin, *1, 2 Thessalonians*, 278.
28. Malherbe, *Moral Exhortation*, 135.
29. Weima, *1–2 Thessalonians*, 607.
30. Witherington III, *Paul Quest*, 86.
31. Bujo, *Foundations*.
32. Castelli, *Imitating Paul*, 13.
33. Castelli, 22.
34. Malherbe, *Letters to the Thessalonians*, 58.
35. Menken, *2 Thessalonians*, 134.
36. Getty, "Imitation of Paul," 278.
37. Menken, *2 Thessalonians*, 134.

his converts to imitate him (1 Thess 1:6). Paul shaped his communities by gathering them around himself and offering himself as an example of what he taught. Apparently, this was common among moral philosophers such as Musonius Rufus or Seneca.[38] Malherbe remarks "The pattern provided by a teacher's life was prized because it lent concreteness to his teaching, thereby making it more persuasive."[39]

The problem of the ἄτακτοι is spelt out beginning in verse 7. He reveals their problem by demonstrating the missionary team example, with whom the ἄτακτοι are apparently at loggerheads. Paul reminds the community that it is "necessary to imitate us" (δεῖ μιμεῖσθαι ἡμᾶς). The word μιμεῖσθαι can be translated as "to use as a model, imitate, emulate, follow."[40] Two of the uses of this word are in 2 Thess 3:7 and 9. The other uses are found in Hebrews where the writer calls on the audience to "imitate their (leaders') faith" (Heb 13:7) and in 3 John where the author calls on the audience "not to imitate what is evil but what is good" (1:11). What is clear from these examples is that it is a person who is to be imitated and those who imitate model their lives after the one they imitate. The idea of μιμεῖσθαι in verses 7 and 9 forms an *inclusio* that addresses Paul's example.[41]

Paul's audience was mostly Gentile (1 Thess 1:9) and hence did not know how they were to behave in their new faith, especially how to do life together with their brothers and sisters. As Scott J. Hafemann remarks, "the Thessalonians needed a more compressive understanding of the contents of faith as well as the ethos it required."[42] As such, Timothy's visit, and Paul's own visit, and Paul's letters are all ways in which Paul seeks to teach them the gospel.[43] Paul knows that it is not enough to simply teach. He offered his example so that they can imitate him. As such he models for them the life of the kingdom into which they come; such life is nothing short of cruciform life-giving love.[44] Imitating Paul does not mean Paul is the only example to be imitated as suggested by Furnish who does this to advance his case that the

---

38. Malherbe, *Paul and the Thessalonians*, 52.
39. Malherbe, 53.
40. μιμέομαι, BDAG: 651; μιμέομαι, TBDAG: 1349.
41. Weima, *1-2 Thessalonians*, 606.
42. Hafemann, *Paul's Message and Ministry*, 192–93.
43. Hafemann, 192–93.
44. Johnson, *1 and 2 Thessalonians*, 218.

two letters are from two different authors.[45] In some way to follow Paul and his followers is also to follow Christ – the paradigm par excellence (1 Cor 11:1). For Paul "sees himself as one who is in Christ, as one who is but a servant or messenger of Christ, who is embedded in the body of Christ, who is what he is by the grace of God."[46]

The relationship between Paul and his followers is not "hierarchical and asymmetrical" as suggested by Castelli.[47] In fact "Paul models himself on the narrative pattern of Christ's life of self-sacrificial giving,"[48] and this model does not leave space for any power play. Paul, then, is not obsessed with having his own followers but is calling people to follow Christ and he himself is a paradigm of what that means.[49] Paul discusses how he did not make use of his "right" (ἐξουσία) to claim support from the Thessalonians, but rather chose to forgo his right (v. 9). It is indeed true that, unlike the disorderly, "if anyone could have been excused for declining to labour, on the ground that he was preoccupied with religious hopes and interests, it was he."[50] Paul is acting in a cruciform way; that is, following Christ who emptied himself (Phil 2:5–11). Paul demonstrates his example in the area of earning his own living and not being a burden to whom he ministered. As such "Paul's life could not be distinguished from what he preached: he verified his gospel ... So by imitating him, the Thessalonians joined him in that giving of self for others."[51]

The imitation that the Thessalonians are to carry out has a specific context: namely, not being idle (οὐκ ἠτακτήσαμεν). Paul uses the perfect tense to convey the sense that what they did still has implications for the present. In verse 8 Paul speaks of his work while in Thessalonica; this helps us to understand what he means by ἠτακτήσαμεν. Paul and the missionary team were not idle among the Thessalonians; they earned their upkeep. Rigaux captures the sense in which Paul provided an example when he says "Paul

---

45. Furnish, *1 Thessalonians*, 175.
46. Witherington, *Paul Quest*, 86; Brian Rosner also asserts that "For Paul, the cross is not just the way of salvation and the supreme demonstration of God's righteousness and love, but the paradigmatic pattern for the life of Christians." Rosner, "Paul's Ethics," 217.
47. Castelli, *Imitating Paul*, 22.
48. Witherington, *Paul Quest*, 86.
49. Jenks, *Paul and His Mortality*, 195. Jenks further notes "his passion was that they should follow Christ and imitate his passion for imitating Christ" (Jenks, 195).
50. Denney, *Epistles to the Thessalonians*, 377.
51. Malherbe, *Paul and the Thessalonians*, 54.

is an example because he worked day and night and because he was not dependent on anyone."[52] Given that Paul is a missionary, the questions arise, how are the Thessalonians to imitate someone whose life situation is different from theirs? Stephen E. Fowl's suggestion is "non-identical repetition."[53] In other words they are to imitate the apostles in a way that takes their *Sitz im Leben* and vocation seriously.[54] Getty, while recognizing the vital aspect of community building implicit in the idea of imitation asserts that the love command "helps the new community of believers to define themselves over against the outsiders. Models of this unlimited love are exemplified in the Apostle, in Christ himself and in the mission to the Gentiles."[55]

Thematic similarities between 1 Thessalonians 4:11–12 and 2 Thessalonians 3:6–15 have long been noted. Close textual similarities can also be seen between 2 Thessalonians 3:8 and 1 Thessalonians 2:9.[56] It has been suggested that the passage does show signs of literary dependence from 1 Thessalonians; however, the structure is different and it seems to be dictated by the concerns of community life and how to address the problem of the disorderly members.[57] The differences between the two texts can be seen in that our present text does not mention the love or gospel proclamation or the voluntary nature of Paul's work, which are the epitome of 1 Thessalonians 2:8; what is rather central in our present text is Paul's concern not to be a burden.[58]

A continuation between verse 7 and verse 8 is evident; verse 8 is stated as a reason why the Thessalonians should imitate Paul and his companions. Paul's evidence is that they did not "eat anyone's bread without paying for it" "δωρεὰν ἄρτον ἐφάγομεν παρά τινος." The word translated "without pay" is δωρεάν, which can also be translated "gift, present or bounty."[59] Literally, Paul is saying that they did not eat anyone's bread and considered it a gift. The missionary team paid for their sustenance and did not allow the community

---

52. Rigaux, *Saint Paul*, 706. Author's own translation.
53. Fowl, "Christology and Ethics," 148.
54. Gorman, *Becoming the Gospel*, 90; See also Johnson, "Sanctification." Johnson asserts that "This pattern of life exhibited by Paul is a 'non-identical' repetition of that exhibited by Christ." Johnson, "Sanctification," 284.
55. Getty, "Imitation of Paul," 282.
56. Richard, *First and Second Thessalonians*, 386.
57. Richard, 387.
58. Malherbe, *Letters to the Thessalonians*, 451.
59. Δωρεάν, *LSJ*: 464.

to bear their cost. In other words, they did not live off fellow Christians while at Thessalonica.[60] Paul understands that to fail to work results in becoming dependent on others, which is not in keeping with what it means to live in the community of the people of God.

The phrase "to eat bread" is a Semitic expression which does not mean literally eating bread but to "get a living" rather than simply "get a meal,"[61] or "receiving basic daily needs."[62] Its use is found in 2 Samuel 9:7 when David says to Mephibosheth, son of Jonathan "you shall eat bread at my table continually" (2 Sam 9:7). David was telling Mephibosheth that he shall get his daily supplies from his house.[63] By not eating anyone's bread, Paul walks in the tradition of Samuel who could ask "Whose ox have I taken? Or whose donkey have I taken? Or whom have I defrauded? Whom have I oppressed? Or from whose hand have I taken a bribe to blind my eyes with it?" (1 Sam 12:3). Just like Israel who answered, "You have not defrauded us or oppressed us or taken anything from the hand of anyone" (1 Sam 12:4), the Thessalonians could also answer in the affirmative had Paul asked.[64]

In using the phrase, Paul means that he did not get his upkeep from his converts. This certainly does not mean Paul never accepted hospitality while at Thessalonica but that he did not depend on others for his livelihood.[65] Paul may have lodged with Jason, but in this he did not act like the idlers who wanted to receive support δωρεὰν; in other words, without paying for it.[66] Martin is right when he says "Paul did not accept anything as a gift from the church (he did not eat 'freely') and apparently did not allow the church to remunerate him for the gospel ministry he performed for their benefit."[67] Paul's understanding of the gospel informed his position on receiving support. Since the gospel was received freely, so it must also be given freely.[68]

---

60. Marshall, *1 and 2 Thessalonians*, 221–22.
61. Morris, *Epistles of Paul*; Frame, *Critical and Exegetical Commentary*, 302.
62. Weima, *1–2 Thessalonians*, 609.
63. Weima, 609.
64. Shogren, *1 and 2 Thessalonians*, 326.
65. Morris, *Epistles of Paul*, 254.
66. Frame, *Critical and Exegetical Commentary*, 302.
67. Martin, *1, 2 Thessalonians*, 278.
68. Martin, 278.

The rest of the verse captures 1 Thessalonians 2:9 almost verbatim. Paul reminds them of how they "undertook toilsome and rigorous manual labour at all available moments day and night so that they could avoid being a burden to any believers [sic]."[69] Paul worked so that he and his co-workers might not be a burden (ἐπιβαρῆσαί). The word which means "'weigh down, burden' denotes material support such as the provision of food, lodging, and financial remuneration."[70] Paul's practice of Christian love led him to this policy of self-support. Such a policy ensured that the reputation of the gospel and that of the evangelists remained intact.[71] For Paul, the ideal is for members of the community to eat their own bread.[72] In 1 Corinthians 9:12 the reason he does not accept support is so that he does not "put an obstacle in the way of the gospel of Christ" (1 Cor 9:12). This aspect is most evident in 1 Thessalonians 2:1–12 where Paul is defending his integrity while preaching the gospel. There he is aware of the charlatans whose goal in preaching was money and δοχα (glory).[73] It is clear that Paul and his co-workers had more than one reason for working to provide for their needs.[74] As such he could draw upon it and use it as needed when addressing community concerns.

Paul sees the behaviour of the disorderly idle as burdening others in the community. They must stop doing so as it is not in harmony with how Paul conducted himself.[75] Such a way of life is at loggerheads with the apostles. As Christina M. Kreinecker has noted, "The conscious 'not wanting to be burdened' reveals an affirmative interest in the congregation, which, as can be seen in the following verse, has a broader meaning, namely to encourage the congregation to act in a similar manner in an exemplary manner."[76] Similarly, Best holds that "Those who do not work are a burden on the community and threaten its life and mission, if not its very existence; they fail to love their neighbours as themselves."[77]

---

69. Nicholl, *From Hope to Despair*, 169.
70. Weima, *1–2 Thessalonians*, 611.
71. Paige, *1 & 2 Thessalonians*; Demarest, *Communicator's Commentary*, 142.
72. Richard, *First and Second Thessalonians*, 380.
73. Weima, *1–2 Thessalonians*, 610.
74. Green, *Letters to the Thessalonians*, 348.
75. Weima, *1–2 Thessalonians*, 611.
76. Kreinecker, *2. Thessaloniker*, 204. Author's own translation.
77. Best, *First and Second Epistles*, 339.

After Paul left the city, he expected his converts to support his ministry, as seen when he received support from Philippi while in Thessalonica (Phil 4:15–16).[78] Peterman is correct in stating that "Paul's unique relationship with the Philippians is not merely a social one. He has received their financial aid because he sees that they have a partnership which advances the gospel."[79] Consequently, Paul's self-support was not an issue of individualism or even selfish pride but a way to ensure that the gospel was not hindered and the Christian community not abused.[80] The result is that "Paul presents a powerful example of himself that functions as not only an explicit challenge for the Thessalonians believers to imitate . . . but also an implicit rebuke for the idle members of the church, whose conduct is strikingly at odds with that of their spiritual father."[81]

The *inclusio*, opened in verse 7, comes to a close in verse 9 where Paul completes his thought. Paul says they did not work as a matter of necessity but because they wanted to give the Thessalonians an example to follow. In fact, the missionary team had every right to be supported, but they decided to forgo it so that they could offer themselves as a model to follow. The word translated "right" is ἐξουσία which can also be translated "power, authority to do a thing."[82] The apostles had the right to support but chose to work rather than to make use of their right.[83] As such "Their personal commitment to self-support not only modelled self-sufficiency; it also showed that they were concerned for the welfare of the congregation."[84]

Paul's exhortations are to the community members who do not have a claim to be supported by the community the same way he and his co-workers have. Bruce captures the rhetorical effect when he writes "But if those who were entitled to be supported by others chose rather to support themselves, how much more should those who had no such entitlement earn their own living!"[85] Paul had no problem in affirming his full rights and also waiving

---

78. Everts, "Testing a Literary-Critical Hermeneutic," 297.
79. Peterman, *Paul's Gift*, 121.
80. Weatherly, *1 & 2 Thessalonians*, 294.
81. Weima, *1–2 Thessalonians*, 611.
82. ἐξουσία, *LSJ*: 599.
83. Paige, *1 & 2 Thessalonians*, 257.
84. Elias, *1 and 2 Thessalonians*, 322.
85. Bruce, *1 & 2 Thessalonians*, 206; See also Weima, *1–2 Thessalonians*, 612.

those rights when they stood in the way of the gospel.[86] He reveals to his audience that he worked even though he had the right not to work since he was entitled to support from the church.[87] As such his "example becomes an imperative for the disorderly of the congregation."[88] Paul's act is synonymous with the pattern exemplified by Christ's story (Phil 2:6–8) albeit in a different context.[89] Regardless of other reasons Paul may have worked, in this case, he openly uses his example to instil in his audience a life of cruciformity.[90]

In summary, Paul (like an African elder) draws on the missionary team's way of life in Thessalonica to address the problem of the ἀτάκτοι. He demonstrates that he and his team were not idle while in Thessalonica, they did not eat anyone's food without pay; instead, they worked for their upkeep. Paul did not do this because he did not have the authority but to offer an example of cruciform living. It is evident that those who are living in idleness are not functioning as they should in the community. For Paul community requires that each person earns their own bread; for it is not loving to sponge off others in the community. Communal life for Paul has no place for the ἀτάκτως.

6.5 Paul's Διδαχη on Work and Eating in 2 Thessalonians 3:10: "A Lazy Person Kills the Whole Community"

Paul begins by reminding the Thessalonians of his teaching concerning work. This teaching was given as a command (παραγγέλλομεν).[91] The imperfect tense informs us that this is not something that Paul said casually or merely mentioned once; rather, this was deliberate, and Paul did it consistently while he was with them. It is quite possible that Paul was intentional because for him this issue relates to community formation.[92] As to the origin of this maxim, it has been suggested that it has its roots in Genesis 3:19.[93] Rabbi Abbabu is

---

86. Morris, *Epistles of Paul*, 255.
87. Weima, *1–2 Thessalonians*, 612.
88. Green, *Letters to the Thessalonians*, 349.
89. Johnson, *1 and 2 Thessalonians*, 218.
90. Johnson, 218.
91. Green, *Letters to the Thessalonians*, 349.
92. Wanamaker, *Epistles to the Thessalonians*, 385.
93. Milligan, *St. Paul's Epistles*, 115.

said to have said in his commentary on Genesis 1:2 "If I do not work, I do not eat" (Genesis Rabbah 2:2).[94] Yet it must be noted that Paul's statement differs from Genesis Rabbah in that in Thessalonians it is an imperative and its concern has to do with an unwillingness to work, which is not the case in GR.[95]

Deissmann considered the phrase "a bit of good old workshop morality, a maxim applied no doubt hundreds of times by industrious workmen as they forbade a lazy apprentice to sit down to dinner."[96] Other scholars see it as a Greek proverb, and others as a dictum originating from Paul himself. It is possible that it originates with Paul and it expresses his understanding of the scriptures.[97] Best speculates that "It may have been a popular proverb (Jewish or Hellenistic) taken over by the primitive church or adapted from one, or it may have been created by Christians."[98] The dictum can also be equated to what Pseudo-Phocilides 30–40 BC says in the *Sentences*: "work hard so that you can live from your own means; for every idle man lives from what his hands can steal."[99] We do not have compelling evidence to suggest that Paul is drawing from any source. As such, we are in agreement with those who suggest that this phrase originates with Paul. For Paul the phrase represents God's will for his people.[100] It is also consistent with what is natural – if one does not work, they have nothing to eat. Failure to work contradicts not only the law of God but the law of nature.[101]

Contextual evidence in Thessalonians demonstrates that Paul is not just teaching a work ethic as is the case in the sources we have cited above since his admonitions have a context of people who deliberately have chosen not to work. In the Thessalonian correspondence the ἄτακτοι are unwilling to work and the exhortations are aimed at them (1 Thess 4:9–12; 5:12–14; 2 Thess 3:6–15). These people "refuse to work" even when opportunities for work are

---

94. Richard, *First and Second Thessalonians*, 381.
95. Marshall, *1 and 2 Thessalonians*, 223.
96. Morris, *Epistles of Paul*, 256.
97. Frame, *Critical and Exegetical Commentary*, 304; Morris, *Epistles of Paul*, 256.
98. Best, *First and Second Epistles*, 338.
99. Pseudo Focílides, *Sentences of Pseudo-Phocylides*, 153:99.
100. Williams, *1 & 2 Thessalonians*, 156.
101. Geoghegan, *Attitude Towards Labour*, 156.

available.¹⁰² Those who cannot work for one reason or another, especially the poor, Paul expects to be provided for, but those who refuse to work should not be allowed to eat (Gal 6:10; Eph 4:28; 1 Tim 5:2–8; Titus 3:14 – the collection is further evidence).¹⁰³ As Nicholl notes "The stress is clearly on unwillingness to work; it refers not to those who cannot, but to those who will not work. Apparently, the ἄτακτοι were unwilling to work."¹⁰⁴ Let us now discuss what occasioned the problem of the disorderly.

6.5.1 What is the Occasion for the ἄτακτοι?

It is critical to be clear about the specific context that occasioned the disorderliness at Thessalonica in order to understand the dictum. Various suggestions have been proposed as the proper context for the problem of not working. Richard Ascough proposes that "the injunction . . . pertains to a ban of the disorderly from ritualized commensality, the kind of commensality that takes place periodically (perhaps at set times) and provides participants with a means for individual and collective identity."¹⁰⁵ In this sense, "The Pauline prohibition on participation would thus not deprive the offender(s) from ever eating, which would, over time, become a death sentence."¹⁰⁶ Ascough's application of data from the voluntary associations to the church is commendable. Nevertheless, he has allowed the voluntary associations to be a kind of procrustean bed that determines the interpretation of the text. This interpretation is true of the voluntary associations but not of the church. It is certain that when Paul is talking about eating, it is ordinary eating, not sacred meals. The connection between work and eating makes it evident that Paul is talking about ordinary meals. There is no evidence to suggest that the disorderly have any other problem apart from failure to work.

Some scholars have read this text from the perspective of patron-client relationships.¹⁰⁷ For instance, Green suggests that Paul, by telling the patrons not to let anyone who does not work eat, liberates them from their patronal

---

102. Contra Russell, "Idle in 2 Thess," 112; Weima, *1–2 Thessalonians*, 615; Green, *Letters to the Thessalonians*, 349.

103. Weima, *1–2 Thessalonians*, 616; Weatherly, *1 & 2 Thessalonians*, 293.

104. Nicholl, *From Hope to Despair*, 169.

105. Ascough, "Of Memories and Meals," 67.

106. Ascough, 67.

107. Witherington, *1 and 2 Thessalonians*, 252.

responsibility.[108] Bruce W. Winter has also argued that it is patronage that Paul addresses in 2 Thessalonians 3:10; for Winter, Paul does not seek its "transformation" but its "abolition."[109] In this system, the patron's responsibilities to the client were continual responsibility, so long as the client returned appropriate χαριτας.[110] The gratitude given is in some way "a form of solicitation," and the lack thereof was considered "the greatest crime."[111] Simply put, to receive a gift was to put oneself in debt. One could only relieve oneself of the debt through giving a counter-gift or favour.[112] For Green, Paul then does not want this kind of relationship in which some people are indebted to others. It is indeed true that Paul does not desire that anyone should be indebted perpetually; Paul certainly does not support patronage. However, if people are clients of these patrons (some who may not be members of the church) in what way do these exhortations affect them?

Winter rightly mentions that clients were drawn from the upper levels of society and not the lower levels.[113] Given that recent scholarship has affirmed that the Thessalonian Christians were drawn from mostly artisans, such characterization does not leave space for patrons. All the evidence used by scholars who hold this view to support the existence of patrons in Thessalonica is drawn from Acts of Apostles, Colossians and Philemon (Acts 20:5, cf 27:2, Col 4:10 and Phlm 24). Nothing in the Thessalonian letters themselves indicate that there were any patrons. According to Jewett, if meals "were being provided by upper-class patrons, it would be relatively immaterial whether particular guests were gainfully employed or not."[114] Jewett surmises that church members who lived in tenement buildings without a patron met for services in one of the workshop sections within the *insula*.[115] As such it was not the patrons who provided meeting place, but members shared their space, or else rented space was used.[116] The people in question then are not the up-

---

108. Green, *Letters to the Thessalonians*, 350.
109. Winter, *After Paul Left*, 185.
110. Green, *Letters to the Thessalonians*, 350.
111. Seneca, *Epistles* 1.10.3–4; Peterman, *Paul's Gift*, 67.
112. Peterman, *Paul's Gift*, 83.
113. Winter, *After Paul Left*, 188.
114. Jewett, "Tenement Churches," 23–43, 38.
115. Jewett, *Paul the Apostle*, 80.
116. Jewett, 80.

per- or middle-class patron but the urban artisans who were mostly slaves or former slaves and the leadership was primarily "charismatic and egalitarian."[117]

Jewett's position is that the meals in question are the agape meals (what he calls *agapaic communalism* following Gerd Theissen), or love feasts, which the lower class labourers shared in the tenement or *insulae* where they lived.[118] Jewett's proposal seems to do justice to Paul's dictum; clients would certainly not have been considered as not working considering the kind of services they rendered their patrons.[119] The agape meals provide a context in which it is possible to refuse participation to a member of the community who is not working and therefore not contributing to the production of these meals. Such a practice of pooling resources to make a banquet is not without precedent within the Christian tradition. In the late fourth century such a practice is described by John Chrysostom, who calls on his fellow Christians, drawing on the example of poor Christians; "Let us enter into fraternities and partnerships in this matter; and as the poor do in their feasts, when each one alone would not be able to furnish a complete banquet; when they all meet together, they bring their contribution to the feast; so also let us act."[120] Let us now discuss in detail meals in the early church so as to understand how the dictum relates to them.

6.5.2 Meals in Early Christian Communities

We have presented the three options that scholars have proposed as the proper context for the dictum. The first option, ritualized commensality, does not fit the data we have; nothing in the text suggests a ritual meal. The second option of meals coming from patrons still does not do justice to the fact that the disorderly are not working. The third option, the agape meals provided by all the members, seems to fit the data we have in the Thessalonian correspondence. We shall now should discuss more specifically these communal meals. Given the proximity in which people lived with each other "we should

---

117. Jewett, 80.

118. Jewett, "Tenement Churches," 23–43; Jewett, "Gospel and Commensality," 240.

119. Bruce Winter who is a proponent of the patron-client explanation for the disorderly lists a number of functions that clients did for their patrons. These include the morning salutation, attending at court with the patron, financial and business errands, accompanying the patron to the public baths, and help with the elections for civic offices. Winter, *After Paul Left*, 188–89.

120. Chrysostom, *Homilies*, 417–18.

not overlook the possibility of a strong sense of community among such neighbors."[121] The community must have had prerogatives over the frequent daily meals of its members.[122] As Reta Halteman Finger has observed "food can only be withheld in a community that eats meals together regularly, not just once a week."[123] This fact addresses the question of enforceability; how is it possible that the community could enforce "let them not eat"? The injunction "[he/she] should not eat" μηδὲ ἐσθιέτω (imperative mood) only makes sense when read with communal meals as the background.[124] The issue here is not "independent self-support of individuals and families." Rather it presupposes a "communal or familial system."[125] This, however, is not to say the passage cannot apply to the former. Since the dictum is given to the community (μηδὲ ἐσθιέτω plural), Paul's concern in this passage is the communal life of the congregation. The conduct of the disorderly endangers the very existence of the community through failing to participate fully in the life of the community.[126] It does not augur well for Paul to have some working in a workshop below and others only taking part in communal meals above.[127]

Scholars have suggested that there is a possibility that the Christian communities in Thessalonica and Corinth could have had more opportunities for eating together especially when compared to voluntary associations or clubs.[128] As Crossan and Reed argue, "early Christians brought whatever they had and shared it among one another."[129] The ἀσύμβολον δεῖπνον (private dinner) was a common practice in classical Greece to the Roman Empire; the dinner guests were required to bring their own food, which was shared by the group.[130] A related dinner by subscription was ἔρανος (potluck dinner), and in this dinner

---

121. Wallace-Hadrill, "*Domus* and *Insulae*," 18.
122. Jewett, "Tenement Churches," 31.
123. Finger, *Widows and Meals*, 75.
124. Ascough, "Of Memories and Meals," 58–59; Wilson-Reitz, "2 Thessalonians," 205.
125. Jewett, "Tenement Churches," 38; see also Bridges, *1 & 2 Thessalonians*, 10.
126. Best, *First and Second Epistles*, 399.
127. Thiselton, *1 and 2 Thessalonians*, 264.
128. Gregson, *Everything in Common?*, 129; Theissen, *Social Setting*, 153; Banks, *Paul's Idea of Community*, 81.
129. Crossan and Reed, *In Search of Paul*, 339.
130. For Winter the Corinthians allowed the secular culture of how the private dinners were conducted to influence how they were done in the church. Winter, *After Paul Left*, 157.

guests were required to foot the bill of the meals.[131] Since the meal was made possible by contributions from the members, each individual was required to contribute their fair share.[132] It is possible that the motivation for such communal meals might have been to cater for less fortunate brothers and sisters in the community.[133] Fiona J. R. Gregson observes that these communal meals were held in Corinth and were widespread in Thessalonica.[134] At Thessalonica food is shared and intimate relationships develop out of such practice, and the responsibility to work arises from the need for such meals. Consequently, as individuals and together as a community, members of the house church are summoned to do good.[135] The expectation then is that if one refuses to work and fails to contribute to the community basket, that individual should be forbidden from participating in communal meals.[136]

The meals in Pauline communities were a means of expressing the unity among its members; as such, the meal was in the words of Banks "a truly social occasion."[137] Similarly, Jewett asserts that "the tenement churches in Thessalonica developed *koinonia* in the form of sharing the results of daily labor."[138] The sharing of material possessions which took place voluntarily resulted in communal meals shared by the community.[139] In the Thessalonian correspondence, the connection between meals and work is evident. It can then be argued that the results of work are part of the glue that holds the community together.[140] As Stegemann and Stegemann note "social meals replicate social positions and relationships of people . . . Thus meals can be understood as mirrors of social systems and social relationships. They reflect the

---

131. Coutsoumpos, *Paul and the Lord's Supper*, 1–2; Lampe, "Corinthians Eucharistic Dinner," 1–3; Jewett, "Tenement Churches," 41.

132. Lanuwabang, *Exclusion and Judgment*, 10.

133. Jewett, "Tenement Churches," 39–42; McRay, *Paul*, 397.

134. Gregson, *Everything in Common?*, 129; Jewett, *Paul the Apostle*, 77–84; Elias, *1 and 2 Thessalonians*, 323.

135. Gregson, *Everything in Common?*, 246.

136. Gregson, 250.

137. Banks, *Paul's Idea of Community*, 98; see also Wright, *Paul and His Recent Interpreters*, 256.

138. Jewett, "Tenement Churches," 43.

139. Banks, *Paul's Idea of Community*, 87.

140. Goody, *Cooking, Cuisine, and Class*, 37–47; Neyrey, "Meals, Food, and Table," 160, 174.

fundamental values and thus the related boundaries of groups."[141] It cannot be true that the value Paul attaches to work is that it "makes a man independent" as suggested by William Neil.[142] Independence may be a result of what work may bring; however, it is not the goal. Paul has communal concerns in his exhortation concerning work. As Hudson notes, "As much as the elite used banqueting events to affirm their individual social statuses, so, too, did the sub-elite use convivial dining to construct and maintain an anonymous yet united community identity."[143]

The result was that an egalitarian congregational structure emerged.[144] This non-hierarchical understanding of the early Christian community is also supported by Peter Lampe, who recognizes "the irrelevance of ethnic, legal, social-economic, and gender differences" given that in Paul's churches the community members were to exist in equality.[145] What made a difference for these Christians was their different mental context in contradistinction to their actual social context, and in their gathering, the mental context morphed to become their actual social context.[146] There is no doubt that eating and drinking *together* helped to bridge the divisions among these early Christians. Subsequently what emerged was "equalitarian participation and contribution where food was communal and shared among banqueters."[147] Let us focus on the proposal that Paul's goal here is community formation.

6.5.3 Exclusion of the ἄτακτοι from Participation in Communal Meals

In African traditional society, as in other societies, food has the potential for reinforcing religious and ethnic boundaries.[148] The fact that food brings

---

141. Stegemann and Stegemann, *Jesus Movement*, 268.
142. Neil, *Epistle of Paul*, 197.
143. Hudson, "Changing Places," 693.
144. Jewett, *Paul the Apostle*, 77–86.
145. Lampe, "Language of Equality," 78. Lampe recognizes that such irrelevancy did not mean the early Christians discarded their social context, they continued to fulfil their various vocations (κλῆσις), and Paul encouraged them to do so (1 Cor 7). Lampe writes "Whatever worldly status the environment placed on Christians, the baptized should voluntarily accept these worldly roles in light of the quickly approaching eschaton." Lampe, "Language of Equality," 79.
146. Lampe, "Language of Equality," 78–80.
147. Hudson, "Changing Places," 693.
148. Mintz and Du Bois, "Anthropology of Food," 107.

people together and cements social relations has long been noted.[149] The concept of community was dependent on eating and drinking together.[150] Karen Madeira makes an important distinction between the nutritive and non-nutritive aspects of food.[151] It is in the category of non-nutritive that social relations fall; in other words, food provides the nutrients for social cohesion. Shirin Edwin asserts with reference to West Africa, "The non-nutritive function of food and its social symbolism constitutes the basis for community, relationships and identity."[152] When, however, one is excluded from participating in a meal, one must have done something that required exclusion from the meals. Through participation in communal meals, one knows one is accepted, since food is a means of communication, as noted by Mary Douglas.[153]

In most African communities, men and young boys, women and young girls eat together respectively. Eating together means they do not just eat at the same time but that they eat from a common dish.[154] Cohen affirms this when he writes "Never once in Nigeria, except among Europeans, did I ever see people eat alone."[155] Similarly, the Shona people have a proverb: *Hukama igasva hunozadzikiswa nekudya* which literally translates "Relations are incomplete unless people have eaten together." Not only is food eaten with those one is biologically related to, but also with non-relatives, who include business and political associates. As such, food not only cements social relations but economic and political connections as well.[156] Eating together does not happen by accident; it must have been arranged prior to the dining, which presupposes the existence of a close-knit organization with "rules, intentions, and

---

149. Douglas, "Deciphering a Meal," 61–81; Mintz and Du Bois, "Anthropology of Food," 107; Ascough, "Communal Meals," 210–11.

150. Edwin, "Subverting Social Customs," 40–41.

151. Madeira, "Cultural Meaning."

152. Edwin, "Subverting Social Customs," 41.

153. Mary Douglas explains "If food is treated as a social code, the message it encodes will be found in the pattern of social relations being expressed. The message is about different degrees of hierarchy, inclusion and exclusion, boundaries and transactions across the boundaries." Douglas, "Deciphering a Meal," 61; Edwin, "Subverting Social Customs," 41.

154. Newman, "History and Culture," 1336; Kifleyesus, "Muslims and Meals," 253.

155. Cohen, "Everyday Life," 34.

156. Osseo-Asare, *Food Culture*, 26.

goals animating the sharing of meals."[157] This precludes, however, those who drop by and find their host at meals, or travellers who are accorded hospitality.

The people who eat alone in Africa are the social misfits and those who are excluded because of health conditions – for instance, leprosy.[158] Eating alone is considered best fit for animals but not for human beings.[159] The social pariahs eat alone so that they can experience what it means to be alone. Since the orientation everyone receives is that to be with others is what life should be about, when they are condemned to eat alone, they find life unbearable.[160] Consequently, they are made to reform their ways so that they are able to participate again in communal meals.[161] The exclusion from communal meals is not a permanent exclusion; it is meant to reform the ways of the person who has transgressed the rules of the community. We can say then that one is excluded so that they are included. Concerning food, Douglas's words are pertinent: "One cannot share the food prepared by people without sharing in their nature."[162] Neither did one eat and avoid the obligations that came with eating,[163] "since cooperation in food procurement is essential to social organization."[164] If one did not meet the obligations of eating together prior to the meal, then they were excluded from the meal. As such Paul's dictum makes sense to African people steeped in communal worldviews.

In summary, we have discussed 2 Thessalonians 3:10 and based on our investigation we were able to establish that the dictum is enforceable to the extent the community hosts communal meals on a regular basis. Participation in the communal meal requires one to contribute the result of their labour to the community. None of our sources (including the African worldview) reveal a situation in which one is allowed to participate in communal life without contributing to the well-being of the community. This proves our hypothesis: namely, that work plays a role in community formation in the Thessalonian

---

157. Edwin, "Subverting Social Customs," 42; Anigbo, *Commensality*, 7–8.
158. Cohen, "Everyday Life," 34; Fischler, "Commensality, Society and Culture," 539.
159. Fischler, "Commensality, Society and Culture," 539.
160. Moyo, "Material Things," 53; Kirwen, *Missionary and the Diviner*, 72.
161. Turner, *Forest of Symbols*; Goody, *Cooking, Cuisine, and Class*; Goody, *Parenthood and Social Reproduction*.
162. Douglas, *Purity and Danger*, 126.
163. Lanuwabang, *Exclusion and Judgment*, 3.
164. Fischler, "Commensality, Society and Culture," 530.

correspondence. As such if one does not work and so fails to contribute one is to be denied participation. Yet, this denial is actually aimed at community formation. It is not that the community is to cut all ties with these people, but that they are to maintain ties sufficient for the redemption of the disorderly. Even in denying communal meal participation, Paul's interests are the well-being of the community. If there is no food (result of work) there will not be communal meals, and if there are no meals, then there is no commensality which creates community for "Food assembles and binds together."[165]

6.6 Paul's Paradigm and Its Application – 2 Thessalonians 3:11-12

Paul now turns to the application of what he has said concerning the situation of the disorderly idlers (vv. 11–12).[166] Paul has invoked the tradition he gave them in his teaching that addresses the problem of the disorderly.[167] The present tense participle περιπατοῦντας suggests that the issue is an ongoing problem, which should be appropriately rendered "continuing to walk."[168] These "some" are not only idle but insubordinate, and the NIV translates "We hear that some among you are idle and disruptive."[169] Verse 11 is significant in that it mentions the ἄτακτοι and identifies their problem specifically as μηδὲν ἐργαζομένους.

Paul addresses these remarks to the congregation for "idleness is an affair of the brotherhood . . . and the brethren as a whole are responsible for the few."[170] Johnson holds that Paul refuses to make this issue a private affair since "the health and holiness of the church is at stake" consequently making it a public concern.[171] The play on words, ἐργαζομένους and περιεργαζομένους,

---

165. Garnsey, *Food and Society*, 6.

166. Best, *First and Second Epistles*, 339; Fee, *First and Second Letters*, 33; Weima, *1-2 Thessalonians*, 616.

167. Weima, *1-2 Thessalonians*, 617.

168. Weima, 617; Ellicott, *St. Paul's Epistles*, 131. Ellicott states "In cases like the present the predicative participle is not merely equivalent to infinitive mood but is idiomatically used as marking the state or action used as marking the state or action as now in existence, and coming before the observation of the writer," Ellicott, 131.

169. Weima, *1-2 Thessalonians*, 617.

170. Frame, *Critical and Exegetical Commentary*, 305.

171. Johnson, *1 and 2 Thessalonians*, 220.

has long been noted by commentators.[172] The word περιεργαζομένους comes from περιεργάζομαι which can be translated as "to be intrusively busy, be a busybody, meddler."[173] The NIV captures the phrase "they are not busy, but busybodies." As Beverly Roberts Gaventa says the Greek speaks of those "not working but working around."[174]

Busybodies are then people who do not concern themselves with their own work but are busy with other people's work.[175] They clearly get busy with "things that are not their concern."[176] Martin explains the double jeopardy these people find themselves in when he writes "These people were not 'busy,' that is, engaged in productive activities (*ergazomai*), but were 'busybodies,' that is, engaged in unproductive activities (*periergazomai*)."[177] Similarly, Holmes remarks "It is not that these people were inactive, but that they were active in an unproductive, irresponsible, and disruptive manner."[178] Both idle and disorderly are contained in the phrase "not busy but busybodies."[179] The issue then with the ἄτακτος is not simply about what they have not done but what they have done. Not working has led them to do what is socially unacceptable.[180]

The closest use of this word in the New Testament appears in 1 Timothy where the writer is talking about widows "who learn to be idle [ἀργαὶ] . . . not merely idle [ἀργαὶ], but also gossips and busybodies [περίεργοι]" (1 Tim 5:13). Not only do these widows move from house to house but they also talk about what they should not. Even though in 1 Timothy a different word for "idle" (ἀργαὶ) is used, the relation with our passage is clear; both talk about being idle and being a busybody. In Acts 19:19 the word is used of those who "practice magic" (περίεργα πραξάντων), the implication being that their craft (magicians) involves meddling in other people's affairs. What is clear from these uses is that nothing gets accomplished by those who "work around"

---

172. Menken, *2 Thessalonians*, 136.
173. περιεργάζομαι, BDAG: 800; περιεργάζομαι, LSJ: 1373.
174. Gaventa, *First and Second Thessalonians*, 128–29.
175. Gaventa, 128–29.
176. Stegemann and Stegemann, *Jesus Movement*, 403.
177. Martin, *1, 2 Thessalonians*, 282.
178. Holmes, *1 and 2 Thessalonians*, 273.
179. Weima, *1-2 Thessalonians*, 618.
180. Paige, *1 & 2 Thessalonians*, 259.

rather they simply "go beyond work." The only thing they do is get involved in other people's lives in a negative way. The ἄτακτοι are characterized by not being willing to work or rather not working and also as περιεργαζομένοι.[181] The problems these people create are not good for the community. Through being disorderly they do not contribute to the well-being of the community and by being busybodies they actually destroy the community.

The busybodies can also be explained as those who do not occupy themselves with their own business and whose preoccupation is "to search out everyone's business."[182] The people Paul is discussing consumed their time meddling in other people's concerns instead of meaningful employment.[183] As Beale notes "not only are they passively out of order by not busying themselves with proper work, but they are actively unruly by busying themselves with wrong activities."[184] As such Paul understands that to be a Christian is not to meddle in other people's affairs but to engage in tasks that benefit the community.[185]

The question that arises relates to what these people were doing that was meddlesome. Some scholars have suggested that the ἄτακτοι had become unpleasant street preachers.[186] However, we have no evidence that Paul has any problem with preaching the gospel and that he may have seen it as a social problem.[187] Some have suggested that these people are acting on behalf of the patrons in political affairs.[188] Green represents those who hold this position: "The problem is rather the involvement of the clients in public assembly where they supported the causes of their patrons, entangling themselves in issues that were properly none of their concern."[189] Our categorization of

---

181. Ascough, "Of Memories and Meals," 58–59.

182. Richard, *First and Second Thessalonians*, 390; Demosthenes, *Orations*, I:i.32.28; Polybius, *Histories*, VI:18.51.2; Theophrastus, *Characters*, 13; Plutarch, *Moralia. On Being a Busybody*, 516–18; Lucian, *Icaromenippus*, 20; Epictetus, *Discourses*, 3.22.97.

183. Nicholl, *From Hope to Despair*, 170.

184. Beale, *1–2 Thessalonians*, 251.

185. Witherington, *Work*, 43.

186. Barclay, "Conflict in Thessalonica," 522–23.

187. Paige, *1 & 2 Thessalonians*, 259.

188. Winter, *Seek the Welfare*, 50–51; Green, *Letters to the Thessalonians*, 351; Witherington, *1 and 2 Thessalonians*, 247–49.

189. Green, *Letters to the Thessalonians*, 351.

the Thessalonian community as artisans does not agree with a patron-client explanation since patrons never made use of artisans as clients.

According to Ascough this text "provides the community with advice and motivation rather than with detailed disciplinary procedures."[190] For Ascough the disorderly behaviour is to be understood from the perspective of worship, that is those in associations who are disorderly in the context of worship. He writes "Such inscriptions give an indication of the type of disturbances that could occur at a meeting (fighting, disruptions of order and ceremony, abuse of others) along with guidance on how to deal with such disturbances (fines and floggings)."[191] It is our contention that Ascough has allowed the evidence from the association records to dictate his reading of the situation at Thessalonica. It is not clear how he can connect work and worship. If the disorderly are disorderly during worship how does that make them fail to work?

The result of the meddling of these ἄτακτοι was that they become a "nuisance to both Christians and the wider community."[192] Bridges points to the problem of busybodies when she says "Artisan's work demands quiet, creative space. A person who is busily talking in the workshop, chatting mindlessly about the affairs of others, is a deterrent to the creative productivity of an artist colony."[193] Following A. Roosen,[194] Nichol has noted that what is at issue here is not religious work but "irreligious prying into matters which do not concern them."[195] This could have been done to both believers and unbelievers.[196]

Regardless of what one might think about the specific situation of the ἀτάκτως, what is clear from the text is that what the ἀτάκτως are doing is not work, it is busyness that disrupts rather than benefits the community.[197] Paul understands that "troublesome meddling is in direct proportion to a person's

---

190. Ascough, "Thessalonian Christian Community," 321.
191. Ascough, "Of Memories and Meals," 60.
192. Paige, *1 & 2 Thessalonians*, 256; Bridges remarks "The artisan without any work to do created a nuisance in the community" (Bridges, *1 & 2 Thessalonians*, 256).
193. Bridges, *1 & 2 Thessalonians*, 256.
194. Roosen, *De brieven van Paulus aan de Tessalonicenzen*, 167–68.
195. Nicholl, *From Hope to Despair*, 170.
196. Nicholl, 170.
197. Holmes, *1 and 2 Thessalonians*, 272.

time away from his or her post of responsibility."[198] Instead of consuming their time in what Holmes calls "pseudo-work or unproductive busyness and meddling" these people should involve themselves in "productive self-supporting activities" as the apostles modelled.[199] The result of working will be that the believers will provide for themselves through hardworking and will not be dependent on the largess of the Christian community.[200]

Paul is apparently concerned about communal relations in the church. He is aware that a few people have the capacity to fracture the community. The behaviour of the ἄτακτοι can have the effect of hindering the community from engaging faithfully in the *missio Dei*. Those who can support themselves should do so and free the church to provide for those who cannot do so, whether in or outside the church.[201] Malherbe is right when he remarks

> Paul's interest in this section is not primarily in the economic policy of the church. It is, rather, in mutual responsibility within the church, which some Thessalonians were threatening by being disorderly and meddlesome. His own behavior was exemplary for its orderliness and self-giving concern for others and constituted the tradition by which they were to conduct themselves.[202]

In verse 12 Paul makes use of the word παραγγέλλομεν as he did in verse 6; this time it is supported by παρακαλοῦμεν. Not only are they commanded, but they are also encouraged. The object of παραγγέλλομεν καὶ παρακαλοῦμεν is "such persons" namely the ἄτακτοι. Paul shifts his focus to those who are walking disorderly; he says, "such people." The command and encouragement are given ἐν κυρίῳ Ἰησοῦ Χριστῷ (in the Lord Jesus Christ) just as he did in verse 6. They are commanded to do their work quietly (ἡσυχίας ἐργαζόμενοι). The word translated by the NIV as "settle down" ἡσυχίας recalls its use in 1 Thessalonians 4:11 where it is usually translated "quietness" – this speaks of the manner in which these the disorderly are to earn their support.

---

198. Palmer, *1 and 2 Thessalonians*, 74.

199. Holmes, *1 and 2 Thessalonians*, 274.

200. Nicholl, *From Hope to Despair*, 170; Bruce, *1 & 2 Thessalonians*, 92; Marshall, *1 and 2 Thessalonians*, 279.

201. Johnson, *1 and 2 Thessalonians*, 216.

202. Malherbe, *Letters to the Thessalonians*, 457.

The contrast with their practice of being busybodies is evident when the meaning of ἡσυχία is taken into consideration.²⁰³ In the words of Wanamaker, "Paul undoubtedly intended the practice of 'working with quietness' as an alternative to the indolent members' tendency to meddle in other people's business (v. 11)."²⁰⁴ Not only are the disorderly to do self-sufficient work but they are to do it "with quietness."²⁰⁵ The participle ἐργαζόμενοι is the means through which they are able to eat their "own bread" quietly.²⁰⁶ Both injunctions address the two problems of not being busy but busybodies.²⁰⁷ Weima terms "working with quietness" the "much-needed antidote."²⁰⁸ The rest of the passage is directed to the whole congregation rather than the leaders and the wayward alone; for the issue is severe enough to warrant the entire community's involvement.²⁰⁹ In all his letters, Paul never addresses his remarks to a few select people who have different responsibilities than the rest of the congregants.²¹⁰

Not only are they to "work quietly" but also to "eat their own bread." The contrast with verse 8 where they eat bread freely is evident.²¹¹ Paul wants these people to move from eating bread free of charge to eating ἑαυτῶν ἄρτον "own bread." They have been living off the largess of others, now they are asked to eat the fruit of their own labour.²¹² Yet as cautioned by Jewett we must avoid the "individualistic and capitalistic slant that disguises the link to the communal meal."²¹³ The reflexive pronoun ἑαυτῶν is plural. It agrees with "such people" (τοῖς δὲ τοιούτοις). It should not be understood as one person earning their own bread and eating it but working for bread and contributing to the communal meal and eating together. This reading does

---

203. Weatherly, *1 & 2 Thessalonians*, 297.
204. Wanamaker, *Epistle to the Thessalonians*, 287.
205. Weima, *1–2 Thessalonians*, 621.
206. Blight, *Exegetical Summary*, 285.
207. Contra Frame, *Critical and Exegetical Commentary*, 307.
208. Weima, *1–2 Thessalonians*, 612; see also Martin, *1, 2 Thessalonians*, 283.
209. Weima, *1–2 Thessalonians*, 619.
210. Banks, *Paul's Idea of Community*, 136–38.
211. Bruce, *1 & 2 Thessalonians*, 207.
212. Morris, *Epistles of Paul*, 258.
213. Jewett, *Paul the Apostle*, 85. This is the same direction that Verlyn D. Verbrugge has taken when they agree that Paul is saying "mind your own business and work to provide for yourself and your family," Verbrugge, *Paul & Money*, 216.

not speak of each family being "economically independent" but the focus is the entire community, which must avoid reliance on a few within the community.²¹⁴ Our position is contrary to that taken by Fee who thinks that Paul is not concerned about idleness; it is our contention that he is since that is the pretext for περιεργαζομένους.²¹⁵ Besides, Paul is also concerned about the disruption of the community shalom by the disorderly.²¹⁶ Paul does not wish that certain members of the community carry alone the burden of feeding the community. As such every individual must play a part in contributing to communal welfare.²¹⁷

In summary, Paul has spelt out the implications of following his example. Those who are living in idleness, not working but meddling, are commanded to work quietly and in the process earn their daily bread. It is clear in that Paul has concerns about idleness for it becomes the pretext for meddling in other people's affairs. Second, Paul has a problem with idleness because it results in people who do not earn their daily bread. Not earning one's bread is not consistent with the example Paul demonstrated. If Paul's example were based on the gospel, it would follow that those living in a disorderly manner were not in line with the gospel of Jesus Christ. For "Paul's understanding of community is nothing less than the gospel itself in corporate form!"²¹⁸ It is in the "Lord Jesus Christ" that they are commanded to work. To be part of the community of Jesus then requires one to work for their daily bread. Work then not only demonstrates love but builds community as well.²¹⁹ We now turn to the issue of chastising the disorderly in the community.

---

214. Jewett, *Paul the Apostle*, 85.
215. Fee, *First and Second Letters*, 335.
216. Fee, 335.
217. Wanamaker, *Epistle to the Thessalonians*, 278–79.
218. Banks, *Paul's Idea of Community*, 190.
219. Elias, *1 and 2 Thessalonians*, 166.

6.7 Discipline on Account of Refusing to Work in 2 Thessalonians 3:13–15

These verses (vv. 13–15) are usually taken as relating to the entire letter, particularly in the older commentaries.[220] A number of recent scholars, however, are of the opinion that 3:13–16 is related to the preceding section on the question of disorderly behaviour.[221] The phrase "But you" is very telling. Even Menken acknowledges that "The conjunction 'but' opposes the exhortation to the preceding injunction to the disorderly ones."[222] Similarly, Nicholl understands verses 14–15 as part of 6–12 since there is no other issue in the letter which warrants discipline.[223]

Before he gives instructions on what to do with those who disobey his commands, in verse 13 Paul returns to addressing the entire community after addressing "such persons" in verse 12.[224] The contrast between "such persons" and ὑμεῖς, "you" (in an emphatic position) is evident.[225] Again he calls them ἀδελφοί and exhorts them to "not be weary in doing what is right" (μὴ ἐγκακήσητε καλοποιοῦντες) (2 Thess 3:13.) The word ἐγκακήσητε comes from ἐγκακέω which can be translated as to "become weary, tired, lose heart, despair."[226] What they are not to become weary of is καλοποιοῦντες. The word καλοποιοῦντες is a participle with its root in καλοποιέω which is translated "making beautiful, creating beauty."[227] It can also be translated "do what is right, good."[228] The aorist subjunctive conveys the sense "Do not begin now to be slack."[229] Ceslas Spicq states that it is a "Christian technical term to express the unflagging pursuit of the goal of service to neighbor or of apostolic ministry as well as the 'tautness' of the determined heart that does not let up,

---

220. Trilling, *Der Zweite Brief an die Thessalonicher*, 154–55; Milligan, *St. Paul's Epistles*, 116; Wanamaker, *Epistles to the Thessalonians*, 288.
221. Menken, *2 Thessalonians*, 141; Malherbe, *Letters to the Thessalonians*, 459.
222. Menken, *2 Thessalonians*, 141.
223. Nicholl, *From Hope to Despair*, 170.
224. Verbrugge has noted that "This means that the whole church is to take this seriously by keeping an eye on the person who persists going down a wrong path. They are to watch that person, so they can avoid him," (Verbrugge, *Paul & Money*, 217).
225. Verbrugge, *Paul & Money*, 217.
226. ἐγκακέω, *SLGNT*: 54.
227. καλοποιέω, *LSJ*: 869.
228. καλοποιέω, *BDAG*: 504.
229. Best, *First and Second Epistles*, 342.

do not lose courage."[230] Paul understands that love issues forth in service. The labour of love is dictated by the neighbour's needs which are met by the act of service motivated by love.[231]

The participle "in well doing" can mean "doing what is right" (generally) or "doing good toward others" possibly the ἀτάκτως.[232] Some scholars argue for "do what is right" as the possible meaning of the participle. They opine that Paul does not want the Christian community to react without love to the brothers and sisters who have abused their generosity.[233] The other explanation is that Paul wants the Christian community to continue providing support to the genuinely needy.[234] The latter seems to fit the context of the ἀτάκτως. As such, καλοποιοῦντες, relates to "benevolent acts extended to the rebellious idlers" as suggested by Weima who acknowledges that Paul is clear "to keep away from" (v. 6) and "not associate with" (v. 14) disorderly members.[235]

Galatians 6:9 is essential for an understanding of verse 13, for the two words we are dealing with here appear there too. The text in Galatians reads τὸ δὲ καλὸν ποιοῦντες μὴ ἐγκακῶμεν, and in 2 Thessalonians it reads μὴ ἐγκακήσητε καλοποιοῦντες. Whereas in Galatians the two words καλὸν and ποιέω appear separately, in 2 Thessalonians they have been combined to form a participle. In Galatians, ἐγκακῶμεν is a present subjunctive first-person plural and in 2 Thessalonians ἐγκακήσητε is an aorist subjunctive second-person plural, μὴ negatives both of them. Regardless of these morphological differences, the Galatians passage is critical in that its context is the Jerusalem collection, Galatians 6:6–10 calling on the community to take part in the collection.[236] It follows then that in Thessalonians, where the two words appear together, "doing good" must have something to do with taking care of those who cannot take care of themselves. Jewett is right when he notes that good

---

230. Spicq, "Les Thessaloniciens," 1:339.

231. Furnish, *1 Thessalonians*, 205.

232. Martin, *1, 2 Thessalonians*, 284.

233. Martin, 284–85.

234. Malherbe, *Letters to the Thessalonians*, 484; Green, *Letters to the Thessalonians*, 353; Witherington, *1 and 2 Thessalonians*, 255; Martin, *1, 2 Thessalonians*, 284.

235. Weima, *1-2 Thessalonians*, 623.

236. Hurtado, "Jerusalem Collection," 53; Bruce, *1 & 2 Thessalonians*, 266; Lyons, *Galatians*, 376.

"in this instance refers to supporting a community whose life centres in a Love Feast dependent on the contributions of each member."[237] Work then is an essential aspect of providing for members of the community who cannot provide for themselves.

Paul does not want the responsible members of the community to copy the behaviour of the indolent members.[238] In other words, Paul wants the working members of the community to continue to do so. Working for their own bread is good, and therefore they should continue to work.[239] Working is not an end in itself, but a means to seek the welfare of the city as they do good to others through sharing their financial resources.[240] Similarly, R. C. H. Lenski agrees:

> It means what 1 Thess 4:11 states after the injunction to be quiet; the καλόν or "excellent thing" the Thessalonians are to do is "to attend to their business" (if they are merchants), "to work with their hands" (if they are craftsmen or labourers). Nothing is to unsettle them when they are doing this "excellent thing."[241]

As Miroslav Volf notes, Paul wants "to make sure that no able people live justifiably from other's people's work, and that those who are unable to work still have their basic needs met."[242]

As Paul draws to the end of this exhortation, he provides the community with a viable way to address the problem of the ἀτάκτως if it persists. Paul says with a conditional Εἰ δέ τις, (if anyone) "does not obey what we say in this letter, [σημειοῦσθε] take note of that person" (v. 14 ESV). The word σημειοῦσθε comes from σημειόω which is translated "mark for oneself, note down"[243] or "take special notice of."[244] The congregation should "take special notice" of the wayward person; he, however, does not specify what that entails. Paul probably wants the community to "call out" the disorderly and

---

237. Jewett, *Paul the Apostle*, 85.
238. Wanamaker, *Epistles to the Thessalonians*, 288.
239. Beale, *1–2 Thessalonians*, 258.
240. Winter, "If a Man Does," 314.
241. Lenski, *Interpretation*, 455.
242. Volf, *Work in the Spirit*, 149.
243. σημειόω, *LSJ*: 1593.
244. σημειόομαι, *BDAG*: 921.

to do it publicly.²⁴⁵ Rigaux is of the opinion that it is not important how the individuals are noted; what is, however, important is that the community acts appropriately in relation to the "des member délinquants."²⁴⁶ The reason for noting someone is συναναμίγνυσθαι "so as not to associate with him."²⁴⁷ The word comes from συναναμίγνυμι which is translated "to mix up together or mingle or associate with."²⁴⁸ The mixing up is usually in reference to persons.²⁴⁹

In Hosea the word is used of Ephraim who, it is said, "mixes himself with the peoples" (Hos 7:8); the context being that Ephraim has become corrupt particularly because he associates with foreigners who consume his strength, yet does not realize it. The problem with Ephraim seems to be mixing with the wrong people. As such "Paul's point, as in 3:6, is not so much absolute isolation of the righteous from the ungodly but vigilance on the part of the faithful not to allow such people to influence others."²⁵⁰ John Calvin interpreted this word to mean excommunication; however, this reflects more his ecclesial context rather than what the text says.²⁵¹ Excommunication does not seem to be on the radar here.²⁵²

In the New Testament, the word is used only in 1 Corinthians 5 where Paul calls on the Corinthians not to "associate [μὴ συναναμίγνυσθαι] with sexually immoral persons" (1 Cor 5:9). The reference here is to the man who is living with his father's wife. In verse 11 of that chapter more people are added to the equation: we are "not to associate [μὴ συναναμίγνυσθαι] with anyone who bears the name of brother or sister who is sexually immoral or greedy, or is an idolater, reviler, drunkard, or robber" (1 Cor 5:11). Verse 11 is even more critical for our purposes since it adds "do not even eat [συνεσθίειν] with such a one." In 2 Thessalonians Paul has already discussed the issue of eating especially with those who eat bread without payment. He has also instructed

---

245. Byron, *1 and 2 Thessalonians*, 299; Bassin says "C'est une manière pour des frères de considérer comme responsables de leur frère" (Bassin, *Epîtres de Paul*, 272).

246. Rigaux, *Saint Paul*, 713.

247. Weima, *1-2 Thessalonians*, 625.

248. συναναμίγνυμι, BDAG: 784.

249. Weatherly, *1 & 2 Thessalonians*, 299.

250. Beale, *1-2 Thessalonians*, 260.

251. Calvin, *1, 2 Thessalonians*, 108; Bassin remarks "Pas plais qu'au v. 6, il n'est question à proprement parler d'excommunication ou de quelque chose qui y ressemblerait" (in Bassin, *Epîtres de Paul*, 271).

252. Green, *Letters to the Thessalonians*, 345.

the Thessalonians not to allow those who do not work to eat. Now he says mark that person so that you do "not associate with him." 1 Corinthians helps us understand what συναναμίγνυσθαι entails.[253] Since meals were intimate occasions, one is not to eat with those who are not behaving properly. This is true of Qumran: "At the congregational meal, the offender must eat alone, an appropriate punishment for a person who has refused to work in order to eat (cf. 1QS 6.24–7:27;8:21–24)."[254] Since we are also dealing with the issue of food here, it follows that συναναμίγνυσθαι has to do with withholding table fellowship with this person.[255]

The congregation is called upon to stop some form of contact with people who disobey Paul's rule.[256] Fee is probably right when he says "private fellowship may not have been included in the ban."[257] However, the person under discipline was to be "shunned in terms of close fellowship in the believing community."[258] Best states that Paul's exhortation relates to his teaching on the community as the body of Christ: as such "the loafers have injured the life of the body and so the body must act."[259] Paul's purpose for "not mixing up" with the disorderly people is "in order that they may be ashamed" (ἵνα ἐντραπῇ) (v. 14). The root word is ἐντρέπω and it means "to cause to turn (in shame), to shame or to show deference to a person in recognition of special status . . . respect" or "being turned in upon oneself."[260] Both meanings are present in the New Testament: "respect" is present in the Gospels and "shame" is used in the Epistles, and 2 Thessalonians 3:14 is no exception.

---

253. In 1 Corinthians 5 the incestuous man is to be handed to Satan so that he can reform and in turn not allow Satan to infiltrate the community. This act will return the man back to the community, Moses, "Physical and/or Spiritual," 191.

254. Witherington, *1 and 2 Thessalonians*, 255; Wanamaker, *Epistle to the Thessalonians*, 289.

255. Johnson, *1 and 2 Thessalonians*, 221; Verbrugge opines that what we have here is an issue of "complete or disfellowshipping of someone," citing 1 Cor. 5:9,11. This position does not resonate with verse 15 which requires that these people be treated as brothers. Verbrugge, *Paul & Money*, 218.

256. Holmes, *1 and 2 Thessalonians*, 275.

257. Fee, *First and Second Letters*, 226; Weima, *1–2 Thessalonians*, 626.

258. Fee, *First and Second Letters*, 226.

259. Best, *First and Second Epistles*, 345.

260. ἐντρέπω, BDAG: 340–41.

In an honour and shame society, the command not to associate with a person is important.[261] The aforementioned was a typical method in the ancient world of ensuring that social norms were adhered to. Without respect and honour, a person was devoid of self-worth.[262] Honour has to do with publicly acknowledging one as belonging to the group and shame is public recognition of a person as out of step with the group's accepted norms. People were socialized to seek honour and avoid shame at all cost.[263] As Witherington notes "Shaming in an honor and shame culture could be a very effective behavior modification technique, but it would also arouse deep emotions and usually controversy."[264]

Given that they had "turned from idols to serve God" (1 Thess 1:9), the church became their social group and to be shamed by the group to which one belongs is, in the words of Weima, to be "in a highly precarious position."[265] To be in such a situation is to face a double jeopardy, having been shamed by their pagan fellow citizens (1 Thess 2:14) and being shamed by their new social group – the church.[266] As Green states "these Christians lived as social pariahs in the city of Thessalonica and had come into the new Christian family, the church. Therefore, the separation of the disorderly believer from the new family would have been devastating."[267] This strategy was bound to be effective; one cannot remain without a group which provide social support. Yet "The non-association [v. 14] does not involve cutting off all forms of contact with that person (excommunication), since the corrective commands in the following verse presuppose some degree of ongoing interaction."[268] Bridges has pointed out that shaming someone did not only have psychological implications but resulted in economic sanctions as well. Given that it was expensive for one person to purchase all the tools they needed, an isolated individual was unlikely to flourish; resultantly the isolated artisan could not

---

261. Malina, *New Testament World*, 28–62.

262. Paige, *1 & 2 Thessalonians*, 261; Fee, *First and Second Letters*, 337; Green, *Letters to the Thessalonians*, 355.

263. DeSilva, "Honor and Shame," 166–68; Byron, *1 and 2 Thessalonians*, 300.

264. Witherington, *1 and 2 Thessalonians*, 255; see also Fee, *First and Second Letters*, 338.

265. Weima, *1–2 Thessalonians*, 626.

266. Weima, 626.

267. Green, *Letters to the Thessalonians*, 345.

268. Weima, *1–2 Thessalonians*, 625; see also Shogren, *1 and 2 Thessalonians*, 330.

make ends meet.²⁶⁹ Discipline was necessary for Paul in that it was the means for social sanction and a way to delineate the boundaries between insiders and outsiders.²⁷⁰

In verse 15 the conjunction καὶ opens the concluding phrase and scholars are surprised since they expect the adversative particle ἀλλὰ.²⁷¹ This should not surprise us, however, since Paul does not want to contrast verse 14 with verse 15, for "The actions enjoined in verse 14 are just as kindly intentioned as those in this verse."²⁷² Beale reveals our modern puzzlement with these two verses when he says "it is difficult to determine how these verses line up with a traditional notion of excommunication. Any answer to the question must explain how the apparently disparate statements of 3:14 and 15 are to be reconciled."²⁷³ In Paul's world, the two verses do not need harmonization, they fit perfectly. Withholding of intimate association is consistent with treating one as a brother or sister. It was evident to Paul "that if someone were debarred from the church community, then in many people's minds this would be tantamount to having declared that person an enemy of the community."²⁷⁴ These people continue to be members of the community of faith. As such, they should not give up on speaking to them so that they may change their wayward behaviour.²⁷⁵ As such, every rebellious brother or sister, regardless of their idle behaviour are still brothers and sisters and are to be treated as such not as "an enemy" (v. 15).²⁷⁶

Paul says the person is not to be regarded as ὡς ἐχθρὸν but νουθετεῖτε ὡς ἀδελφόν. The word ἐχθρός is translated "hated, hateful, detested."²⁷⁷ The hate or hated is usually in relation to persons or things and a sense of hostility can be present.²⁷⁸ In the Pauline corpus we hear of enemies (ἐχθροὶ) of God, (Rom 5:10; 11:28), the enemy as death (1 Cor 15:25, 26) and enemies of the

---

269. Bridges, *1 & 2 Thessalonians*, 258.
270. South, *Disciplinary Practices*.
271. Fee, *First and Second Letters*, 338.
272. Morris, *Epistles of Paul*, 261; see also Weima, *1–2 Thessalonians*, 627.
273. Beale, *1–2 Thessalonians*, 259.
274. Wanamaker, *Epistle to the Thessalonians*, 289.
275. Menken, *2 Thessalonians*, 142; Green, *Letters to the Thessalonians*, 356.
276. Weima, *1–2 Thessalonians*, 605.
277. ἐχθρός, *TBDAG*: 884.
278. ἐχθρός, *LSJ*: 748.

cross (Phil 3:18). These people in Paul's understanding are those who have nothing to do with God and they are opposed to anything that is godly. In Romans 12:20 Paul instructs the Roman church on how to live with enemies. He writes "if your enemies (ὁ ἐχθρός) are hungry, feed them; if they are thirsty, give them something to drink." In Paul's perspective, the enemy is to be treated well rather than with hostility. Then the question is, in our passage, what does Paul mean when he says do not regard the person ὡς ἐχθρὸν but ὡς ἀδελφόν? Paul is not saying they actually treat their enemies with hostility but how an enemy would be treated in ordinary circumstances. Yet Christians do not live in ordinary circumstances; they are ἐν Χριστῷ, they are the ones who feed the enemy and do good to the enemy (Rom 12:20).[279]

Marcus Aurelius in his *Meditations* speaking on dealing with someone rude in the gymnasium states "We keep an eye on him, not though as an enemy, not from suspicion of him but with good-humoured avoidance."[280] Yet it is evident that Aurelius had no concern for the reform of the person in question.[281] For Paul, proper discipline should have its aim as the redemption of the wayward person. Discipline is to be done "as a brother or sister" which means that "it must be exercised in love."[282] It is not coincidental that 2 Thessalonians 3:6–15 begins (v. 6) and ends (v. 15) with the non-vocative "brother/sister." The *inclusio* is not just a literary marker but also acts "thematically to highlight the 'brotherly/sisterly' or loving way that discipline ought to be carried out in the church."[283] Malherbe is right to note that Paul expected the letter carrier to explain the details of what they were to do with the disorderly or that the church was to figure out procedures of dealing with the disorderly. What was important for Paul was that his instructions were put into practice.[284]

In summary, for Paul, those who are living as responsible members of the community must continue to do so. This means they must continue working and doing good. Doing good pertains to providing for the less fortunate of the community who deserve to be supported and not the disorderly who must

---

279. Mtukwa, *God in His Place*.
280. Marcus Aurelius, *Meditations*.
281. Moffatt, "2 Thessalonians," 328; Bruce, *1 & 2 Thessalonians*, 211.
282. Marshall, *1 and 2 Thessalonians*, 229.
283. Weima, *1–2 Thessalonians*, 628.
284. Malherbe, *Letters to the Thessalonians*, 460.

work. The issue of the ἀτάκτως is essential to Paul; it is vital to the extent that it calls for the discipline of the persons who are living in that way. Those who do not work cannot participate fully as members of the community; as such, the community should "not associate" with such persons, especially in communal meals. Such people have already cut themselves off from the community by failing to contribute meaningfully to community life through their work. The issue is severe enough to warrant being admonished (νουθετεῖτε), albeit as a brother or sister and not as an enemy. Such admonition has as its aim the full restoration of the errant brother or sister to full membership in the community with benefits and responsibilities.[285] Yet it must not be forgotten that the reason the community is to discipline the disorderly is that they are not working. Work is an important part of communal life which warrants discipline when one fails to do it as a member of the Christian community.

6.8 Conclusion

In 2 Thessalonians 3:6–15 Paul addresses the problem of the disorderly. The passage has elements that are at home within the African setting. The disorderly people are those who fail to take part in work parties, the lazy ones who kill the community by their laziness. Paul, like an African elder, invokes his way of life in order to teach the Thessalonians how they must live. We also saw that people were forbidden to take part in communal meals if they were deviant, and when the circumstances were right they could take part in meals. The disorderly are those who live contrary to the natural order of working to meet one's needs. Paul presented to them the missionaries as the way members of the community are to behave. The example of the missionaries is one which does not involve eating other people's food without making a contribution. For Paul, the community requires that each person earn their own bread; for it is not loving to depend on others' resources in the community. Communal life for Paul has no place for the ἀτάκτως. Paul commands that the disorderly should be forbidden from eating communal meals. Participation in the communal meal requires one to contribute the result of their labour to the community.

---

285. Nicholl, *From Hope to Despair*, 171.

It is evident that work is critical for community formation. If there is no work, there will not be any meals, and if there are no meals, then there is no community. Those who are working for their upkeep are to continue doing so and are not to tire. They, however, are not "to associate" with the disorderly to redeem them back to communal life. The disorderly remains "a brother/sister" and not "an enemy." Discipline is to be carried out on those who are disorderly first, because they do not work, and as such they do not contribute to communal life, and second, because they destroy community through meddling in other people's affairs. It is clear from our analysis of 2 Thessalonians that work plays a significant role in community formation for the people of God at Thessalonica.

CHAPTER 7

Conclusion

7.1 Summary and Conclusions

In this study, we have argued that in Paul's exhortations on work there is an inextricable link between work and community. We first stated our hypothesis, namely, that work plays a role in community formation by looking at the African worldview. Since the study was done using ABH, African traditional community was offered as the context for our method. First, among most Africans contributions to the community were encouraged. Whether one looks at work parties in different tribes or working as an extended family one sees the fact that people worked together and encouraged each and every member to play their part. Second, when one looks at ceremonies or other community group activities, each member was encouraged to contribute so that their ceremony could take place. One could never think of showing up empty-handed.[1] Third, one does not work only for self; one works so that they can have something to share with members of the community. Production is not an end in itself, but a means to an end. As we have established in our interpretation of 2 Thessalonians, one is not only to work for their food but so that they can share with others in the community.

Our study took the position that the people behind the Dead Sea Scrolls were the sectarian community that domiciled at Qumran. The community required its members to come with their wealth (what one owned as well as one's ability to earn through work). The community required that members

---

1. Gelfand, *Genuine Shona*, 151.

contribute "knowledge, power, and wealth" (1QS 1 11–15). Wealth (holistically understood as inclusive of work) was a prominent symbol of community unity.[2] By extension, work, which is what brings about wealth, is a way to bring the community together. In this sense, the community was interested in the whole person and not part of the person. Archaeological evidence strongly suggests that the sectaries made scrolls, pottery, soap and also cultivated dates, grain, sheep, goats, and cattle. Agriculture may have played a significant role at Qumran, and, if so, it provided most of the work the sectaries did.

Our survey of the scrolls also revealed that the community has much to say about money and work. Regulations are provided as to when work is not to be done – that is, on Sabbath – and whom to consult and obey in such matters of work and money. Also, the community punished those who failed to report their earnings truthfully; these were excluded from the communal meals. Participation at the community table is connected with working with the earnings thereof. Even though we do see the interplay of work and community in Qumran, the type of community that was created was an exclusive community. Not everyone was welcome in this community. This, for us, provides a significant difference between the communities we see Paul nurturing and the one the sectaries enjoined.

We examined the Greco-Roman perspective on work and community. We set out to find out if work played any role in community formation. The household and the associations were seen to be crucial – particularly in the guilds, where we see communities which were founded by people who worked in the same trade. Even the associations that had nothing to do with the trades also encouraged service from their members in the form of leadership and contributions for the running of the association. As such, a connection between work and community is evident in voluntary associations. The philosophical schools, Epicurean in particular, were a kind of anomaly in that work does not seem to play a major role in the life of the community. They seem to have been taken care of by benefactors and to a certain extent friends and slaves. Members of the school don't seem to have integrated work and the pursuit of philosophy.

In First Thessalonians we examined 1 Thessalonians 2:9; 4:9–12; 5:12–14a. All the texts confirm our hypothesis that Paul's exhortations on work are

---

2. Murphy, *Wealth in the Dead Sea*, 154.

aimed at community formation. Paul's ministry in Thessalonica showed us that his work was done in a workshop where he also had the audience for the gospel. The reason he worked was out of consideration for others in the community – not to be a burden (1 Thess 2:9). Our second text (1 Thess 4:9–12) demonstrated that there is a connection between love and work. Work is a demonstration of love for others in the community – both internal and external. The third text revealed that individuals within the community offered themselves to serve the community through their varied acts of service. They were then to be recognized for their work they do, and those who were living in a disorderly way were required to follow the example of the community servants. Community life would be unimaginable without people who work for the community. We concluded then that 1 Thessalonians demonstrates a relationship between work and community. Parallels between the African worldview and this text include the fact that a visitor should not continue to be a guest: they must contribute to the local economy in one way or another (1 Thess 2:9). Concerning love, we demonstrated that just like in 1 Thessalonians 4:9–12 love is not a feeling but concrete actions done for another. Yet within the African setting love needs to be extended to include the outsider, one who does not belong to the clan. Respecting the elders is an aspect that is valued in African society – these elders are those who are worth respect because of what they do for the community. Acts of service are to be honoured and imitated (1 Thess 5:12–14).

In Second Thessalonians 3:6–15 we looked at the problem of the disorderly. The disorderly are those who live contrary to the natural order of working to meet one's needs. Paul presented the missionaries as the way members of the community are to behave. The example of the missionaries is one that does not involve eating other people's food without contributing. For Paul, the community requires that each person earn their own bread; for it is not loving to eat the resources of others in the community. Communal life for Paul has no place for the ἀτάκτοι. Paul commands that the disorderly should be forbidden from eating the communal meals. Participation in the communal meal requires one to contribute from the result of their labour to the community. Various elements from the African worldview were seen in this text. These include disciplining those who do not take part on the work organized by their age group (the disorderly), the call to imitate the elders and the ancestors, the depiction of eating after a work party, and the disciplining of the deviants within the community.

We have argued throughout this study that Paul's interest is community formation. If that were the case, in what way would denying a member of the community promote community? Studies in the sectarian scrolls revealed that the newcomer was not allowed to eat the communal meal until they had gone through all the stages of becoming a member.[3] In addition, wealth functioned as a way to delineate who was in and who was out; in other words, it was "one of the distinctive boundary markers of the community."[4] This can be seen to be the case in 1QHodayot XVIII 22–30, 33–35. It is likely then that the scrolls provide precedence for withholding participation in community meals until the conditions are right for participation (cf. 1QS 6.24–7:27;8:21–24).[5] Denying a person participation in a communal meal in view of the fact that their property is not yet with the community is crucial for our purposes. In the same manner the ἄτακτοι cannot participate since they have nothing to bring to the table because they are not being productive. However, whereas at Qumran the issue is purity, for Paul it is work and its results. Refusal of participation in community meals is not permanent, since one is allowed to take part once requirements for participation are fulfilled.

Similarly, in the Greco-Roman associations,[6] the members were aware that the continued existence of their association depended on their contributions.[7] For instance, regarding worshippers of Diana, members take turns to provide dinner, and members who fail to comply are to pay thirty sesterces to the treasury. Subsequently, the one who is next in line will provide, and the one who failed will provide in the place of the one who did it in his place. The meals are the glue of the society's existence, and if they are not offered, the society ceases to be a society.[8] The purpose of the symposium was not just to eat food, as noted by Plutarch citing Hagias the Greek poet: "we invite

---

3. Murphy, 153.
4. Murphy, 213.
5. Jewett, "Tenement Churches," 35.
6. Jewett, 35.
7. *CIL* XIV 2112, 195.
8. *CIL* XIV 2112, 197. For people to eat someone has to pay, and for one to pay, they must have work. Barclay addresses the financial sources of the associations when he says, "The 'associations' only came into existence by the donation of money-whether from a single benefactor (living or dead), by the subscription of a number of founder-members, or by the

each other not for the sake of eating and drinking, but for drinking *together* and eating *together*."[9] The symposium should not only benefit the stomach but the mind as well, since "A guest comes to share not only meat, wine, and dessert, but conversation, fun, and the amiability that leads to friendship."[10] Accordingly "we should not let a party break up before we have made a new friend and well-wisher among the other guests and fellow diners"[11] Plutarch recommends. This picture is further supported by evidence from Roman language as represented in banquet imagery.[12]

In the Greco-Roman context there is a sense in which a guest was discouraged from thinking of oneself and one's invitees as "an army living off enemy country."[13] The banquet was not an opportunity to plunder; as such, one needed to be considerate in extending invitations to others when invited. In a sense, every dinner guest was aware that he "Who offers sacrifice at Delphi must buy meat for himself."[14] Even though we do not have evidence from extant sources to suggest that guests were required to bring something to the dinner except in private dinners, it is true that reciprocity was required. This reciprocity meant that "dinners were a kind of gift exchange."[15] To be invited is to owe a debt to the friend who has extended you an invitation.[16]

The Bacchic society required its members to pay their monthly dues for drinks, failure of which resulted in being excluded from the fellowship meal.[17] There is a possibility that if a member was no longer able to meet their obligation to the association, giving up their membership was the only option, as was the case with Epiodoros of Karanis Egypt. However, should the said member be in a position to keep up with membership obligations, they were naturally permitted to assume membership again. It emerges here that food itself is a pretext for the higher goal of social interaction. As such,

---

collection of membership-dues from those who made up the 'associations.'" Barclay, "Money and Meetings."

9. Plutarch, *Moralia, Volume VIII*, 643:185.
10. Plutarch, 660:293.
11. Plutarch, 660:293.
12. Hudson, "Changing Places," 665.
13. Plutarch, *Moralia, Volume VIII*, 708:65.
14. Plutarch, 708:67.
15. Finger, *Widows and Meals*, 173.
16. Moxnes, "Social Context," 386.
17. *IG* II² 1368, 13–16.

the provision of food is essential. We have so far considered the Sectarian scrolls and Greco-Roman philosophers and voluntary associations and have established that meals were a critical part of community life. In all the sources considered there is precedence for withholding participation to members and a requirement to contribute towards the meals or to reciprocate by inviting those who invite you to these meals.

It is evident that work is critical for community formation. If there is no work, there will not be any meals, and if there are no meals, then there is no community. Those who are working for their upkeep are to continue doing so and are not to tire. They, however, are not "to associate" with the disorderly to redeem them back to communal life. The disorderly remains "a brother/sister" and not "an enemy." Discipline is to be imposed on those who are walking in a disorderly way, primarily because they do not work and as such they do not contribute to communal life, and secondarily because they destroy community through meddling in other people's affairs. It is clear from our analysis of the 2 Thessalonians that work plays a significant role in community formation for the people of God at Thessalonica.

Our method ABH has proved fruitful, for the questions we brought to the text emanated from it. We were able to ask if work plays a part in community formation. Fresh insights have emerged from the Thessalonian correspondence. We have been able to see that work plays a positive role in community formation. Unlike previous interpretations, which have only focused on the role work plays in Paul's ministry, we have been able to detect that Paul's vision of work entails community formation. In the process we observed the following: first, as we have noted above, the African community is an exclusive community whereas the Christian community is an inclusive community. The Christian gospel will need to help the African community embrace all of humanity as members of one's community rather than those of one's tribe. This means in an African setting, the results of one's labour can be given to someone of a different tribe and not just to one's kith and kin. Second, the African perspective on labour does not perceive work as drudgery; this is evidenced by the community singing songs of rejoicing while working. The words Paul uses to describe work (the κόπος group of words) do not fall into the category of something one enjoys but something one dreads. This is a place where the African worldview can make a contribution in restoring the beauty and the joy of work.

7.2 Contributions

This study challenges the long-held interpretation of Paul's exhortations on work that focus on Paul's work as a strategy only for preaching the gospel. Scholarship has overlooked the role of work in community formation. Instead of seeing work only from an instrumental perspective, this study suggests that for Paul there are higher goals in his working and that of the community; namely, community formation. The study also challenges the individualistic reading of Paul's work exhortations, and it sets them within their proper context, which is communitarian. Paul's call to individuals to work for their own daily bread has a communal meal context in view in which he considers it improper to eat without contributing.[18] This study makes a distinction between people who are not able to work and those who do not wish to work. Paul's focus is on those people who can work but choose not to work. As such, work, as understood by Paul, contributes to our understanding of Paul's ecclesiology. For Paul, the εκκλησιά consists of working people.

The study does not pit the eschatological against the sociological explanations for the attitude of the for the ατάκτοι. We recognize the impact of both eschatological and sociological factors on the disorderly. The study also contributes to our reading of the Thessalonian correspondence; the study revealed that the relationship between the two letters of Paul to the Thessalonians regarding what they say about work and community is quite close. This is offered as further evidence for the Pauline authorship of 2 Thessalonians. In addition, this study demonstrates that African biblical hermeneutics can be used fruitfully to interpret the biblical texts. This hermeneutic is a much-needed correction to methods that do not make community central in the interpretation of the text.

7.3 Further Studies

Future researchers will need to explore the issue of the Lord's Supper in light of Paul's requirement for all to contribute. It will be interesting to explore the Thessalonian letters in the light of in 1 Corinthians 9. Paul's view of work is a bit ambivalent and some scholars have concluded that Paul disparages work in his Corinthian letters. Is this view tenable in light of the findings of this

---

18. See Jewett, "Tenement Churches."

study concerning the positive relationship between work and community? Reading Paul's approach to ministry from a communal perspective could also yield significant results. ABH could be used to look at Paul's missionary practices and his relationship with co-workers. This study has demonstrated that ABH has much to offer in the interpretation of the biblical text.

Bibliography

Primary Sources

Achilles Tatius. *Leucippe and Clitophon*. Translated by S. Gaselee. Loeb Classical Library 45. Cambridge, MA: Harvard University Press, 1969.

Aelius Aristides. *Dionysiaca*. Translated by W. H. D. Rouse. Loeb Classical Library. Cambridge, MA: Harvard University Press, 1940.

———. *Orations*. Edited and translated by Michael Trapp. Loeb Classical Library 533. Cambridge, MA: Harvard University Press, 2017.

Philostratus. *Apollonius of Tyana, Volume III: Letters of Apollonius. Ancient Testimonia. Eusebius's Reply to Hierocles*. Edited and translated by Christopher P. Jones. Loeb Classical Library 458. Cambridge, MA: Harvard University Press, 2006.

Aristotle. *Art of Rhetoric*. Translated by J. H. Freese. Loeb Classical Library 193. Cambridge, MA: Harvard University Press, 1926.

———. *Nicomachean Ethics*. Translated by H. Rackham. Loeb Classical Library 73. Cambridge, MA: Harvard University Press, 2015.

———. *Politics*. Translated by H. Rackham. Loeb Classical Library 264. Cambridge, MA: Harvard University Press, 1932.

Cicero. "De Re Publica." In *On the Republic. On the Laws*, 2–287. Translated by Clinton W. Keyes. Loeb Classical Library 213. Cambridge, MA: Harvard University Press, 1928.

Clement of Alexandria. *Stromata*. Translated by William Wilson. From *Ante-Nicene Fathers*, vol. 2. Edited by Alexander Roberts, James Donaldson, and A. Cleveland Coxe. Buffalo, NY: Christian Literature Publishing, 1885. Revised and edited for New Advent by Kevin Knight. https://www.newadvent.org/fathers/0210.htm.

Cornelius Nepos. "Excerpt from the Book of Latin Historians. Atticus." In *On Great Generals. On Historians*, 282–325. Translated by J. C. Rolfe. Loeb Classical Library 467. Cambridge, MA: Harvard University Press, 1929.

Demosthenes. *Orations, Volume I*. Translated by J. H. Vince. Loeb Classical Library 238. Cambridge, MA: Harvard University Press, 1930.

Dio Cassius. *Roman History*. Translated by Earnest Cary and Herbert B. Foster. Loeb Classical Library 32. Cambridge, MA: Harvard University Press, 1927.

Diogenes. *Thirteen New Fragments of Diogenes of Oenoanda*. Translated by Martin Ferguson Smith. Wien: Verlag der Österreichischen Akademie der Wissenschaften, 1974.

Diogenes Laertius. *Lives of Eminent Philosophers, Volume I: Books 1–5*. Translated by R. D. Hicks. Loeb Classical Library 184. Cambridge, MA: Harvard University Press, 1925.

Dionysius of Halicarnassus. *Roman Antiquities*. Translated by Earnest Cary. Loeb Classical Library 319. Cambridge, MA: Harvard University Press, 1937.

Epictetus. *Discourses*. Translated by W. A. Oldfather. Loeb Classical Library 131. Cambridge, MA: Harvard University Press, 1925.

Epicurus. *Epicurus, the Extant Remains: With Short Critical Apparatus, Translation, and Notes*. Translated by Cyril Bailey. Westport, CT: Hyperion Press, 1980.

Epicurus. *Principal Doctrines*. Translated by R. D. Hicks, n.d. The Internet Classics Archive, http://classics.mit.edu/Epicurus/princdoc.html.

Galen. *Thrasybulus*. Edited and translated by Ian Johnston. Loeb Classical Library 536. Cambridge, MA: Harvard University Press, 2018.

Hallo, William W., and K. Lawson Younger, eds. "Epic of Creation (1.111) (Enuma Elish)." In *Context of Scripture: Canonical Compositions from the Biblical World*, 390–402. Translated by Benjamin R. Foster. Boston: Brill, 2003.

Homer. *Iliad, Volume I*. Translated by A. T. Murray. Loeb Classical Library 170. Cambridge, MA: Harvard University Press, 1924.

Homer. *Odyssey*. Translated by A. T. Murray. Loeb Classical Library 104. Cambridge, MA: Harvard University Press, 1919.

Horace. *Satires*. Translated by H. Rushton Fairclough. Loeb Classical Library 194. Cambridge, MA: Harvard University Press, 1926.

Josephus, Flavius. *Jewish Antiquities*. Translated by Louis H Feldman, Ralph Marcus, H. St. J. Thackeray, and Allen Paul Wikgren. Cambridge, MA: Harvard University Press, 2015.

———. *The Works of Josephus: Complete and Unabridged*. Translated by William Whiston. Peabody, MA: Hendrickson, 1987.

Lucian. *Icaromenippus, or The Sky-Man*. Translated by A. M. Harmon. Loeb Classical Library 54. Cambridge, MA: Harvard University Press, 1915.

———. *Lucian*. Translated by A. M. Harmon, K. Kilburn, and M. D. Macleod. London: Heinemann, 1913.

———. *The Runaways*. Translated by A. M. Harmon. Loeb Classical Library 302. Cambridge, MA: Harvard University Press, 1990.

Marcus Aurelius. *Meditations*. Translated by C. R. Haines. Loeb Classical Library 58. Cambridge, MA: Harvard University Press, 1916.

Musonius Rufus. *Stoic Fragments*. Translated by Cora E. Lutz. New Delhi, India: Isha Books, 2013.

Philo of Alexandria. *On Flight and Finding*. Translated by F. H. Colson and G. H. Whitaker. Loeb Classical Library 275. Cambridge, MA: Harvard University Press, 1934.

———. *On the Creation*. Translated by F. H. Colson and G. H. Whitaker. Loeb Classical Library 226. Cambridge, MA: Harvard University Press, 1929.

———. *The Works of Philo: Complete and Unabridged*. Translated by Charles Duke Yonge. Peabody, MA: Hendrickson, 1995.

Plato. *Commentatio ad Legg*. Translated by Godofredus Stallbaum. IV. Lipsiae: Staritz, 1845.

———. *Epistles*. Translated by R. G. Bury. Loeb Classical Library 234. Cambridge, MA: Harvard University Press, 1929.

———. *Lysis. Symposium. Gorgias*. Translated by W. R. M. Lamb. Loeb Classical Library 166. Cambridge, MA: Harvard University Press, 1925.

———. *Republic*. Edited and translated by Chris Emlyn-Jones and William Preddy. Loeb Classical Library 237. Cambridge, MA: Harvard University Press, 2013.

———. *Timaeus*. Translated by Chris Emlyn-Jones. Loeb Classical Library 234. Cambridge, MA: Harvard University Press, 1929.

Pliny the Elder. *The Natural History of Pliny*. Translated by John Bostock and Henry T. Riley. London: H. G. Bohn, 1855.

Plutarch. *Lives*. Translated by Bernadotte Perrin. Loeb Classical Library 98. Cambridge, MA: Harvard University Press, 1919.

———. *Moralia, Volume VIII*. Translated by P. A. Clement and H. B. Hoffleit. Loeb Classical Library 424. Cambridge, MA: Harvard University Press, 1969.

———. *Moralia. Advice to Bride and Groom*. Translated by Frank Cole Babbitt. Loeb Classical Library 222. Cambridge, MA: Harvard University Press, 1928.

———. *Moralia. On Being a Busybody*. Translated by W. C. Helmbold. Loeb Classical Library 337. Cambridge, MA: Harvard University Press, 1939.

———. *Moralia. Reply to Colotes in Defence of the Other Philosophers*. Translated by Benedict Einarson and Phillip H. De Lacy. Loeb Classical Library 428. Cambridge, MA: Harvard University Press, 1967.

———. *On Brotherly Love*. Translated by W. C. Helmbold. Loeb Classical Library 337. Cambridge, MA: Harvard University Press, 1939.

Polybius. *The Histories*. Translated by W. R. Paton, F. W. Walbank, Christian Habicht, and S. Douglas Olson. Loeb Classical Library 128. Cambridge, MA: Harvard University Press, 2012.

Pseudo Focílides. *The Sentences of Pseudo-Phocylides*. Translated by Pieter Willem van der Horst. Leiden: Brill, 1978.

Quintilian. *The Institutio Oratoria*. Translated by Harold Edgeworth Butler. Loeb Classical Library 124. Cambridge, MA; London: Harvard University Press, 1995.

Seneca, Lucius Annaeus. *Epistles*. Translated by Richard M Gummere. Loeb Classical Library 75. Cambridge, MA: Harvard University Press, 1917.

Sextus Empiricus. *Against the Professors*. Translated by R. G. Bury. Loeb Classical Library 382. Cambridge, MA: Harvard University Press, 1949.

Strabo. *Geography*. Translated by Horace Leonard Jones and J. R. Sitlington Sterrett. Loeb Classical Library 49. Cambridge, MA: Harvard University Press, 2005.

Suetonius. *Lives of Illustrious Men. Grammarians and Rhetoricians. Grammarians*. Translated by J. C. Rolfe. Loeb Classical Library 38. Cambridge, MA: Harvard University Press, 1914.

Martínez, Florentino García, and Eibert J. C. Tigchelaar, eds. *The Dead Sea Scrolls Study Edition*. 2 vols. 2nd ed. Leiden: Brill, 1999.

Theophrastus. *Characters. Mimes. Sophron and Other Mime Fragments*. Translated by Jeffrey Rusten and I. C. Cunningham. Loeb Classical Library 225. Cambridge, MA: Harvard University Press, 2002.

Varro, M. Terentius. *On Agriculture*. Translated by M. Porcius Cato, William Davis Hooper, and Harrison Boyd Ash. Loeb Classical Library 283. Cambridge, MA: Harvard University Press, 1999.

Xenophon. *Oeconomicus*. Translated by Sarah B. Pomeroy. Oxford: Clarendon, 1994.

———. *The Whole Works of Xenophon*. Translated by Maurice Ashley Cooper, Edward Spelman, William Smith, Sarah Fielding, James Welwood, Richard Graves, Richard Bradley, Walter Moyle, and Thomas Stanley. Philadelphia: T. Wardel, 1845.

Secondary Sources

Aasgard, Reidar. *"My Beloved Brothers and Sisters!": Christian Siblingship in Paul*. London: T&T Clark, 2004.

———. "'Role Ethics' in Paul: The Significance of the Sibling Role for Paul's Ethical Thinking." *New Testament Studies* 48, no. 4 (2002): 513–30. doi:10.1017/S0028688502000310.

Abbott-Smith, G. *A Manual Greek Lexicon of the New Testament*. London: Forgotten Books, 2015.

Adamo, David Tuesday. *Explorations in African Biblical Studies*. Eugene, OR: Wipf & Stock, 2001.

Agrell, Göran. *Work, Toil and Sustenance: An Examination of the View of Work in the New Testament, Taking into Consideration Views Found in Old Testament, Intertestamental, and Early Rabbinic Writings.* Lund: H. Ohlsson, 1976.

Anigbo, Osmund A. C. *Commensality and Human Relationship among the Igbo: An Ethnographic Study of Ibagwa Aka, Igboeze L.G.A. Anambra State, Nigeria.* Nsukka: University of Nigeria Press, 1987.

Applebaum, Herbert A. *The Concept of Work: Ancient, Medieval, and Modern.* Albany: State University of New York Press, 1992.

Aringo, Margaret. "Work in the Old Testament and in African Tradition: Implications for Today." In *Interpreting the Old Testament in Africa*, edited by Mary N. Getui, Knut Holter, and Victor Zinkuratire, 171–74. New York: Lang, 2001.

Asano, Atsuhiro. *Community-Identity Construction in Galatians: Exegetical, Social-Anthropological and Socio-Historical Studies.* New York: T&T Clark, 2005.

Ascough, Richard S. "Communal Meals." In *The Oxford Handbook of Early Christian Ritual*, edited by Risto Uro, Juliette J. Day, Rikard Roitto, and Richard E. DeMaris, 204–19. Oxford: Oxford University Press, 2018.

———. "Forms of Commensality in Greco-Roman Associations." *Classical World* 102, no. 1 (2008): 33–45. doi:10.1353/clw.0.0038.

———. "Of Memories and Meals: Greco-Roman Associations and the Early Jesus-Group at Thessalonikē." In *From Roman to Early Christian Thessalonikē: Studies in Religion and Archaeology*, edited by Laura Salah Nasrallah, Charalambos Bakirtzēs, and Steven J. Friesen, 49–72. Cambridge, MA: Harvard University Press, 2010.

———. "Paul and Associations." In *Paul in the Greco-Roman World: A Handbook, Volume 1*, edited by J. Paul Sampley, 68–89. London: Bloomsbury, 2016.

———. "The Thessalonian Christian Community as a Professional Voluntary Association." *Journal of Biblical Literature* 119, no. 2 (2000): 311–28. doi:10.2307/3268489.

———. "Voluntary Associations and Community Formation: Paul's Macedonian Christian Communities in Context." PhD Thesis, University St. Michael's College, 1997.

Aune, David C. "Trouble in Thessalonica: An Exegetical Study of 1 Thess 4:9–12, 5:12–14 and 2 Thess 3:6–15 in Light of First Century Social Conditions." ThM Thesis, Regent College, 1989. doi:10.2986/tren.048-0035.

Austin, M. M., and Pierre Vidal-Naquet. *Economic and Social History of Ancient Greece: An Introduction.* Berkeley: University of California Press, 1980.

Bahemuka, Judith Mbula. *Our Religious Heritage.* Surrey: Thomas Nelson & Sons, 1983.

Bailey, John A. "Who Wrote II Thessalonians?" *New Testament Studies* 25, no. 2 (1979): 131–45. doi:10.1017/S0028688500004239.

Balla, Marta, and Gunneweg Jan. "Was the Qumran Settlement a Mere Pottery Production Center? What Instrumental Neutron Activation Revealed?" In *Holistic Qumran: Trans-Disciplinary Research of Qumran and the Dead Sea Scrolls*, edited by Jan Gunneweg, Annemie Adriaens, and Joris Dik, 39–61. Leiden: Brill, 2010.

Balthasar, Hans Urs von. *Thessalonicher- Und Pastoralbriefe Des Heiligen Paulus*. 2nd ed. Freiburg: Johannes, 1992.

Banks, Robert J. *Paul's Idea of Community: The Early House Churches in Their Cultural Setting*. Grand Rapids, MI: Baker Academic, 2012.

Barclay, John M. G. "Conflict in Thessalonica." *Catholic Biblical Quarterly* 55, no. 3 (1993): 512–30.

———. *Paul and the Gift*. Grand Rapids, MI: Eerdmans, 2015.

———. "Money and Meetings: Group Formation among Diaspora Jews and Early Christians." In *Vereine, Synagogen und Gemeinden im kaiserzeitlichen Kleinasien*, edited by Andreas Gutsfeld and Dietrich-Alex Koch, 113–27. Tübingen: Mohr Siebeck, 2006.

Barton, Stephen C. "Christian Community in the Light of I Corinthians." *Studies in Christian Ethics* 10, no. 1 (1997): 1–15. doi:10.1177/095394689701000101.

Bassin, François. *Les Epîtres de Paul aux Thessaloniciens*. Vaux-sur-Seine: Edifac, 1991.

Batluck, Mark. "Paul, Timothy and Pauline Individualism: A Response to Malina." In *Paul and His Social Relations*, edited by Stanley E. Porter and Christopher D. Land, 35–56. Boston: Brill, 2013. doi:10.1163/9789004244221_004.

Barrett, David B. *Schism and Renewal in Africa: An Analysis of Six Thousand Contemporary Religious Movements*. Nairobi: Oxford University Press, 1968.

Bauer, Walter, and Felix Wilbur Gingrich. *Shorter Lexicon of the Greek New Testament*. Chicago: University of Chicago Press, 1965.

Baumann, Gerlinde. "Ancient Egyptian Ma'at or Old Testament Deed-Consequence Nexus as Predecessors of Ubuntu?" *Verbum et Ecclesia* 36, no. 2 (2015): 1–4. doi:10.4102/ve.v36i2.1429.

Baumgarten, Albert. "Graeco-Roman Voluntary Associations and Ancient Jewish Sects." In *Jews in a Graeco-Roman World*, edited by Martin Goodman, 93–112. Oxford: Oxford University Press, 1998.

Baur, Ferdinand Christian. *Paul the Apostle of Jesus Christ: His Life and Works, His Epistles and Teachings*. Translated by Eduard Zeller, A. Menzies, and Frederick Crombie. Peabody, MA: Hendrickson, 2003.

Beale, G. K. *1-2 Thessalonians*. Downers Grove, IL: InterVarsity Press, 2003.

———. *We Become What We Worship: A Biblical Theology of Idolatry*. Downers Grove, IL: InterVarsity Press, 2008.

Beardslee, W. A. *Human Achievement and Divine Vocation in the Message of Paul*. London: SCM Press, 1961.

Best, Ernest. *The First and Second Epistles to the Thessalonians*. Peabody, MA: Hendrickson, 2003.

Bilder, Per. "The Common Meal in the Qumran Essene Communities." In *Meals in a Social Context: Aspects of the Communal Meal in the Hellenistic and Roman World*, edited by Inge Nielsen and Hanne Sigismund Nielsen, 145–66. Aarhus: Aarhus University Press, 2001.

Blight, Richard C. *An Exegetical Summary of 1 & 2 Thessalonians*. Dallas, TX: Summer Institute of Linguistics, 1989.

Bornkamm, Gunther. *Paul*. Minneapolis: Fortress Press, 1970.

Bradley, Keith. *Discovering the Roman Family Studies in Roman Social History*. New York: Oxford University Press, 1991.

———. *Slavery and Society at Rome*. Cambridge: Cambridge University Press, 1994. doi:10.1017/CBO9780511815386.

Rick, Brennan. *Lexham Analytical Lexicon to the Greek New Testament*. Bellingham, WA: Lexham Press, 2011.

Bridges, Linda McKinnish. *1 & 2 Thessalonians*. Macon, GA: Smyth & Helwys, 2008.

Briones, David E. *Paul's Financial Policy: A Socio-Theological Approach*. London: Bloomsbury, 2015.

Broodryk, Johann. *Ubuntu: Life Lessons from Africa*. Pretoria: Ubuntu School of Philosophy, 2002.

Brooke, George. "The Scrolls and the Study of the New Testament." In *The Dead Sea Scrolls at Fifty: Proceedings of the 1997 Society of Biblical Literature Qumran Section Meetings*, edited by Robert A. Kugler and Eileen M. Schuller, 61–78. Atlanta, GA: Scholars Press, 1999.

Bruce, F. F. *1 & 2 Thessalonians*. Word Biblical Commentary 45. Waco, TX: Word, 1982.

———. *Paul: Apostle of the Free Spirit*. Exeter: Paternoster, 1977.

———. *Paul and His Converts; 1 and 2 Thessalonians, 1 and 2 Corinthians*. London: Lutterworth, 1962.

———. "St Paul in Macedonia: 2. The Thessalonian Correspondence." *Bulletin of the John Rylands University Library* 62, no. 2 (1980): 337–54.

Bujo, Bénézet. *Foundations of an African Ethic: Beyond the Universal Claims of Western Morality*. New York: Crossroad, 2001.

Bohannan, Paul. "The Tiv of Nigeria." In *Peoples of Africa*, edited by James Lowell Gibbs, 513–46. Prospect Heights, IL: Waveland Press, 1988.

Burke, Trevor J. *Family Matters: A Socio-Historical Study of Kinship Metaphors in 1 Thessalonians*. London: T&T Clark, 2003.

———. "Paul's New Family in Thessalonica." *Novum Testamentum* 54, no. 3 (2012): 269–87. doi:10.1163/156853612X632471.

Byron, John. *1 and 2 Thessalonians*. Grand Rapids, MI: Zondervan, 2014.

Calvin, Jean. *1, 2 Thessalonians*. Edited by Alister McGrath and J. I. Parker. Wheaton, IL: Crossway, 1999.

Castelli, Elizabeth A. *Imitating Paul: A Discourse of Power*. Literary Currents in Biblical Interpretation. Louisville: Westminster John Knox Press, 1991.

Chambo, Filimao Manuel. "Metadidonai as Ethical Principle on Material Possessions According to the Gospel of Luke (3:10–14) and the Book of Acts." PhD Thesis, University of Johannesburg, 2008.

Chang, Kei Eun. *The Community, the Individual and the Common Good: To Idion and to Sympheron in the Greco-Roman World and Paul*. London: Bloomsbury, 2015.

Charlesworth, James H. "Community Organization." In *Encyclopedia of the Dead Sea Scrolls*, edited by Lawrence Schiffman and James C. Vanderkam, 133–39. Oxford University Press, 2000.

Chrysostom, John. *Homilies*. Vol. 11 of *A Select Library of the Nicene and Post-Nicene Fathers of the Christian Church, First Series*. Peabody, MA: Hendrickson, 1994.

———. *On the Priesthood, Ascetic Treatises, Select Homilies and Letters, Homilies on the Statues*. Vol. 9, *A Select Library of the Nicene and Post-Nicene Fathers of the Christian Church, First Series*. Plymouth: Christian Literature Co., 1889.

Chuwa, Leonard Tumaini. *African Indigenous Ethics in Global Bioethics: Interpreting Ubuntu*. Advancing Global Bioethics 1. New York: Springer, 2014. doi:10.1007/978-94-017-8625-6.

Cohen, Ronald. "Everyday Life in Africa." *International Journal* 17, no. 1 (1961): 34–39. doi:10.2307/40198551.

Cohick, Lynn. *Women in the World of the Earliest Christians: Illuminating Ancient Ways of Life*. Grand Rapids, MI: Baker Academic, 2014.

Collins, John J. *Beyond the Qumran Community: The Sectarian Movement of the Dead Sea Scrolls*. Grand Rapids, MI: Eerdmans, 2010.

———. "Introduction." In *Religion in the Dead Sea Scrolls*, edited by John J. Collins and Robert A. Kugler, 1–8. Grand Rapids, MI: Eerdmans, 2000.

Collins, Raymond F. *Studies on the First Letter to the Thessalonians*. Leuven: University Press-Uitgeverij Peeters, 1984.

Coutsoumpos, Panayotis. *Paul and the Lord's Supper: A Socio-Historical Investigation*. New York: Lang, 2005.

Crossan, John Dominic, and Jonathan L. Reed. *In Search of Paul: How Jesus' Apostle Opposed Rome's Empire with God's Kingdom: A New Vision of Paul's Words & World*. London: SPCK, 2005.

Danker, Frederick W., Walter Baur, William F. Arndt, and F. Wilbur. *Greek-English Lexicon of the New Testament and Other Early Christian Literature*. 3rd ed. Chicago: University of Chicago Press, 2000.

Dautzenberg, G. "Der Verzicht auf das Apostolische Unterhaltsrecht: Eine Exegetische Untersuchung Zu 1 Kor 9." *Bihlica* 50, no. 2 (1969): 212–32.
De Vos, Craig Steven. *Church and Community Conflicts: The Relationships of the Thessalonian, Corinthian, and Philippian Churches with Their Wider Civic Communities*. Atlanta, GA: Scholars Press, 1999.
De Witt, Norman W. *Saint Paul and Epicurus*. Minneapolis: University of Minnesota Press, 1954.
Deissmann, Adolf. *Light from the Ancient East: The New Testament; Illustrated by Recently Discovered Texts of the Graeco-Roman World*. London: Forgotten Books, 2012.
Demarest, Gary W. *The Communicator's Commentary 1, 2 Thessalonians, 1, 2 Timothy, Titus*. Communicator's Commentary Series 9. Waco, TX: Word Books, 1984.
Denney, James. *The Epistle to the Thessalonians*. London: Hodder & Stoughton, 1880.
Derrida, Jacques. "The Time of the King." In *The Logic of the Gift: Toward an Ethic of Generosity*, edited by Alan D. Schrift, 121–47. New York: Routledge, 1997.
DeSilva, David A. "Honor and Shame in the Gospel of Matthew [Review] / Jerome H. Neyrey." *Andrews University Seminary Studies* 38, no. 1 (2000): 166–68.
Dibelius, Martin. *An Die Thessalonicher I-II: An Die Philipper*. Erklärt von D. Dr. Martin Dibelius. Tübingen: Mohr, 1925.
———. *An die Thessalonicher I-II: An die Philipper*. Tübingen: Mohr, 1937.
Dimant, Divorah. "The Scrolls and the Study of Early Judaism." In *The Dead Sea Scrolls at Fifty: Proceedings of the 1997 Society of Biblical Literature Qumran Section Meetings*, edited by Robert A. Kugler and Eileen M. Schuller, 43–60. Atlanta, GA: Scholars Press, 1999.
Donfried, Karl P. *Paul, Thessalonica, and Early Christianity*. London: Continuum, 2002.
Donlan, Walter. "Reciprocities in Homer." *The Classical World* 75, no. 3 (1982): 137–75. doi:10.2307/4349350.
Douglas, Mary. "Deciphering a Meal." *Daedalus* 101, no. 1 (1972): 61–81.
———. *Purity and Danger: An Analysis of Concepts of Pollution and Taboo*. London: Routledge, 2002.
Downs, David J. "Is God Paul's Patron: The Economy of Patronage in Paul's Theology." In *Engaging Economics: New Testament Scenarios and Early Christian Reception*, edited by Bruce W. Longenecker and Kelly D. Liebengood, 129–56. Grand Rapids, MI: Eerdmans, 2009.
———. *The Offering of the Gentiles: Paul's Collection for Jerusalem in Its Chronological, Cultural, and Cultic Contexts*. Wissenschaftliche Untersuchungen Zum Neuen Testament 248. Tübingen: Mohr Siebeck, 2008.
Durant, Will. *Story of Philosophy*. New York: Simon & Schuster, 2012.

Edwin, Shirin. "Subverting Social Customs: The Representation of Food in Three West African Francophone Novels." *Research in African Literatures* 39, no. 3 (2008): 39–50. doi:10.2979/RAL.2008.39.3.39.

Elias, Jacob W. *1 and 2 Thessalonians*. Scottdale: Herald Press, 1995.

Deutsch, Eliot. "Community as Ritual Participation." In *On Community*, edited by Leroy S. Rouner, 15–26. Notre Dame: University of Notre Dame Press, 1991.

Ellicott, C. J. *St. Paul's Epistles to the Thessalonians: With a Critical and Grammatical Commentary, and Revised Translation*. London: Longman, 1880.

Ellingworth, Paul, and Eugene Albert Nida. *A Handbook on Paul's Letters to the Thessalonians*. UBS Handbook Series. New York: United Bible Societies, 1976.

Elliott, John Hall. *What Is Social-Scientific Criticism?* New Testament Series. Minneapolis: Fortress Press, 1993.

Ellis, E. Earle. "Paul and His Co-Workers: For the Very Rev. Professor James S. Stewart on His Seventy-Fifth Birthday." *New Testament Studies* 17, no. 4 (1971): 437–52. doi:10.1017/S0028688500024139.

Esler, Philip Francis. *The First Christians in Their Social Worlds: Social-Scientific Approaches to New Testament Interpretation*. London: Routledge, 1994.

Evans, Robert Maxwell. "Eschatology and Ethics: A Study of Thessalonica and Paul's Letters to the Thessalonians." Dissertation, Princeton, NJ, McMahon Printing Co., 1968.

Everts, Janet Meyer. "Testing a Literary-Critical Hermeneutic: An Exegesis of the Autobiographical Passages in Paul's Epistles." PhD Thesis, Duke University, 1988.

Fee, Gordon D. *The First and Second Letters to the Thessalonians*. Grand Rapids, MI: Eerdmans, 2009.

Ferdinando, Keith. *The Triumph of Christ in African Perspective: A Study of Demonology and Redemption in the African Context*. Carlisle: Paternoster Press, 1999.

Ferkiss, Victor C. *Africa's Search for Identity*. Cleveland: World Publishing, 1966.

Finger, Reta Halteman. *Of Widows and Meals: Communal Meals in the Book of Acts*. Grand Rapids, MI: Eerdmans, 2007.

Finley, M. I. *Economy and Society in Ancient Greece*. Edited by Brent D. Shaw and Richard P. Saller. New York: Viking Press, 1982.

Fiorenza, Elizabeth Schussler. *In Memory of Her: A Feminist Theological Reconstruction of Christian Origins*. New York: Crossroad, 1994.

Fischler, Claude. "Commensality, Society and Culture." *Social Science Information* 50, no. 3–4 (2011): 528–48. doi:10.1177/0539018411413963.

Fortes, Meyer, and Jack Goody. *Religion, Morality and the Person*. Cambridge: Cambridge University Press, 2011.

Foster, Paul. "Who Wrote 2 Thessalonians? A Fresh Look at an Old Problem." *Journal for the Study of the New Testament* 35, no. 2 (2012): 150–75. doi:10.1177/0142064X12462654.
Fowl, Stephen E. "Christology and Ethics in Phippians 2:5–11." In *Where Christology Began: Essays on Philippians 2*, edited by Ralph P. Martin and Brian J. Dodd, 140–53. Louisville, KY: Westminster John Knox Press, 1998.
Frame, James E. *A Critical and Exegetical Commentary on the Epistles of Saint Paul to the Thessalonians*. Edinburgh: Clark, 1912.
Freed, Edwin D. *The Morality of Paul's Converts*. London: Equinox Publishing, 2005.
Friesen, Steven J. "Poverty in Pauline Studies: Beyond So-Called New Consensus." *Journal for the Study of the New Testament* 26, no. 3 (2004): 323–361.
———. "Second Thessalonians, the Ideology of Epistles, and the Construction of Authority: Our Debt to the Forger." In *From Roman to Early Christian Thessalonikē: Studies in Religion and Archaeology*, edited by Laura Nasrallah Salah, Charalambos Bakirtzis, and Steven J. Friesen, 189–212. Cambridge, MA: Harvard University Press, 2010.
Furnish, Victor Paul. *1 Thessalonians, 2 Thessalonians*. Abingdon New Testament Commentaries. Nashville: Abingdon, 2007.
———. *Theology and Ethics in Paul*. Louisville, KY: Westminster John Knox Press, 2009.
Gager, John G. *Kingdom and Community: The Social World of Early Christianity*. Englewood Cliffs, NJ: Prentice-Hall, 1975.
———. *Reinventing Paul*. Oxford: Oxford University Press, 2000.
Garnsey, Peter. *Food and Society in Classical Antiquity*. Cambridge, UK: Cambridge University Press, 1999. doi:10.1017/CBO9780511612534.
Gaston, Lloyd. "Pharisaic Problems." In *Approaches to Ancient Judaism 4*, edited by Jacob Neusner. Missoula: Scholars Press, 1993.
Gatumu, Kabiro wa. *The Pauline Concept of Supernatural Powers: A Reading from the African Worldview*. Eugene, OR: Wipf & Stock, 2009.
Gaventa, Beverly Roberts. *First and Second Thessalonians*. Louisville, KY: Westminster John Knox, 1998.
Gelfand, Michael. *The Genuine Shona: Survival Values of an African Culture*. Rhodesia: Mambo Press, 1973.
Geoghegan, Arthur T. *The Attitude Towards Labor in Early Christianity and Ancient Culture*. Washington, DC: Catholic University of America Press, 1945.
Getty, M. A. "The Imitation of Paul in the Letters to the Thessalonians." In *The Thessalonian Correspondence*, edited by Raymond F. Collins, 277–87. Leuven: University Press, 1990.
Glad, Clarence E. *Paul and Philodemus: Adaptability in Epicurean and Early Christian Psychagogy*. Leiden: Brill, 1995. doi:10.1163/9789004267275.

Goff, Matthew. "Review of *All the Glory of Adam: Liturgical Anthropology in the Dead Sea Scrolls; To Increase Learning for the Understanding Ones: Reading and Reconstructing the Fragmentary Early Jewish Sapiential Text 4QInstruction; Wealth in the Dead Sea Scrolls and the Qumran Community*." *Journal of Biblical Literature* 122, no. 1 (2003): 165–75. doi:10.2307/3268099.

Goodman, Martin, and Jane Sherwood. *The Roman World, 44 BC–AD 180*. London, New York: Routledge, 1997.

Goody, Esther N. *Parenthood and Social Reproduction: Fostering and Occupational Roles in West Africa*. Cambridge, New York: Cambridge University Press, 2007.

Goody, Jack. *Cooking, Cuisine, and Class: A Study in Comparative Sociology*. Cambridge University Press, 1982. doi:10.1017/CBO9780511607745.

Gorman, Michael J. *Becoming the Gospel: Paul, Participation, and Mission*. The Gospel and Our Culture Series. Grand Rapids, MI: Eerdmans, 2015.

———. *Cruciformity: Paul Narrative Spirituality of the Cross*. Grand Rapids, MI: Eerdmans, 2001.

Gow, A. S. F., and D. L. Page. *The Greek Anthology*. Cambridge: Cambridge University Press, 1965.

A Greek-English Lexicon. Henry George Liddell and Robert Scott. Oxford: Clarendon, 2006.

Green, Gene L. *The Letters to the Thessalonians*. Grand Rapids, MI: Eerdmans, 2002.

Gregson, Fiona J. R. *Everything in Common? The Theology and Practice of the Sharing of Possessions in Community in the New Testament*. Eugene, OR: Pickwick, 2017.

Gunn, David M. "Narrative Criticism." In *To Each Its Own Meaning: An Introduction to Biblical Criticisms and Their Applications*, edited by Stephen R. Haynes and Steven L. McKenzie, 201–29. Louisville, KY: Westminster John Knox, 1999.

Gunneweg, Jan. "Introduction to 'Soap at Qumran.'" In *Holistic Qumran: Trans-Disciplinary Research of Qumran and the Dead Sea Scrolls*, edited by Jan Gunneweg, A. Adriaens, and Joris Dik, 163–70. Leiden: Brill, 2010. doi:10.1163/ej.9789004181526.i-210.94.

Gupta, Nijay K. *1-2 Thessalonians A New Covenant Commentary*. Cambridge. London: Lutterworth Press, 2017.

Gyekye, Kwame. *An Essay on African Philosophical Thought: The Akan Conceptual Scheme*. Philadelphia: Temple University Press, 1995.

Hafemann, Scott J. *Paul's Message and Ministry in Covenant Perspective: Selected Essays*. Eugene, OR: Cascade, 2015.

Hanna, Robert. *A Grammatical Aid to the Greek New Testament*. Grand Rapids, MI: Baker Book House, 1983.

Harland, Philip A. *Associations, Synagogues, and Congregations: Claiming a Place in Ancient Mediterranean Society*. Minneapolis, MN: Fortress Press, 2003.
von Harnack, Adolf. "Das Problem des zweiten Thessalonicherbriefs." In *Sitzungsberichte der Königlich-Preussischen Akademie der Wissenschaften*, 560–78. Berlin, 1910.
Harrington, Daniel S. J. *Wisdom Texts from Qumran*. London: Routledge, 2003.
Hartley, Helen-Ann M. "'We Worked Night and Day That We Might Not Burden Any of You' (1 Thessalonians 2:9) Aspects of the Portrayal of Work in the Letters of Paul, Late Second Temple Judaism, the Greco-Roman World and Early Christianity." PhD, Thesis Oxford University, 2004.
Hays, Richard B. *Echoes of Scripture in the Letters of Paul*. New Haven, CT: Yale University Press, 2008.
Helyer, Larry R. *Exploring Jewish Literature of the Second Temple Period: A Guide for New Testament Students*. Downers Grove, IL: InterVarsity Press, 2002.
Hengel, Martin. "Qumran and Hellenism." In *Religion in the Dead Sea Scrolls*, edited by John J. Collins and Robert A. Kugler, 46–56. Grand Rapids, MI: Eerdmans, 2000.
Hiebert, D. Edmond. *The Thessalonian Epistles: A Call to Readiness*. Chicago, IL: Moody Press, 1982.
Hill, Judith Lynn. "Establishing the Church in Thessalonica." Unpublished Thesis, Duke University, 1990.
Hirschfeld, Yizhar. *Qumran in Context: Reassessing the Archaeological Evidence*. Peabody, MA: Hendrickson, 2005.
Hock, Ronald F. *The Social Context of Paul's Ministry: Tentmaking and Apostleship*. Philadelphia: Fortress Press, 1980.
———. *The Working Apostle: An Examination of Paul's Means of Livelihood*. New Haven: Fortress, 1979.
———. "The Workshop as a Social Setting for Paul's Missionary Preaching." *Catholic Biblical Quarterly* 41, no. 3 (1979): 438–50.
Holladay, William Lee. *A Concise Hebrew and Aramaic Lexicon of the Old Testament: Based upon the Lexical Work of Ludwig Koehler and Walter Baumgartner*. Leiden: Brill, 2000.
Holmes, Michael W. *1 and 2 Thessalonians: From Biblical Text . . . to Contemporary Life*. Grand Rapids, MI: Zondervan, 1998.
Hooker, Morna Dorothy. *Paul: A Beginner's Guide*. Oxford: Oneworld Publications, 2012.
Horrell, David G. *Solidarity and Difference: A Contemporary Reading of Paul's Ethics*. London: T&T Clark, 2005.
Horrell, David G, Cherryl Hunt, and Christopher Southgate. *Greening Paul: Rereading the Apostle in a Time of Ecological Crisis*. Waco, TX: Baylor University Press, 2010.

Hubbard, Moyer V. *Christianity in the Greco-Roman World: A Narrative Introduction*. Peabody, MA: Hendrickson, 2010.

Hudson, Nicholas F. "Changing Places: The Archaeology of the Roman 'Convivium.'" *American Journal of Archaeology* 114, no. 4 (2010): 663–95. doi:10.3764/aja.114.4.663.

Hurtado, Larry W. "The Jerusalem Collection and the Book of Galatians." *Journal for the Study of the New Testament* 2, no. 5 (1979): 46–62. doi:10.1177/0142064X7900200503.

Huttunen, Niko. *Paul and Epictetus on Law: A Companion*. London: T&T Clark, 2009.

Ilogu, Edmund. *Christianity and Ibo Culture*. Leiden: Brill, 1974.

Jashemski, Wilhelmina Mary Feemster. *The Gardens of Pompeii. Vol. 1*. New Rochelle, NY: Caratzas Brothers, 1979.

Jefferies, Daryl F. *Wisdom at Qumran: A Form-Critical Analysis of the Admonitions in 4QInstruction*. Gorgias Dissertations Near Eastern Studies 3. Piscataway, NJ: Gorgias Press, 2002.

Jeffers, James S. *The Greco-Roman World of the New Testament Era: Exploring the Background of Early Christianity*. Downers Grove, IL: InterVarsity Press, 1999.

Jenks, R. Gregory. *Paul and His Mortality: Imitating Christ in the Face of Death*. Bulletin for Biblical Research Supplements 12. Winona Lake, IN: Eisenbrauns, 2015.

Jewett, Robert. "Gospel and Commensality: Social and Theological Implications of Galatians 2.14." *Journal for the Study of the New Testament, Supplement Series* 108 (1994): 240.

———. *Paul the Apostle to America: Cultural Trends and Pauline Scholarship*. Louisville, KY: Westminster John Knox, 1994.

———. "Tenement Churches and Communal Meals in the Early Church: The Implications of a Form-Critical Analysis of 2 Thessalonians 3:10." *Biblical Research* 38 (1993): 23–43.

———. *The Thessalonian Correspondence: Pauline Rhetoric and Millenarian Piety*. Philadelphia: Fortress, 1986.

Johnson, Andy. "The Sanctification of the Imagination in 1 Thessalonians." In *Holiness and Ecclesiology in the New Testament*, edited by Kent E. Brower and Andy Johnson, 275–92. Grand Rapids, MI: Eerdmans, 2007.

———. *1 and 2 Thessalonians*. The Two Horizons New Testament Commentary. Grand Rapids, MI: Eerdmans, 2016.

Jones, Catherine M. "Theatre of Shame: The Impact of Paul's Manual Labour on His Apostleship in Corinth." PhD Thesis, University of Toronto, 2013.

Jones, Nicholas F. *The Associations of Classical Athens: The Response to Democracy*. New York: Oxford University Press, 1999.

Jonker, Louis. "Towards a 'Communal' Approach for Reading the Bible in Africa." In *Interpreting the Old Testament in Africa: Papers from the International Symposium on Africa and the Old Testament in Nairobi, October 1999*, edited by Mary N. Getui, Knut Holter, and Victor Zinkuratire, 77–88. New York: Lang, 2001.

Kamalu, Chukwunyere. *Foundations of African Thought: A Worldview Grounded in the African Heritage of Religion, Philosophy, Science, and Art*. London: Karnak House, 1990.

ΚΑΡΑΒΙΔΟΠΟΥΛΟΥ ΙΩΑΝΝΗ. "Φιλαδελφία» (Α' Θεσ. 4,9). Η Παύλεια Παραίνεση Για Κοινωνική Συμπεριφορά Των Χριστιανων." Pages 191–208 in *ΟΙ ΔΥΟ ΠΡΟΣ ΘΕΣΣΑΛΟΝΙΚΕΙΣ ΕΠΙΣΤΟΛΕΣ ΤΟΥ ΑΠΟΣΤΟΛΟΥ ΠΑΥΛΟΥ ΠΡΟΒΛΗΜΑΤΑ ΦΙΛΟΛΟΓΙΚΑ ΙΣΤΟΡΙΚΑ ΕΡΜΗΝΕΥΤΙΚΑ ΘΕΟΛΟΓΙΚΑ*. ΘΕΣΣΑΛΟΝΙΚΗ: ΕΚΔΟΣΕΙΣ Π.ΠΟΥΡΝΑΡΑ, 2000.

Kenyatta, Jomo. *Facing Mount Kenya*. School Edition. Nairobi: Heinemann Kenya, 2011.

Khoza, Reuel J. *Attuned Leadership: African Humanism as Compass*. Johannesburg: Penguin Books, 2011.

———. *Let Africa Lead: African Transformational Leadership for 21st Century Business*. Johannesburg: Vezubuntu, 2006.

Kifleyesus, Abbebe. "Muslims and Meals: The Social and Symbolic Function of Foods in Changing Socio-Economic Environments." *Africa: Journal of the International African Institute* 72, no. 2 (2002): 245–76. doi:10.3366/afr.2002.72.2.245.

Kirwen, Michael C. *The Missionary and the Diviner: Contending Theologies of Christian and African Religions*. Maryknoll, NY: Orbis Books, 1987.

Kithinji, Ciriaka. "In Search of an African Identity." In *Social and Religious Concerns of East Africa: A Wajibu Anthology*, edited by G. J. Wanjohi and G. Wakuraya Wanjohi, 273–78. Nairobi: Paulines Publications, 2005.

Kittel, Gerhard, and Gerhard Friedrich, eds. *Theological Dictionary of the New Testament*. Translated by Geoffrey W. Bromiley. 10 vols. Grand Rapids, MI: Eerdmans, 1964–1976.

Kloppenborg, John S. "Civic Identity and Christ Groups." In *Jewish and Christian Communal Identities in the Roman World*, edited by Yair Furstenberg, 87–115. Ancient Judaism and Early Christianity 94. Leiden: Brill, 2016. doi:10.1163/9789004321694_005.

———. "Collegia and Thiasoi: Issues in Function, Taxonomy and Membership." In *Voluntary Associations in the Graeco-Roman World*, edited by John S. Kloppenborg and S. G. Wilson, 43–62. London: Routledge, 1996.

———. "Membership Practices in Pauline Christ Groups." *Early Christianity* 4, no. 2 (2013): 183–215. doi:10.1628/186870313X13667164610110.

Kloppenborg, John S., Richard S. Ascough, and Philip A. Harland. *Greco-Roman Associations: Texts, Translations, and Commentary*. Berlin: de Gruyter, 2011.

Kloppenborg, John S., and S. G. Wilson. *Voluntary Associations in the Graeco-Roman World*. London: Routledge, 1996.

Knibb, Michael A. "Community Organization in the Damascus Document." In *Encyclopedia of the Dead Sea Scrolls*, edited by Lawrence Schiffman and James C. Vanderkam, 136–38. Oxford University Press, 2000.

———. *The Qumran Community*. Cambridge: Cambridge University Press, 1987. doi:10.1017/CBO9780511621352.

Kreinecker, Christina M. *2. Thessaloniker*. Papyrologische Kommentare zum Neuen Testament Bd. 3. Göttingen: Vandenhoeck & Ruprecht, 2010.

Krentz, Edgar. "2 Thessalonians." In *The Blackwell Companion to the New Testament*, edited by David C. Aune, 515–25. Malden, MA: Blackwell, 2010. doi:10.1002/9781444318937.ch29.

Kümmel, Werner Georg. *Introduction to the New Testament*. London: SCM Press, 1987.

Kunene, Musa Victor. *Communal Holiness in the Gospel of John: The Vine Metaphor as a Test Case with Lessons from African Hospitality and Trinitarian Theology*. Carlisle: Langham Monographs, 2012.

Lake, Kirsopp. *The Text of the New Testament*. London: Rivingtons, 1911.

Lakoff, George. *Metaphors We Live By*. Taipei: Crane, 1985.

Lampe, Peter. "The Corinthians Eucharistic Dinner Party: Exegesis of the Cultural Context *(1 Cor. 11:17–34)*." *Affirmation* 4, no. 2 (1991): 1–15.

———. "The Language of Equality in Early Christian House Churches." In *Early Christian Families in Context: An Interdisciplinary Dialogue*, edited by David L. Balch and Carolyn Osiek, 73–83. Grand Rapids, MI: Eerdmans, 2003.

Lanuwabang, Jamir. *Exclusion and Judgment in Fellowship Meals: The Socio-Historical Background of 1 Corinthians 11:17–34*. Eugene, OR: Pickwick, 2016.

Last, Richard. *The Pauline Church and the Corinthian Ekklēsia: Greco-Roman Associations in Comparative Context*. New York: Cambridge University Press, 2016.

Leaney, Alfred Robert Clare. *The Rule of Qumran and Its Meaning: Introduction, Translation, and Commentary*. London: SCM Press, 1966.

Lenski, R. C. H. *The Interpretation of St. Paul's Epistles to the Colossians, to the Thessalonians, to Timothy, to Titus and to Philemon*. Minneapolis: Augsburg Fortress, 1937.

Liddell, Henry George, Robert Scott, Henry Stuart Jones, and Roderick MacKenzie. *A Greek-English Lexicon: With a Revised Supplement 1996*. Oxford: Clarendon Press, 1996.

Lightfoot, J. B. *The Apostolic Fathers: A Revised Text with Introductions, Notes, Dissertations, and Translations*. Hildesheim: Olms, 1973.

———. *Notes on the Epistles of St. Paul: (I and II Thessalonians, I Corinthians 1–7, Romans 1–7, Ephesians 1:1–14)*. Grand Rapids, MI: Zondervan, 1957.
Liu, Jinyu. "Pompeii and *Collegia*: A New Appraisal of the Evidence." *Ancient History Bulletin* 22 (2008): 53–69.
Lloyd, P. C. "The Yoruba of Nigeria." In *Peoples of Africa*, edited by James Lowell Gibbs, 547–82. Prospect Heights, IL: Waveland Press, 1988.
Loba-Mkole, Jean-Claude. "Rise of Intercultural Biblical Exegesis in Africa" *HTS Theological Studies* 64, no. 3 (2008): 1347–64. doi:10.4102/hts.v64i3.77.
Long, A. A. *Hellenistic Philosophy: Stoics, Epicureans, Sceptics*. 2nd ed. Berkeley, CA: University of California Press, 1986.
Longenecker, Bruce W. *Remember the Poor: Paul, Poverty, and the Greco-Roman World*. Grand Rapids, MI: Eerdmans, 2010.
Lüdemann, Gerd. *Paul, Apostle to the Gentiles: Studies in Chronology*. Philadelphia: Fortress, 1984.
Lünemann, Gottlieb. "Critical and Exegetical Handbook to the Epistles of St Paul to the Thessalonians." In *Critical and Exegetical Hand-Book to the Epistle to the Ephesians and the Epistle to Philemon*, edited by Heinrich August Wilhelm Meyer, Maurice J. Evans, William Purdle Dickson, and Henry Eyster Jacobs, 248. Edinburgh: T&T Clark, 1978.
Lyons, George. *Galatians: A Commentary in the Wesleyan Tradition*. Kansas City: Beacon Hill, 2012.
———. *Pauline Autobiography: Toward a New Understanding*. Atlanta, GA: Scholars Press, 1985.
MacDonald, Margaret. "Reading the New Testament Household Codes in Light of New Research on Children and Childhood in the Roman World." *Studies in Religion/Sciences Religieuses* 41, no. 3 (2012): 376–87.
———. *At Work in the Field of Birth: Midwifery Narratives of Nature, Tradition, and Home*. Nashville: Vanderbilt University Press, 2007.
Madeira, Karen. "Cultural Meaning and Use of Food: A Selective Bibliography (1973–1987)." In *Cooking by the Book: Food in Literature and Culture*, edited by Schofield, Mary Anne, 207–15. Bowling Green, OH: Bowling Green State University Popular Press, 1989.
Mafeje, Archie. "The Ideology of 'Tribalism.'" *The Journal of Modern African Studies* 9, no. 2 (1971): 253–61.
Magesa, Laurenti. *African Religion: The Moral Traditions of Abundant Life*. Maryknoll, NY: Orbis Books, 1997.
Magness, Jodi. *The Archaeology of Qumran and the Dead Sea Scrolls*. Grand Rapids, MI: Eerdmans, 2003.
Malherbe, Abraham J. *Moral Exhortation: A Greco-Roman Sourcebook*. Philadelphia: Westminster, 1989.

———. *The Letters to the Thessalonians: A New Translation with Introduction and Commentary.* New York: Doubleday, 2000.

———. *Paul and the Thessalonians.* Philadelphia: Fortress, 1987.

———. *Paul and the Thessalonians: The Philosophic Tradition of Pastoral Care.* Philadelphia: Fortress, 1987.

Malina, Bruce J. *The New Testament World: Insights from Cultural Anthropology.* Louisville, KY: Westminster John Knox, 2002.

Manus, Ukachukwu Chris. *Intercultural Hermeneutics in Africa: Methods and Approaches.* Biblical Studies in African Scholarship Series. Nairobi, Kenya: Acton Publishers, 2003.

Marshall, I. Howard. *1 and 2 Thessalonians: A Commentary.* Vancouver: Regent College, 2002.

Martin, D. Michael. *1, 2 Thessalonians.* The New American Commentary 33. Nashville, TN: Broadman & Holman, 1995.

Martínez, Florentino García, and Eibert J. C. Tigchelaar. *The Dead Sea Scrolls.* Grand Rapids, MI: Eerdmans, 1999.

Martínez, Florentino García, Julio Trebolle Barrera, and Wilfred G. E. Watson. *The People of the Dead Sea Scrolls.* Leiden: Brill, 1995.

Mathews, Mark D. *Riches, Poverty, and the Faithful: Perspectives on Wealth in the Second Temple Period and the Apocalypse of John.* Monograph Series (Society for New Testament Studies) 154. Cambridge: Cambridge University Press, 2013.

Marxsen, Willi. *Der erste Brief an die Thessalonicher.* Zûrich: Theologischer Verlag, 1979.

Matsinhe, David Mario. "Masculinities in an African Context: The Case of Mozambique." Unpublished master's thesis, University of Calgary, 2004.

Mbithi, Philip M., and Rasmus Rasmusson. *Self-Reliance in Kenya: The Case of Harambee.* Uppsala: Scandinavian Institute of African Studies, 1977.

Mbiti, John S. *African Religions and Philosophy.* Nairobi: East African Educational Publications, 2015.

McCready, Wayne O. "*Ekklēsia* and Voluntary Associations." In *Voluntary Associations in the Graeco-Roman World*, edited by John S. Kloppenborg and Stephen G. Wilson, 101–19. London: Routledge, 2002.

McRay, John. *Paul: His Life and Teaching.* Grand Rapids, MI: Baker Academic, 2007.

Meeks, Wayne A. *The First Urban Christians: The Social World of the Apostle Paul.* New Haven, CT: Yale University Press, 1983.

———. *The Origins of Christian Morality: The First Two Centuries.* New Haven, CT: Yale University Press, 1993.

Meggitt, Justin J. *Paul, Poverty and Survival.* Edinburgh: Bloomsbury T&T Clark, 2000.

Menken, M. J. J. *2 Thessalonians*. New Testament Readings. London: Routledge, 1994.

———. "Paradise Regained or Still Lost? Eschatology and Disorderly Behaviour in 2 Thessalonians." *New Testament Studies* 38, no. 2 (1992): 271–89.

Merrill, Eugene H. *Deuteronomy*. The New American Commentary 4. Nashville, TN: Broadman & Holman, 1994.

Metuh, Emefie Ikenga. *God and Man in African Religion: A Case Study of the Igbo of Nigeria*. London: G. Chapman, 1981.

Milligan, George. *St. Paul's Epistles to the Thessalonians: The Greek Text*. London: Macmillan & Co., 1908.

Mintz, Sidney W., and Christine M. Du Bois. "The Anthropology of Food and Eating." *Annual Review of Anthropology* 31 (2002): 99–119.

Mitchell, Margaret M. "1 and 2 Thessalonians." In *The Cambridge Companion to St. Paul*, edited by James D. G. Dunn, 51–66. Cambridge Companions to Religion. Cambridge: Cambridge University Press, 2003.

Miquez, Nestor O. *The Practice of Hope: Ideology and Intention in 1 Thessalonians*. Minneapolis: Fortress, 2012.

Mitchell, Margaret M. "Concerning peri de in 1 Corinthians." *Novum Testamentum* 31, no. 3 (1989): 229–256.

Moffatt, James. "2 Thessalonians III 14, 15." *Expository Times* 21 (1909): 328.

———. "First and Second Epistle to the Thessalonians." In *The Expositor's Greek Testament*, vol. 4, edited by W. Robertson Nicoll, 26–29. Franeker: Wever, 1936.

Montanari, Franco. *The Brill Dictionary of Ancient Greek*. Boston, MA: Brill, 2015.

Moore, A. L. *1 and 2 Thessalonians*. London: Nelson, 1969.

Morris, Leon. *The Epistles of Paul to the Thessalonians: An Introduction and Commentary*. 2nd ed. Tyndale New Testament Commentaries. Leicester: Inter-Varsity Press, 1984.

Moses, Robert E. "Physical and/or Spiritual Exclusion? Ecclesial Discipline in 1 Corinthians 5." *New Testament Studies* 59, no. 2 (2013): 172–91.

Moxnes, Halvor. "The Social Context of Luke's Community." *Interpretation* 48, no. 4 (1994): 379–89.

Moyo, Ambrose. "Material Things in African Society: Implications for Christian Ethics." In *Moral and Ethical Issues in African Christianity: Exploratory Essays in Moral Theology*, edited by J. N. K. Mugambi, 49–57. 2nd ed. African Christianity Series 3. Nairobi: Acton Publishers, 1999.

Mtukwa, Gift. *God in His Place: Paul's Teaching of Non-Violence in Romans 12:17–21*. Saarbrücken: Lap Lambert Academic Publishing, 2016.

———. "A Reconsideration of Self-Support in Light of Paul's 'Collection for the Saints' (1 Cor. 16:1)." *Africa Journal of Evangelical Theology* 33 (2014): 91–106.

———. "Paul's Cruciform Mission in Thessalonica: The Shape of Incarnational Ministry." *Didache* 17, no. 2 (2018): 1–14.
Mulinge, Munyae M., and Gwen N. Lesetedi. "Corruption in Sub-Saharan Africa: Towards a More Holistic Approach." *African Journal of Political Science / Revue Africaine de Science Politique* 7, no. 1 (2002): 51–77.
Murphree, Marshall W. *Christianity and the Shona*. Oxford: Berg, 2004.
Murphy, Catherine M. "The Disposition of Wealth in the 'Damascus Document' Tradition." *Revue de Qumrân* 19, no. 1 (73) (1999): 83–129.
———. *Wealth in the Dead Sea Scrolls and in the Qumran Community*. Leiden: Brill, 2002.
Murphy-O'Connor, J. *Paul: His Story*. Oxford: Oxford University Press, 2004.
———. *St. Paul's Corinth: Text and Archaeology*. Collegeville, MN: Liturgical Press, 2002.
Murray J. Smith. "The Thessalonian Correspondence." In *All Things to All Cultures: Paul among Jews, Greeks, and Romans*, edited by Mark Harding and Alanna Nobbs, 269–301. Grand Rapids, MI: Eerdmans, 2013.
Muzorewa, Gwinyai H. *The Origins and Development of African Theology*. Eugene, OR: Wipf & Stock, 2000.
Mwikamba, Constantine M. "In Search of an African Identity." In *Social and Religious Concerns of East Africa: A Wajibu Anthology*, edited by G. J. Wanjohi and G. Wakuraya Wanjohi, 1–24. Nairobi: Paulines Publications, 2005.
Ndeti, Kivuto. "Elements of Akamba Life." PhD Thesis, Graduate School of Syracuse University, 1974.
Neil, William. *The Epistle of Paul to the Thessalonians*. London: Hodder & Stoughton, 1978.
Newman, James. "The History and Culture of Food in Sub Saharan African and Oceania." In *The Cambridge World History of Food. Vol. 2*, edited by Kenneth F. Kiple and Kriemhild Coneè Ornelas, 1330–70. Cambridge: Cambridge University Press, 2000.
Neyrey, Jerome H. "Meals, Food, and Table Fellowship." In *The Social Sciences and New Testament Interpretation*, edited by Richard L. Rohrbaugh, 159–82. Peabody, MA: Hendrickson, 1996.
Ng, Esther Yue L. "Phoebe as Prostatis." *Trinity Journal* 25, no. 1 (2004): 3–10.
Nicholl, Colin R. *From Hope to Despair in Thessalonica Situating 1 and 2 Thessalonians*. Cambridge: Cambridge University Press, 2004.
Nigdelis, Pantelis M. "Voluntary Associations in Roman Thessalonikē: In Search of Identity and Support in a Cosmopolitan Society." In *From Roman to Early Christian Thessalonikē: Studies in Religion and Archaeology*, edited by Laura Nasrallah Salah, Charalambos Bakirtzēs, and Steven J. Friesen, 13–48. Cambridge, MA: Harvard University Press, 2010.

Nijf, Omno van. *The Civic World of Professional Associations in the Roman East*. Amsterdam: J. C. Gieben, 1997.

Nyiawung, Mbengu D. "Contextualising Biblical Exegesis: What Is the African Biblical Hermeneutic Approach?" *HTS Theological Studies* 69, no. 1 (2013): 1–9.

Oakes, Peter. "Re-Mapping the Universe: Paul and the Emperor in 1 Thessalonians and Philippians." *Journal for the Study of the New Testament* 27, no. 3 (2005): 301–22.

Obeng, Samuel Gyasi. *African Anthroponymy: An Ethnopragmatic and Morphophonological Study of Personal Names in Akan and Some African Societies*. München: Lincom Europa, 2001.

O'Connor, Anthony. "Review: *Circular Migration in Zimbabwe and Contemporary Sub-Saharan Africa* by Deborah Potts." *African Affairs* 110, no. 440 (2011): 510–12.

Oduyoye, M. A. "The Value of African Religious Beliefs and Practices for Christian Theology." In *African Theology En Route*, edited by Kofi Appiah-Kubi and S. Torres, 109–16. Maryknoll, NY: Orbis Books, 1979.

Oeming, Manfred. *Contemporary Biblical Hermeneutics: An Introduction*. Aldershot: Ashgate, 2006.

O'Keefe, Tim. "The Epicureans on Happiness, Wealth, and the Deviant Craft of Property Management." In *Economics & The Virtues: Building a New Moral Foundation*, edited by Mark D. White and Jennifer A. Baker, 37–52. Oxford: Oxford University Press, 2016.

Öhler, Markus. "Cultic Meals in Associations and the Early Christian Eucharist." *Early Christianity* 5, no. 4 (2014): 475–502.

Ojie, A. E. "Democracy, Ethnicity, and the Problem of Extrajudicial Killing in Nigeria." *Journal of Black Studies* 36, no. 4 (2006): 546–69.

Okorie, J. M. "The Pauline Work Ethic in 1 and 2 Thessalonians." *Deltion Biblikon Meleton* 14, no. 1 (1995): 55–64.

Osiek, Carolyn. "The Politics of Patronage and the Politics of Kinship: The Meeting of the Ways." *Biblical Theology Bulletin* 39, no. 3 (2009): 143–52. doi:10.1177/0146107909106758.

Osseo-Asare, Fran. *Food Culture in Sub-Saharan Africa*. Westport, CN: Greenwood, 2005.

Page, D. L, and A. S. F Gow. *The Greek Anthology*. Cambridge: Cambridge University Press, 1968.

Paige, Terence Peter. *1 & 2 Thessalonians: A Commentary in the Wesleyan Tradition*. Kansas City, MO: Beacon Hill Press, 2017.

Palmer, Earl F. *1 and 2 Thessalonians*. A Good News Commentary. San Francisco: Harper & Row, 1983.

Parratt, John. *A Reader in African Christian Theology*. Denver, CO: Academic Books, 2001.
Payne, Philip B. *Man and Woman, One in Christ: An Exegetical and Theological Study of Paul's Letters*. Grand Rapids, MI: Zondervan, 2009.
Peachin, Michael. *The Oxford Handbook of Social Relations in the Roman World*. Oxford: Oxford University Press, 2011.
Perrin-Jassy, Marie France. *Basic Community in the African Churches*. Translated by Jeane Marie Lyons. Maryknoll, NY: Orbis Books, 1973.
Peterman, Gerald W. *Paul's Gift from Philippi: Contemporary Conventions of Gift-Exchange and Christian Giving*. New York: Cambridge University Press, 1997.
Pope John Paul II. *On Human Work: Encyclical Laborem Exercens*. Washington, DC: Office for Publishing and Promotion Services, United States Catholic Conference, 2000.
Porter, Stanley E. "Paul, Virtues, Vices, and Household Codes." In *Paul in the Greco-Roman World: A Handbook*, vol. 2, edited by J. Paul Sampley, 369–90. London: Bloomsbury, 2016.
———. *The Paul of Acts: Essays in Literary Criticism, Rhetoric, and Theology*. Tübingen: Mohr Siebeck, 1999.
Potts, Deborah. *Circular Migration in Zimbabwe and Contemporary Sub-Saharan Africa*. Suffolk: Boydell & Brewer, 2013.
Rayner, William. *The Tribe and Its Successors*. London: Faber, 1962.
Richard, Earl. *First and Second Thessalonians*. Collegeville, MN: Liturgical Press, 1995.
Richards, E. Randolph. *The Secretary in the Letters of Paul*. Tübingen: Mohr Siebeck, 1991.
Rigaux, Béda. *Saint Paul: Les Épitres aux Thessaloniciens*. Études Bibliques. Paris: Librairie Lecoffre, 1956.
Roberts, Colin, Theodore C. Skeat, and Arthur Darby Nock. *The Gild of Zeus Hypsistos*. Cambridge, MA: Harvard University Press, 1936.
Roberts, Mark David. "Images of Paul and the Thessalonians." Unpublished PhD Thesis, Harvard University, 1992.
Rogers, Cleon L. Jr, and Cleon L. Rogers. *The New Linguistic and Exegetical Key to the Greek New Testament*. Grand Rapids, MI: Zondervan, 1998.
Rosner, Brian. "Paul's Ethics." In *The Cambridge Companion to St. Paul*, edited by James D. G. Dunn, 217. New York: Cambridge University Press, 2003.
Roosen, A. *De brieven van Paulus aan de Tessalonicenzen*. Roermond: Romen, 1971.
Rostovtzeff, Michael Ivanovitch. *The Social & Economic History of the Roman Empire*. Oxford: Clarendon, 1926.

Rupp, George. "Communities of Collaboration: Shared Commitments/Common Tasks." In *On Community*, edited by Leroy S. Rouner, 192–208. Notre Dame, IN: University of Notre Dame Press, 1991.

Russell, Bertrand. *History of Western Philosophy*. New York: Routledge, 2004.

Russell, R. "The Idle in 2 Thess 3.6–12: An Eschatological or a Social Problem?" *New Testament Studies* 34, no. 1 (1988): 105–19.

Saller, Richard P. "Household and Gender." In *The Cambridge Economic History of the Greco-Roman World*, edited by Walter Scheidel, Ian Morris, and Richard P. Saller, 88–112. Cambridge: Cambridge University Press, 2007.

———. "Slavery and the Roman Family." In *Classical Slavery*, edited by M. I Finley, 82–110. London: Frank Cass, 1987.

———. "Women, Slaves, and the Economy of the Roman Household." In *Early Christian Families in Context: An Interdisciplinary Dialogue*, edited by David L. Balch and Carolyn Osiek, 185–204. Grand Rapids, MI: Eerdmans, 2003.

Sandmel, Samuel. *Parallelomania: The Presidential Address given before the Society of Biblical Literature and Exegesis in St. Louis, Missouri, December 27, 1961*. Philadelphia: M. Jacobs, 1962.

Scheidel, W, and S. J. Friesen. "The Size of the Economy and the Distribution of Income in the Roman Empire." *Journal of Roman Studies* 99 (2009): 61–91.

Schiffman, Lawrence H. *The Eschatological Community of the Dead Sea Scrolls: A Study of the Rule of the Congregation*. Atlanta, GA: Scholars Press, 1989.

Schmithals, Walter. *Paul & the Gnostics*. Translated by John E. Steely. Nashville, TN: Abingdon, 1972.

Schwartz, Benjamin. "Chinese Culture and Concept of Community." In *On Community*, edited by Leroy S. Rouner, 117–29. Notre Dame, IN: University of Notre Dame Press, 1991.

Sellars, John. "Simon the Shoemaker and the Problem of Socrates." *Classical Philology* 98, no. 3 (2003): 207–16.

Sharples, R. W. *Stoics, Epicureans, and Sceptics: An Introduction to Hellenistic Philosophy*. London: Routledge, 1996.

Shogren, Gary S. *1 and 2 Thessalonians*. Zondervan Exegetical Commentary on the New Testament. Grand Rapids, MI: Zondervan, 2013.

Shorter, Aylward, ed. *African Christian Spirituality*. Maryknoll, NY: Orbis Books, 1980.

Shorter Lexicon of the Greek New Testament. Edited by F. Wilbur Gingrich. Chicago, IL: University of Chicago Press, 1983.

Sindima, Harvey J. *Africa's Agenda: The Legacy of Liberalism and Colonialism in the Crisis of African Values*. Contributions in Afro-American and African Studies 176. Westport: Greenwood Press, 1995.

Sire, James W. *Discipleship of the Mind*. Downers Grove, IL: InterVarsity Press, 1990.

Sithole, Masipula. "Class and Factionalism in the Zimbabwe Nationalist Movement." *African Studies Review* 27, no. 1 (1984): 117–25.

Smith, Claire S. *Pauline Communities as "Scholastic Communities": A Study of the Vocabulary of "teaching" in 1 Corinthians, 1 and 2 Timothy and Titus*. Tübingen: Mohr Siebeck, 2012.

Smith, M. G. "The Hausa of Northern Nigeria." In *Peoples of Africa*, edited by James Lowell Gibbs, 119–56. Prospect Heights, IL: Waveland Press, 1988.

South, James T. *Disciplinary Practices in Pauline Texts*. Lewiston, NY: Mellen Biblical Press, 1993.

Spicq, Ceslas. "Les Thessaloniciens « Inquiets » Etaient-ils Des Paresseux?" *Studia Theologica – Nordic Journal of Theology* 10, no. 1 (1956): 1–13.

———. *Theological Lexicon of the New Testament 1*. Translated by James D. Ernest. Peabody, MA: Hendrickson, 1996.

Stegemann, Ekkehard, and Wolfgang Stegemann. *The Jesus Movement: A Social History of Its First Century*. Translated by O. C. Dean, Jr. Edinburgh: T&T Clark, 1999.

Stegemann, Hartmut. *The Library of Qumran: On the Essenes, Qumran, John the Baptist, and Jesus*. Leiden: Brill, 1998.

Still, Todd D. *Conflict at Thessalonica: A Pauline Church and Its Neighbours*. Sheffield: Sheffield Academic Press, 1999.

Stott, John R. W. *The Message of 1 & 2 Thessalonians: The Gospel & the End of Time*. Edited by J. A. Motyer and Derek Tidball. Leicester: Inter-Varsity Press, 1991.

Swartz, Marc J. "Politics, Ethnicity, and Social Structure: The Decline of an Urban Community during the Twentieth Century." *Ethnology* 35, no. 4 (1996): 233–48.

Tempels, Placide. *Bantu Philosophy*. Translated by Margaret Read and A. Rubbens. Orlando, FL: HBC Publishing, 2010.

Thabede, Dumisani. "The African Worldview as the Basis of Practice in the Helping Professions." *Social Work Social Work/Maatskaplike Werk* 44, no. 3 (2014): 233–45.

The Brill Dictionary of Ancient Greek. Franco Montanari. Leiden: Brill, 2015.

Theissen, Gerd. *The Social Setting of Pauline Christianity*. Edited by J. H. Schutz. Edinburgh: T&T Clark, 1982.

Theological Lexicon of the New Testament. Celas Spicq. Translated by James D. Ernest. Peabody, MA: Hendrickson, 1996.

Thiselton, Anthony C. *1 and 2 Thessalonians Through the Centuries*. Chichester, West Sussex: Wiley-Blackwell, 2010.

Thorley, John. "Subjunctive Aktionsart in New Testament Greek: A Reassessment." *Novum Testamentum* 30, no. 3 (1988): 193–211.

Torrey, E. Fuller. *Witchdoctors and Psychiatrists: The Common Roots of Psychotherapy and Its Future*. New York: Harper & Row, 1986.

Treggiari, Susan. "Lower Class Women in the Roman Economy." *Florilegium: Carleton University Annual Papers on Classical Antiquity and the Middle Ages* 1, no. 1 (1979): 65–86.
Trilling, Wolfgang. *Der Zweite Brief an die Thessalonicher*. Zürich: Benziger, 1980.
Tsouna, Voula. *Philodemus, on Property Management*. Atlanta, GA: Society of Biblical Literature, 2013.
Turaki, Yusufu. *Foundations of African Traditional Religion and Worldview*. Nairobi: WordAlive Publishers, 2006.
Turner, Victor. *The Forest of Symbols: Aspects of Ndembu Ritual*. Ithaca, NY: Cornell University Press, 1967.
Van der Walt, B. J. *Afrocentric or Eurocentric?: Our Task in a Multicultural South Africa*. Potchefstroom, SA: Potchefstroomse Universiteit vir Christelike Hoër Onderwys, 1997.
VanderKam, James. *The Dead Sea Scrolls Today*. Revised ed. Grand Rapids, MI: Eerdmans, 2010.
VanderKam, James, and Peter Flint. *The Meaning of the Dead Sea Scrolls: Their Significance for Understanding the Bible, Judaism, Jesus, and Christianity*. New York: HarperOne, 2014.
Verbrugge, Verlyn D. *Paul & Money: A Biblical and Theological Analysis of the Apostle's Teachings and Practices*. Grand Rapids, MI: Zondervan, 2015.
Vermès, Géza. *The Complete Dead Sea Scrolls in English: Complete Edition*. New edition. London: Penguin Classics, 2004.
———. "The Laws of the Damascus Document: Sources, Traditions and Redaction by Charlotte Hemple." *Journal of Jewish Studies* 56, no. 1 (2005): 177.
Vermès, Géza, and Martin Goodman, eds. *The Essenes: According to the Classical Sources*. Oxford Centre Textbooks, vol. 1. Sheffield: JSOT Press, 1989.
Volf, Miroslav. *Work in the Spirit: Toward a Theology of Work*. New York: Oxford University Press, 1991.
Währisch-Oblau, Claudia, and Henning Wrogemann. *Witchcraft, Demons and Deliverance: A Global Conversation on an Intercultural Challenge*. Zürich: LIT Verlag Münster, 2015.
Wallace-Hadrill, Andrew. "*Domus* and *Insulae* in Rome: Families and Housefuls." In *Early Christian Families in Context: An Interdisciplinary Dialogue*, edited by David L. Balch and Carolyn Osiek, 3–18. Grand Rapids, MI: Eerdmans, 2003.
Wallace, William. *Epicureanism*. London: SPCK, 1908.
Walton, Steve. *Leadership and Lifestyle the Portrait of Paul in the Miletus Speech and 1 Thessalonians*. Cambridge: Cambridge University Press, 2000.
Wanamaker, Charles A. *The Epistles to the Thessalonians: A Commentary on the Greek Text*. New International Greek Testament Commentary. Grand Rapids, MI: Eerdmans, 1990.

Weatherly, Jon A. *1 & 2 Thessalonians*. Joplin, MO: College Press Publishing, 1996.

Weima, Jeffrey A. D. *1–2 Thessalonians*. Grand Rapids, MI: Baker Academic, 2014.

Wenham, Gordon J. *Genesis 1–15*. Word Biblical Commentary 1. Waco, TX: Word Books, 1987.

———. *Rethinking Genesis 1–11: Gateway to the Bible*. The Didsbury Lecture Series. Eugene, OR: Cascade Books, 2015.

White, Michael L. "Paul and the *Pater Familias*." In *Paul in the Greco-Roman World: A Handbook*, vol. 2, edited by J. Paul Sampley, 171–203. New York: Bloomsbury, 2016.

Williams, David John. *1 & 2 Thessalonians*. Grand Rapids, MI: Baker Books, 2011.

Wilson, Monica Hunter. *Good Company: A Study of Nyakyusa Age-Villages*. Boston: Beacon Press, 1963.

Wilson, Stephen G. "Voluntary Associations: An Overview." In *Voluntary Associations in the Graeco-Roman World*, edited by John S. Kloppenborg and Stephen G. Wilson, 23–42. London: Routledge, 2002.

Wilson-Reitz, Megan T., and Sheila E. McGinn. "2 Thessalonians vs. the *Ataktoi*: A Pauline Critique of 'White-Collar Welfare.'" In *By Bread Alone: The Bible through the Eyes of the Hungry*, edited by Sheila E. McGinn, Lai Ling Elizabeth Ngan, and Ahida Calderón Pilarski, 185–208. Augsburg: Fortress, 2014.

Winter, Bruce W. *After Paul Left Corinth: The Influence of Secular Ethics and Social Change*. Grand Rapids, MI: Eerdmans, 2001.

———. "'If a Man Does Not Wish to Work . . .' A Cultural and Historical Setting for 2 Thessalonians 3:6–16." *Tyndale Bulletin* 40, no. 2 (1989): 303–15.

———. *Seek the Welfare of the City: Christians as Benefactors and Citizens*. Grand Rapids, MI Eerdmans, 1994.

Wise, Michael Owen, Martin G. Abegg, and Edward M. Cook. *The Dead Sea Scrolls: A New Translation*. San Francisco: Harper, 2005.

Witherington, Ben III. *The Acts of the Apostles: A Socio-Rhetorical Commentary*. Grand Rapids, MI: Eerdmans, 1998.

———. *1 and 2 Thessalonians: A Socio-Rhetorical Commentary*. Grand Rapids, MI: Eerdmans, 2006.

———. *The Paul Quest: The Renewed Quest for the Jew of Tarsus*. Downers Grove, IL: InterVarsity Press, 1998.

———. *Work: A Kingdom Perspective on Labor*. Grand Rapids, MI: Eerdmans, 2011.

Wright, Christopher J. H. *Living as the People of God: The Relevance of Old Testament Ethics*. Leicester: Inter-Varsity Press, 1983.

Wright, N. T. *Paul and His Recent Interpreters: Some Contemporary Debates*. London: SPCK, 2015.

———. *Paul and the Faithfulness of God*. Minneapolis: Fortress, 2013.

Yankson, Sednak Kojo Duffu Asare. *Africa's Roots in God: The Knowledge of the Creator Embedded in the Indigenous African Culture*. Hempstead, NY: Sanfoka Heritage Books, 2007.

Zeller, Eduard. *The Stoics, Epicureans, and Sceptics*. Translated by Oswald Joseph Reichel. London: Longmans & Co., 1880.

Langham Literature, with its publishing work, is a ministry of Langham Partnership.

Langham Partnership is a global fellowship working in pursuit of the vision God entrusted to its founder John Stott –

> *to facilitate the growth of the church in maturity and Christ-likeness through raising the standards of biblical preaching and teaching.*

Our vision is to see churches in the Majority World equipped for mission and growing to maturity in Christ through the ministry of pastors and leaders who believe, teach and live by the word of God.

Our mission is to strengthen the ministry of the word of God through:
- nurturing national movements for biblical preaching
- fostering the creation and distribution of evangelical literature
- enhancing evangelical theological education

especially in countries where churches are under-resourced.

Our ministry

Langham Preaching partners with national leaders to nurture indigenous biblical preaching movements for pastors and lay preachers all around the world. With the support of a team of trainers from many countries, a multi-level programme of seminars provides practical training, and is followed by a programme for training local facilitators. Local preachers' groups and national and regional networks ensure continuity and ongoing development, seeking to build vigorous movements committed to Bible exposition.

Langham Literature provides Majority World preachers, scholars and seminary libraries with evangelical books and electronic resources through publishing and distribution, grants and discounts. The programme also fosters the creation of indigenous evangelical books in many languages, through writer's grants, strengthening local evangelical publishing houses, and investment in major regional literature projects, such as one volume Bible commentaries like the *Africa Bible Commentary* and the *South Asia Bible Commentary*.

Langham Scholars provides financial support for evangelical doctoral students from the Majority World so that, when they return home, they may train pastors and other Christian leaders with sound, biblical and theological teaching. This programme equips those who equip others. Langham Scholars also works in partnership with Majority World seminaries in strengthening evangelical theological education. A growing number of Langham Scholars study in high quality doctoral programmes in the Majority World itself. As well as teaching the next generation of pastors, graduated Langham Scholars exercise significant influence through their writing and leadership.

To learn more about Langham Partnership and the work we do visit **langham.org**

www.ingramcontent.com/pod-product-compliance
Lightning Source LLC
Chambersburg PA
CBHW051540230426
43669CB00015B/2668